£13.94   3 wks   986.106 LIV

Inside Colombia

DRUGS, DEMOCRACY AND WAR

Grace Livingstone

FOREWORD BY JENNY PEARCE

Rutgers University Press

NEW BRUNSWICK, NEW JERSEY

First published in the United States 2004
by Rutgers University Press, New Brunswick, New Jersey

First published in Great Britain 2003
by Latin American Bureau
1 Amwell Street
London EC1R 1UL

Library of Congress Cataloging-in-Publication Data
Livingstone, Grace.
Inside Colombia : drugs, democracy, and war / Grace Livingstone ; foreword by Jenny Pearce
p.   cm.
Includes bibliographical references and index.
ISBN 0-8135-3442-9 (cloth)—ISBN 0-8135-3443-7 (pbk)
1. Drug traffic—Economic aspects—Colombia.   2. Drug traffic—Social aspects—Colombia.
3. Narcotics, Control of—Colombia.   4. Colombia—Economic conditions—1970-
5. Colombia—History—20th century.   6. Colombia—Politics and government—1946-
7. Colombia—Social conditions—1970-   I. Title.

HV5840.C7L58 2004
986.106'35—dc22   2003066833

British Cataloging-in-Publication information is available from the British Library.

Manufactured in the United States of America

Editing: Marcela López Levy
Cover image: 'Los Papagayos' (1986) Beatriz González de Ripoll
Design and typesetting: Andy Dark
Cover design: Andy Dark

Contents

Acknowledgements

I would like to thank all the Colombians who provided testimonies for this book, many of whom shared painful experiences or risked reprisals by speaking out. Most agreed to have their names published, but we decided not to publish names that have not already appeared in print.

I would like to thank Cifisam, a charity supported by the vicariate of San Vicente de Caguán, which guided me in coca growing areas in southern Colombia. I also owe thanks to the Colombian Commission of Jurists who I pestered incessantly for statistics, the Defensoría del Pueblo's office in Bogotá, CINEP and staff at the gobernación of Cauca and the municipality of Popayán.

In the United States, I would like to thank the Center for International Policy, Human Rights Watch, the Washington Office on Latin America, School of the Americas Watch and the Rand Institute. In London, I would like to thank the press office of the Colombian Embassy which kindly went to great lengths to find information for me. Library staff at the University of London's Institute of Latin American Studies were also exceptionally helpful.

I owe a great debt to Adam Isaacson, of the Center for International Policy, whose website on US involvement in Colombia is unsurpassed and who has generously shared his wide knowledge with me. Similarly, I would like to thank Martin Jelsma, of the Transnational Institute in the Netherlands, which in association with Acción Andina publish some of the best material on the drugs and fumigation available. I would also particularly like to mention Darío González Posso, who has given me great help on environmental and development issues and Bernardo Pérez Salazar who read chapters four and five. Many thanks also to Michael Gillard and Melissa Jones for their help on the BP section and to Diana Rodríguez, who put up with my daily questions about Spanish with great grace. I would also like to thank Mauricio García Durán, Nazih Richani, David Raby and Elsa Nivia. It goes without saying that all errors are my own.

I must also thank all my colleagues at Latin American Newsletters for their support and friendship and Marcela López Levy at Latin America Bureau for her patience and perseverance.

Above all I would like to thank Javier, Olga and Héctor Fabio, in Colombia, for their kindness and generosity. At home, I give love and thanks to Dinah Livingstone, Francis McDonagh and Josh Cedar.

Foreword

WAR AND PEACE: THE COLOMBIAN EPIC

1. *What is power?*

2. *What force produces the movement of the nations?*

(1) *Power is the relation of a given person to other individuals in which the more this person expresses opinions, predictions and justification of the collective action that is performed, the less is his participation in that action.*

(2) *The movement of nations is caused not by power, nor by intellectual activity nor even by a combination of the two as historians have supposed, but by the activity of all the people who participate in the events, and who always combine in such a way that those taking the largest direct share in the event take on themselves the least responsibility and vice versa.*

Morally, the wielder of power appears to cause the event; physically it is those who submit to the power. But as the activity is inconceivable without the physical, the cause of the event is neither in the one nor in the other, but in the union of the two.

Or in other words, the conception of a cause is inapplicable to the phenomena we are examining.

Leo Tolstoy, Second Epilogue, *War and Peace*
London: Macmillan, 1967 pp. 1326-1327

The limits of political analysis – in hindsight

The final paragraph of the book I wrote on Colombia for the Latin America Bureau in 1990 was the following:

> 'The Colombian journalist Antonio Caballero once called Colombia a "political time-bomb". Can an economy that has created only 500,000 jobs in manufacturing, which a leaked World Bank report (July 1989) describes as closed and meeting the needs of only a minority, provide the majority of its population with a humane existence and the means to a livelihood? The archaic political order that has kept that minority in power has proved incapable of taking on this responsibility. The bomb will carry on ticking until it does, or until the left proves itself able to unite the people around an alternative social and political project.'[1]

I do not reproduce this paragraph because I am proud of it. In the five years following the publication of the book in 1990, 10,902 people died for political reasons in Colombia.[2] Amnesty International estimates that 60,000 people have died in Colombia between 1985 and 2003 as a result of the conflict, 80% of them civilians with no involvement in the hostilities.[3] Armed conflict spread to many more parts of the country in the years that followed; the guerrillas increased their presence from 437 municipalities in 1991 to 622 in 1995[4] and to 1,000 in 1999.[5] The FARC increased its combatants from 13,200 in 1989 to 18,000 in 1992.[6] The ELN from 1,800 armed men in 1990 to 4-5,000 in 1996.[7] At the beginning of 2003, intelligence reports pointed to a combined guerrilla force of 22,000.[8] The paramilitary, meanwhile, grew from a few hundred men at the beginning of the 1990s to 4-5,000 by 1995 and 8,000 by the end of the decade[9] with some reports estimating 11,000 by 2002.[10] The prediction quoted in the book about a political time bomb was valid. In my view nothing could be more akin to the impact of an exploding bomb than the death and destruction that Colombia faced in the 1990s, throwing its detritus over everyone, even over those who in the late 1980s, when the book was written, believed they could shelter or were too far to feel the impact.

Colombia's political and economic elite have failed to govern in the interests of all Colombians. They have not constructed a state capable of building a nation which in turn would provide the 'cultural context' for the political activation of citizens and the democratisation of that state.[11]

This failure has had tragic consequences, as the rest of the book makes clear. But what happened to those of the left who tried to propose an alternative vision of state and nationhood? In the mid 1980s many urban middle class intellectuals thought the left might have a viable project for Colombia; they were ambivalent towards the armed opposition and comprehended its logic. The Unión Patriótica, (UP) a project which originated in a bid by the Communist Party and the FARC guerrillas to test the potential for electoral politics and political alliance-building, won the biggest vote in the history of the left in the 1986 presidential election.[11] A decade later, the left in the form of the armed movements had very little social and political support outside historic bases. But they had stronger armies than ever.

A movement for peace amongst social organisations, NGOs and intellectuals gained momentum in the latter half of the 1990s, but had lost it by the end of the decade. By 2002, the Colombian population was prepared to vote in a president on a platform of authority and war. The left wing candidate, Lucho Garzón, with a personal following due to his rejection of armed struggle and his own personality and integrity, could not rally Colombia behind a progressive left politics although he achieved the best result for the left since the elimination of the UP. Not only socialism but democracy and peace had lost their appeal, perhaps temporarily, but no less clearly and significantly.

Inside the Labyrinth was a historical/political analysis written from the perspective of the social activists who were struggling and giving their lives to keep a space open for a radical democratic project of political change. The emphasis of the book was on the exclusionary character of the state and the gap between the 'formal' Colombia of democratic constitutions and electoral competition, and the 'real' Colombia of the majority unable to participate in shaping the course of political life. It looked back to the premature curtailment of a populist momentum around Gaitán in the late 1940s that might have forced change on the old political order and its socio-economic underpinnings. It dealt with the uneven impact of the modernisation project of the 1960s, which was constructed like an extra room on the edifice of the old structure. A compromise was forged between warring political factions of Colombia's ruling elite to allow the country to develop a manufacturing and agro-industrial economy. Thousands moved from countryside to city in the hope of jobs in the new economy, following others expelled in the 1950s through violent party political homogenisation of rural communities. A country that went from 70% rural to 70% urban in the space of three decades, but where traditional political elites kept total control over the spaces for political renovation and social inclusion was doomed to have problems. A significant urban middle class emerged in Colombia in these decades and gained access to education, but not to commensurate employment and political power. The majority urban poor were left to their own devices, to survive as best they might.

Mediators emerged to provide the security and protection the poor needed, but only in return for political support. Party bosses in the rapidly growing cities established what French political sociologist Daniel Pecaut calls the 'logic of protection' which combined political and armed forms of clientelism, with votes exchanged for favours of all kinds. Colombia's two traditional political parties continued to tread their ambiguous path between civil and uncivil mechanisms of political competition, but hung onto political power all the same. The rural poor were abandoned to whichever forces established de facto rule in the villages and hamlets where they lived; many became workers in the new agro-industrial sector as land hunger grew, others migrated to the remaining frontier lands. In the distant zones of peasant colonisation, the FARC guerrillas became the sole authority. Their power and legitimacy amongst peasant farmers in these traditional areas of FARC control derives from the protection they gave and order they maintained in return for a tax on the coca crop earnings that had began to underpin survival for the peasants by the late 1970s.

The FARC were not the only group to make gains from the coca industry. Almost every social class made something out of the enormously lucrative drugs' trade, although some much more than others and ultimately at a cost for the whole of society. The political class increased their vote-buying power and the traditional political parties held onto the support of the relatively small percentage of voting citizens until the evidence that President Samper had funded his electoral campaign of 1994 with cocaine money proved a step too far. The decline of the two traditional parties, Liberal and Conservative, particularly the latter, is one of the notable processes of the 1990s. Significant sectors of the business and banking elite gained in a variety of ways as cocaine dollars lubricated the economy indirectly and sometimes directly, particularly in the financial and real estate sectors. Landowners anxious to get away from FARC-controlled rural areas and the *vacuna*, or guerrilla tax, could sell their lands at highly inflated prices to the new class of *narco-terratenientes* (drug traffickers/landowners).[14] Despite huge disagreements over the impact of drug dollars on the country's exchange rate and balance of payments, many would argue that even the urban middle class benefited from the cheap imported computers, cars and other consumer goods that flooded the markets in the 1980s. The poor benefited also in numerous ways. The drug barons provided the jobs, welfare and entertainment that the state had totally neglected. The Medellín poor did not celebrate the death of its infamous son, Pablo Escobar, in 1993. Drug dollars also created the capacity to buy weapons. This added a lethal factor into cultures already notorious for the violent resolution of disputes and giving power to many who could not gain it in any other way than through the barrel of a gun. Homicides in Medellín, a violent city even in 1980, rose dramatically in the course of the 1990s. There were 42,393 registered homicides in the city between 1992 and 2002.[15]

In terms of the big picture of Colombia's political trajectory of the 1990s, the ruling political and economic elite of Colombia found that the new entrepreneurs of the drugs industry were even more socially and politically conservative than they were. Their killing power was harnessed to the counterinsurgency project. The death squads eliminated social activists, left political opponents (the UP was decimated),[16] social undesirables and demobilised former guerrilla combatants, in the name of re-establishing control and order and eliminating the armed insurgencies. The paramilitary forged regional and local armies funded through the drug trade as well as with the assistance/protection of the armed forces of the state. The United Self Defence Force of Colombia or AUC, which brought disparate private armies together in 1994, had become a brutal and powerful military force by the late 1990s, autonomous from the Colombian army, but sharing its goals and enjoying much practical support from it.[17]

The armed forces were relatively weak by Latin American standards due to the jealous protection of civilian political power by Colombia's two traditional parties. Their main task was to wage the counterinsurgency war. They preferred to do this indirectly rather than directly, an approach which resulted in the deaths of many civilian social activists under suspicion of sympathies with the armed left, while the guerrilla armies, protected in their distant rural enclaves, continued to grow.[18] Nizah Richani has suggested that in fact, there was a 'comfortable impasse' in the war until the late 1990s, which suited the armed forces as well as other armed groups. The argument is that a positive political economy evolved around the armed conflict, with all armed groups gaining from maintaining a low intensity form of combat. On the guerrilla's side, this enabled them to build up a strong financial base from the coca trade, extortion of oil companies, kidnapping and other forms of economic predation. These undoubtedly strengthened the guerrilla groups militarily, but weakened them enormously politically. By the late 1990s their political message was lost in the logic of an increasingly bloody war funded by activities more akin to common crime than a struggle for popular liberation. Distinguished intellectuals, such as Daniel Pecaut, were able to argue that:

> 'One of the reasons why the frontiers between political and non-political violence have become fluid, the same as with organized and disorganised violence, is the fact that all the protagonists with capacity for armed action, direct themselves, as a means or an end, to the control of economic production of the country.'[19]

Middle class professionals who had maintained a latent sympathy for the radical cause in the 1980s found themselves and their relatives under constant fear of kidnapping by the FARC and the ELN a decade later.

But Richani argues that the armed forces also benefited from keeping the level of combat low. He notes the increase in military expenditure from 1.2% of GNP in 1985 to 2.2% in 1996 and to 3.5% in 1999.[20] But these increases went into the military administrative budget and did not improve the military's combat performance. While by 1997 the total number of soldiers amounted to 131,000, only 22,000 were professional soldiers deployed for defensive purposes and for occasional incursions against guerrillas. The rest are in administrative and logistical support positions. The armed forces developed 'an institutional set-up that was relatively comfortable within the context of a civil war.'[21]

The impasse was never 'comfortable' of course for the thousands of non-combatants who lost their lives or who were forced to live under threat and terror from armed groups. And the idea that the war could be contained began to break down in the late 1990s as the paramilitaries launched major offensives into guerrilla territory, while the guerrillas also escalated the war. It was the FARC that lost the most politically. They used the demilitarized zone granted them by President Pastrana in November 1998 as part of the peace process to strengthen their own military power, expand their territorial influence and continue kidnapping and extortion operations against civilians. This abuse of the zone lost them much more moral and political capital than the paramilitaries' brutal assaults on the population. This despite the evidence that the paramilitary right were still responsible for the majority of human rights abuses and massacres, and that they used particularly savage methods to kill their victims.

The guerrillas increasingly came to be seen as the 'cause' of the war and political violence. This violence now exceeded for most Colombians any justification in terms of the real problems facing the country: structural inequality, poverty, political exclusion and repression. Forcible recruitment of children into the guerrilla armies, the sexual abuse of girls and female combatants, summary executions and mass kidnappings caused a level of human suffering in the name of the guerrilla cause that led to widespread repudiation amongst people who might otherwise have sympathised with it. Those who would never sympathise with it were re-legitimised.

Two horrendous 'accidental' mass killings of civilians placed very black marks first against the ELN and then against the FARC. The first was the death in Machuca in 1998 of 73 peasants, 36 of them children, when the ELN blew up the OCENSA oil pipeline. The resulting oil and gas spillage took six minutes to descend a slope, cross the Pocune river and reach the population on the other bank who used open flames for light and cooking. Families were asleep when the lethal mixture ignited. Although the ELN acknowledged responsibility for the act, ELN leader Antonio García subsequently claimed it was sufficient to simply 'acknowledge' the error and insist that units be more careful. The Machuca of the FARC occurred in May 2002 in the Chocó town of Bellavista, Bojayá, while I was staying in Medellín, the nearest city with the hospital facilities to deal with the casualties. A gas cylinder launched by the FARC during a battle with paramilitaries hit the church where the civilian population were taking shelter. The local population, the Church, the Public Defender's Office and the UN Human Rights Office had all warned the military authorities of the impending attack but received no response. Once again, the FARC acknowledged responsibility for the appalling consequences of their action which cost the lives of 119 people, 45 of them children. However, they also put ultimate responsibility on the army for failing to prevent the paramilitary incursion and on the paramilitary at whom the gas cylinder bomb had been aimed, for placing themselves around the church. They had nevertheless launched the gas cylinder bomb, knowing its poor level of accuracy and that civilians were sheltering in the church.

Colombians are left 'comparing' these and other atrocities with those of the paramilitary right, such as that in Chengue, Sucre on January 17, 2002. Human Rights Watch recount how witnesses told government investigators that several Colombian navy units just looked the other way when well-armed paramilitaries entered the village. They assembled the villages in two groups, then as reported in the Washington Post 'one by one, they killed the men by crushing their heads with heavy stones and a sledgehammer. When it was over, twenty-four men lay dead in pools of blood. Two more were found later in shallow graves. As the troops left, they set fire to the village.'[22]

The paramilitary right are a dangerous and nasty monster, borne out of an alliance between landowners, drugs traffickers and army officers. However, they were founded with the intention of defeating the guerrillas, and many of its leaders and combatants had been victims of guerrilla killings. Indeed, the AUC has been particularly successful in drawing in ex-guerillas whose families have suffered at the hands of their former comrades. They also pay their recruits, in a country where unemployment reached its highest ever levels in the late 1990s. Carlos Castaño, the leader of the AUC until 2001, when he stepped down to concentrate on the political side of the movement,[23] skilfully played the political and moral ambiguities surrounding his mission. He has tried to portray the AUC as the heroic force that defends the legitimate order and does what the armed forces have failed to do; he presents it as the saviour of Colombia rather than its inner demon.

The 'comfortable impasse' was over long before Uribe Vélez won the presidency on a hardline anti-guerilla ticket in 2002. The US had already begun to strengthen the military capacity of the armed forces under the umbrella of anti-drugs interdiction and Pastrana's Plan Colombia, which it effectively hijacked. It had also begun to assist in the image-changing operation around the armed forces that would be necessary to justify increasing levels of military assistance to it. US human rights organisations have played a noble role in drawing attention to the ongoing relationship between the army and the paramilitary, the impunity which underlies the abuse of power by the armed forces, and the questionable logic of strengthening this institution before it becomes accountable for its actions to a political authority that cares about the human rights of its citizens. But that has not stopped the US from increasing its military assistance and even agreeing in 2002 to train a brigade to guard the much attacked Caño Limón oil pipeline.

The end of the 'comfortable impasse' makes one reflect on the tragic logic that underpinned it. The belief, for instance, which I heard frequently expressed when researching *Inside the Labyrinth* in the late 1980s, that the Colombian conflict was confined to the distant rural peripheries and given its multipolarity would be unlikely to lead to civil war, which required polarization, or impact on the towns and cities where most people lived. Containment of the problem in these rural areas was the main task, and supping with the devil of private armies and death squads was not considered a moral dilemma for the state. I could not help but be struck by the loss of political opportunities for social and political change in the 1980s that this kind of complacency contributed to. There were peace and reform initiatives in the 1980s, but they faltered against the entrenched defences of the old order, bolstered often by tactical allies in the drugs trade and the ultimate lack of political will of the modernising elite to push beyond a certain point. The Belisario Betancur peace initiative between 1982 and 1985; the Virgilio Barco political reforms to open up municipal political spaces through the direct election of mayors and administrative decentralization as well as his National Rehabilitation Programme (an original project of his predecessor, know by its Spanish acronym, the PNR) for areas affected by violence; César Gaviria's peace process with the M19, Quintín Lame and a majority of the EPL (Ejército Popular de Liberación) and the constitutional reform of 1991.

Each one of these important initiatives was mirrored by a negative counter-process which undermined and wrecked much that was of value. One might think about the armed forces and their allies in the business and landowning elites, who refused to accept Betancur's peace talks with the FARC and M19. They army's incursions into guerrilla territory despite a formal truce, its human rights abuses against those civilians suspected of guerrilla sympathies, and the debacle of the Palace of Justice in 1985,[21] served to strengthen further the scepticism of the armed left towards the sincerity of the state. The political decentralisation of Barco was accompanied by a bloodbath against candidates in the first mayoral election of 1988, resulting in the murder of seven mayors, 28 candidates for mayor, 75 councillors and 19 candidates for the municipal council.[25] The PNR was not pursued with the same energy and social sensitivity by

Barco's successor and evolved into something much more paternalist and far less creative than its earlier phase. Gaviria's peace agreement was followed by the murder of hundreds of demobilised guerrillas. His constitutional reform did give formal Colombia a more progressive constitution but was not followed up by the institutional strengthening and overhaul that would have enabled it to be a practical tool for renovation of the political system.

And these are just some examples of the sabotage of the prospects for serious reform 'from above' in Colombia. The torture, disappearance and murder of social and political activists in the course of the decade weakened those 'from below' who were trying to keep alive the civilian voices in favour of the far-reaching changes needed in the political system and socio-economic structure. The social and civic movements saw their leaderships decimated and many activists killed and/or terrorised. Some may once have been intellectually ambivalent towards the armed movements of the left, but the vast majority were not combatants or even organically linked to the armed movements. Indeed, there were many who sought autonomous spaces for social and political action that both the traditional political elite and the armed left tried to deny them. These are the heroes and heroines of Colombia's struggle for democracy and justice and are the reason that *Inside the Labyrinth* was written.

However, Tolstoy's words at the beginning of this foreword raise a question mark about the overemphasis on power and politics in the book. In hindsight, I would argue that it was necessary but not sufficient to explain the Colombian situation through the lens of a critique of those with political (and economic) power. Tolstoy was concerned with the interaction between those with the power to shape and justify acts of violence and those who actually carry out the acts. A stage further is to look more broadly at the relationship between the powerful and the powerless – those who act violently and those who live within violent contexts. The question of how the powerless respond and adapt to the socio-political context in which they live and in particular to the violence embedded in that context.[26] The powerless are also subjects in this process even though they act in conditions which they do not choose and which they may actively reject.

It is worth reflecting on the idea that the Colombian situation has gone beyond discussion of causality in the sense Tolstoy alludes to. The complex violences of Colombia today are not easily reducible to particular causes. Such analysis is challenging for those who want to attribute blame, and it is of course true that there is greater and lesser responsibility in terms of the Colombian war. Colombia will face problems of transitional justice that will far exceed those confronting all the models of truth and reconciliation commissions that we have seen in the last decade. But my argument is that between the intellectual and actual perpetrators of violence in Colombia there is another story that needs to be understood and confronted if Colombia is ever to build a peaceful and just society. That story concerns the way violence has been embedded in the spaces of socialization that all Colombian citizens are born into and also perpetuate. How can the inter-generational cycle of violence be interrupted in Colombia? What do *all* Colombians (and the international community) have to do to contribute towards such an objective? In the final section, we look at how the violence, war and peace need to be rethought in Colombia

Complex violences and war in Colombia

It is true that the term multipolar violence captures the Colombian conflict better than the term 'civil war' per se.[27] In his most recent book on Colombia, Daniel Pecaut has suggested that while there is still no civil war as such in Colombia, there is a 'war against society.'[28] The problem with such a notion is that it suggests that the problem of Colombia today lies only with its armed actors. There is another argument which suggests that Colombia's complex violences reflect socialisation processes over time and space. These have shaped the evolution of society and state and have a distinctly gendered dynamic. Powerful civilian actors (male and female, but differentially) as well as armed male actors must take a huge share of responsibility for producing and reproducing these processes. But powerless civilian actors (male and female, again differentially) and 'powerless' armed, mostly male, actors have adapted to them as well, and in turn impacted on their reproduction, embedding violence in everyday life and turning it into something conventional and tolerated.

Peace in Colombia will only come when some new configuration of social-political relationships can be constructed that enables both the inter-generational cycle of violence to be interrupted and state-society relations to be reconstructed on the basis of a new logic and normative consensus. These cannot be determined by a small elite, but must involve a democratic and participative process that will undoubtedly challenge vested economic and political interests at present defended through violence, gendered power relationships and everyday life behaviour. A peace agreement between armed actors would not touch the society in the deep way that is needed, although it is an essential precondition for moving forward in Colombia. An authoritarian approach, such as that advocated by President Uribe Vélez, is not only likely to fail, but it is difficult to conceive of a new normative consensus around non-violence, social justice and democracy emerging from it.

Colombia is not the only country today where the distinctions between war, civil war and societal violence have blurred in recent years. Wars no longer take place in clearly demarcated 'theatres'; they are mostly internal conflicts rather than between states; the victims are mainly civilian men, women and children rather than armed male combatants.[29] They appear to be less about the great ideological confrontations of the Cold War, and some even argue they are more about economic agendas than grievances and justice claims.[30] Violence as a broad category of social interaction, in the meantime, has taken new forms and appears to have reached new heights/depths.

The World Health Organisation (WHO) report on global violent deaths in 2000 shows that one third of the 1.7 million violent deaths that year were war related, one fifth were homicides, and just under a half were suicides.[31] They also show that the overwhelming majority of violent deaths take place in low to middle income countries, 1.5 million compared to 149,000 in high income countries. Even these statistics don't necessarily help us clarify the distinction between war-related deaths and political and social violence, a distinction which has been very difficult to maintain in Colombia and elsewhere. The WHO report offers a breakdown of mortality caused by intentional injury by sex, age group and country using the most recent data available between 1990 and 2000. There were, for instance, 43,866 deaths in Brazil according to 1995 figures. Of these, 39,046 were of males, and 20,183 of these were of males between 15 years and 29 years, 12,011 were of males between 30 and 44 years of age.[32] Brazil would not be considered at war, yet its death rate amongst young men is one of the highest in the world, higher even than Colombia.

The comparable figures for Colombia using data from the same year are 24,728 total mortality by intentional injury; 22,685 males, of which 12,169 are aged 15-29 years and 7,272 are 30-44 years. How can we account for these particularly high levels of violence against males aged 15-44? The evidence also shows is committed by other males; most of these homicides are broadly categorised as social rather than political violence in Colombia. There were 300,000 violent deaths of all origins between 1985 and 1995 according to some estimates.[33] Are there links between the social and political violences mixed together in this statistic? Is the social cleansing violence carried out by the paramilitary right against homosexuals, prostitutes and beggars social or political? Is the forced recruitment of children as young as 8 years old by the FARC, social or political? Is there a link between the high levels of male on male killings, and the child abuse and domestic violence, which has also reached extremely high levels in Colombia?[34] Only in recent years has the particular impact of the violence of the war on women been acknowledged by human rights organisations. A space has now opened up for the work of Donny Meertens, for example, on the gender aspects of Colombia's war and the gender implications of internal displacement or of María Clemencia Castro and Carmen Lucia Díaz's gender sensitive work on reintegrated combatants.[35]

Meertens, for example, refers to 'gendered violence' as an 'underground modality that is rarely publicly recognised.'[36] Violence against women is embedded in deep symbolic meanings for armed actors and Meertens has begun to explore how these meanings have changed over time. The civil wars of the nineteenth century, for instance, were armed confrontations between men and the victims were men. But in the period of mid-twentieth century Colombian history, known as *La Violencia*, for the first time there were victims among both sexes, and rape, torture and mutilation of pregnant women as heavily symbolic acts of war against the other side. Today, she argues, maternity is not a motive of violence against women, partly because women are seen increasingly as social and political actors and the culture of the war is more instrumental than ideological. While the percentage of women who are victims of homicide of all kinds is relatively low, between 7 and 8% of the total and slightly higher (between 8 and 11%) as a percentage of political assassination, murder is now the second cause of death for women between 15 and 39 years old.[37] Women also form the largest group amongst the internally displaced, making up 58.2%, according to 1997 estimates. Women and men also experience and cope with displacement differently. Meertens estimates that about a third of refugee households in Colombia are headed by women.[38] In 1994 I spent some time with the widows living in squalor and abandonment in the shantytowns of Monteria, Córdoba. They had fled the violent assassinations of their husbands in Urabá, fleeing at night with as many as five children. My own experience confirmed Meertens' conclusions that the 'magnitude of the personal drama affecting them was striking, but so also was their fortitude in assuming responsibility for the survival of their children and the reconstruction of their lives and social ties.'[39] The question that needs to be asked is how does this experience affect the socialisation space of the families in which their children grow up? How can the male children in particular be prevented from seeking vengeance against their fathers' deaths in the future or developing violent sub-cultures of their own out of the trauma of their childhood? When I was in Monteria, the local people denied displaced children access to local schools, as they were considered the children of 'subversives'. There are profound potential problems of identity in formation at stake here, in which general expectations of masculine and feminine responses will play a major role in terms of the recovery of these children and their ability to contribute to building a more peaceful Colombia.

The research of Meertens and a new generation of feminist and gender aware scholars is opening up these questions. Women themselves are beginning to organise and dare to appear on the streets to protest at the violence and war. In Yopal, Casanare, a town where levels of violence are extremely high, 50 women dared to march in the centre of the town in November 2001 on the International Day of Non-Violence Against Women.[40] In Bogotá, on July 25, 2002, 20,000 women from all over Colombia marched through Bogota to protest against the war, and one of them declared:

> 'Women suffer retaliation because of our love. We are killed for being girlfriends, friends, mothers, sisters, lovers of policemen and soldiers, guerrillas or members of the AUC. We are publicly humiliated because of our clothes, we lose the right to walk freely in the streets, we are selectively assassinated as 'auxiliaries' of the other side.'[41]

The actions of women help open up discussion on the evolution of the family socialisation space in Colombia, a space where even love can be a motivation for assassination, and on how this relates to the ongoing violences in other spaces. Similarly, the work of Clemencia Castro and Lucia Díaz with ex-combatants opens up a whole range of issues around gender, culture and violence. These questions will need to be asked if Colombia's armed actors are ever not only to demobilise but also to deal with their violent pasts in ways that do not reproduce violences in the next generation. They discovered how much harder it is for male rather than female ex-combatants to lay down the gun that has become so much part of their identity that it is almost part of their body. Through their interviews, they found that it is possible for ex-combatants of the guerrillas to rebuild life projects in ways that do not imply an 'an acceptance of the status quo, an accommodation to the inequities and authoritarian logic of the Colombian political system or an attitude of passivity and conformism...With a distance from the authoritarian and anti-libertarian aspects of their history of militancy, many reclaim in their vision of the past and in a prospective political vision of themselves in the future, the validity of an option of social struggle in favour of the interests of the popular sectors.'[12]

These are just some examples of new ways of thinking about violence in Colombia that help build the linkages between the difference violences that make up the Colombian epic.[13] Such new ways of thinking are preconditions, in my view, for a fuller appreciation of the challenges facing Colombia. They do not mean that the political themes are no longer critically important. It just means that the socialisation space of the nation state must be understood alongside the socialisation spaces of the family, the community and associational life, and the violences that have remained embedded in all these spaces in Colombia.[14] It means that perhaps we should consider abandoning our existing forms of categorisation in terms of binary boxes, such as political/social violence, war/peace, private/public. Perhaps the image should be of a continuum of violence, with the most organised violence by armed groups at one end of the spectrum. These armed groups often come out of contexts in which other levels of violence are high, indeed where many perhaps experienced violence in their childhoods.

The gender differentiations must be understood properly and to see how they impact on the high level of male violence against males that the statistics reveal. There are many countries where private violence is high and yet there is no organised public violence; it is necessary to be careful not to read off the one from the other but to explore empirically the connections in given contexts. The explanations must lie in a complex interaction of factors that range from individual experiences of growing up in the family, to community level experiences and the impact of particular nation state formations. In all these spaces of socialisation, identity is formed and shared meanings evolve. If violence remains embedded, tolerated and justified within these spaces, it becomes conventionalised, something normal and expected. Recognising this allows for understanding of the positive actions towards non-violence needed; and what has to happen in the public political sphere as well as the private domestic sphere and in the sphere of community and associational life to facilitate and nurture civil alternatives that do not avoid the substantive issues that divide the society. Ultimately, if violence is not to be perpetuated in Colombia, with old vendettas carried on into new historical moments, participation, tolerance, debate, power realignments in gender, ethnic and class terms must be given a new weight and importance in the society.

The Colombian story has lessons for the contemporary, globally interconnected world in which complementary forms of violence are erupting in many distinct physical locations on the planet and are represented in the increasingly shared cultural reference points of the cinema, the internet and music. Colombia's violences have become a problem for the world and a responsibility of the world, as a result of their links with the exports of drugs and imports of guns. Colombia's elites are battling over how and who will reintegrate Colombia into the global market place to enable it to fulfil its potential as a resource-rich nation. Implicit in much of the political violence today is this struggle between competing civilian and armed elites as well as the war for state integrity between these and the counter-elite of the guerrillas. The paramilitary right have accumulated much land and wealth through primitive, illegal and violent methods and in particular with the forced expulsion of peasants accused of sympathising with the guerrillas. They are looking to legitimise their new wealth. The modernising elite seeks pacification with the de facto assistance of the paramilitary right without allowing them a political stake in the post-war order, though it is likely they will recognise the transfer of wealth. The international community should not ignore these dynamics. The imperative to enter the global market on the present terms of engagement does not help the peace agenda in Colombia; neoliberal economic policies have generated high levels of unemployment in a country which urgently needs to provide alternatives to violence. The global arms trade, drugs consumption, investment patterns, resource extraction and economic realignments through violent expropriations draw international actors into choices that can foster or limit violence. International economic and political engagement with Colombia needs to take the task of peace-building as its driving force and not divorce economic prescription from social reality and thus leave military solutions as the only option from the state and from within society.

However, much of the international community in the wake of September 11th, and led by a belligerent US administration, believes that violence in Colombia can be eliminated with more violence. An authoritarian option imposed from above and outside Colombia will of necessity ignore the efforts of countless Colombians who risk their lives to keep civilian spaces open. They struggle for a Colombia that will not remain under the same kind of political control, defending the same unequal pattern of resource distribution that generated violence in the past. A space for these voices to organise safely, discuss with tolerance of each other in protected public spaces and reflect on the multiple sources of violence in Colombian society is essential if the country is to overcome its past, interrupt the inter-generational cycle of violence and construct a democratic and just peace.

Jenny Pearce, February 2003

Inside Colombia

Introduction

Drugs are not the cause of Colombia's problems, whatever Hollywood or the news might have you think. The conflict began long before the trade in drugs started in Colombia and is rooted in longstanding social inequalities and political exclusion.

The first three chapters of the book look at the history of the war and its human cost. Chapters four and five explain why thousands of poor farmers have taken to growing illicit crops (coca, opium poppies and marijuana) and show the misery caused by the main response, fumigation. The final chapter looks at the United States' role in Colombia. Last but not least, a long section includes facts and figures on everyone who matters in the conflict, a quick reference to all those involved, past and present

This book is an attempt to draw together the most recent research on Colombia and provide a balanced introduction to a country that has suffered more than its fair share of stereotypes and clichés. We include interviews with Colombians on all sides of the conflict; and extracts and material from many sources including human rights organizations, the United Nations, the Colombian ombudsman's office, the Colombian government and security forces, non-governmental organizations and academic work. The aim was for the book to serve as a starting point for further investigation.

The first chapter highlights the grave humanitarian crisis occurring in Colombia. Political life is so polarised in Colombia that there is no agreement about the number of victims, let alone who is responsible for the killings and abuses. We've included, a large amount of statistical data, even though no graph or chart can reflect the level of human suffering they point to. The second chapter provides an overview of Colombian history and, more than any other chapter, relies on other people's work. I owe a debt and an apology to the many historians whose work I have pillaged and ideas I have manhandled into a 30-page précis.

I would particularly like to mention the outstanding collections by Bergquist, Sánchez and Peñaranda, the relevant volumes of the unsurpassed Cambridge History of Latin America and, of course, Jenny Pearce. I encourage the reader to refer to the original works contained in the bibliography. The third chapter focuses on the economy, presenting a picture of inequality, poverty and land hunger, which puts the 40-year civil conflict in its social context.

While the book was being written, the political climate changed both in Colombia and internationally. In February 2002 Colombia's peace process collapsed. In April 2002 Alvaro Uribe Vélez, a man described as Colombia's Ariel Sharon, was elected President. Uribe appealed to the population's disillusion with the peace process and promised to crack down on the rebels, negotiating only from a position of strength. The ease with which Uribe has slotted Colombia's conflict into the global 'war on terror' is worrying, not least because it has allowed a state with the worst human rights record in Latin America to erode civil liberties even further without a murmur from foreign governments. The United Nations' concerns about Uribe's initial security measures are outlined in the first chapter.

Although it is too early to evaluate Uribe's administration (he took office in August 2002) human rights groups had good reason to view it with foreboding. Uribe first came to prominence as a state governor, when he advocated the creation of 'private security and vigilance co-operatives' (*Convivir*). So many of these armed groups evolved into death squads that they were outlawed by the national government in 1999. Uribe was therefore viewed by some as the 'paramilitary candidate' in the 2002 elections – indeed his Liberal opponent, Horacio Serpa, claimed paramilitaries were intimidating voters on his behalf (although not at his behest). Carlos Castaño, the leader of Colombia's largest paramilitary group, the *Autodefensas Unidas de Colombia* (AUC), has also written: 'The social base of the *Autodefensas* consider him their political candidate.'

However, while Uribe shares the paramilitaries' desire to cleanse Colombia of 'subversives', his broader mission is to assert the authority of the state over the whole of Colombia's national territory. Historically, the Colombian State has never controlled the whole country and this is one reason why the rich have so frequently resorted to private security. To defeat the insurgency, the military use the support of irregular forces, which penetrate deeper and instill terror into rural communities. Uribe has announced plans to recruit one million civilian informants and

20,000 rural part-time peasant soldiers, so one can be fairly certain that the problem of illegal paramilitarism, at a local level, will get worse. His ultimate aim is to give the state a monopoly of armed force, so he cannot tolerate (and in this political climate cannot be seen to tolerate) a 10,000-strong national paramilitary organization that is acting with ever-greater autonomy and whose self-aggrandizing leader appears regularly on TV. Uribe has started peace talks with Castaño and it will be no surprise if he and a handful of prominent leaders demobilize, while the rest of the AUC fragments return to being regional paramilitary forces.

To the outsider, the defining image of Colombia is not a paramilitary, but a guerrilla fighter. The book aims to expose the crude lies propagated about the guerrillas while remaining critical of their failings. Two of the most common fallacies about the guerrillas are that they control the drugs trade and are criminals with no political ideals. The guerrilla groups are political organizations formed in reaction to rural poverty, political exclusion and state repression. Nevertheless both main guerrilla groups routinely violate international humanitarian law, most often by kidnapping civilians. No other guerrilla groups in Latin America's history (with the possible exception of Peru's Shining Path) have so systematically violated the rights of the civilian population.

The second half of the book concentrates on the question of drugs. In 1999 I went to southern Colombia to meet coca growers. As I travelled on foot and boat through this remote Amazonian region, it became immediately obvious why it was so hard for these small farmers to make a living from any other crop. There are few roads, only makeshift harbours and no railways. It would cost more to transport a crop of vegetables to the nearest city than a farmer would earn from selling them. When one talks to these hardworking families, who are a bad harvest away from hunger, the rhetoric of waging a 'war' on drugs starts to grate. It becomes plain that the US-promoted solution of spraying farms with herbicides that kill food crops and animals is wholly inappropriate.

Unlike Bolivia and Peru, where the majority of the population is of indigenous descent and chewing coca leaves is a traditional practice, in Colombia most coca is grown by displaced families fleeing poverty and violence. The boom in the cultivation of illicit crops is rooted in rural poverty, land concentration and the globalisation of agriculture. Chapter four looks at the misery caused by chemical spraying and explains why it has failed to stem the flow of drugs. Chapter five traces the genesis of

Plan Colombia, a five-year militarised fumigation programme, hailed as the most ambitious anti-drugs trafficking campaign in history. It presents evidence that in its first year of operation (2000-2001), Plan Colombia harmed the health of thousands of people, killed animals and destroyed food crops and pasture. It argues that by polluting Amazonian rivers with chemicals, Plan Colombia risks causing irreparable environmental damage to a region rich in biodiversity. It questions whether fumigation is the most effective and fairest way to tackle the drugs question when, as the drug appendix shows, the vast majority of cocaine users live in the US and Europe.

If Chapter five takes Plan Colombia at face value as an anti-narcotics initiative, Chapter six considers whether it was, in fact, designed as a counterinsurgency plan to defeat guerrillas in southern Colombia. It considers whether the 'war on drugs' was simply a pretext for continuing US intervention in Latin America from the end of the Cold War. During the Clinton years, Congress banned the government from granting counterinsurgency aid to Colombia and stipulated that military aid could only be used for anti-narcotics purposes. This move stemmed from a desire not to get bogged down in a Vietnam-style war or repeat Reagan's Central American atrocities. Since September 11th 2001 the climate has changed. Congress has approved the first counterinsurgency funds for Colombia since the fall of the Berlin Wall. Hardliners, many of whom were involved in the Iran Contra affair, are back in power at a time when the public seem willing to trade civil liberties for 'security'. Today's anti-terrorist rhetoric is reminiscent of the Cold War, when anti-communism was used to justify support for dictatorships across the Southern Cone, an illegal war in Nicaragua and a scorched-earth campaign in Guatemala so murderous that a national truth commission has defined it as genocide against the Mayan people.

1

Human Rights

Colombia beats many international records. More trade unionists, journalists and mayors are killed here than anywhere else. It has the highest homicide rate in the Americas. Most notoriously, it has the highest kidnapping rate in the world. More than fifty thousand people have died in political violence since 1980 and the death rate is rising.[1] In 1996 there were eight politically-related deaths a day, by 2001 there were 18 a day.[2]

The statistics are so grim and the violence so widespread that it can appear a blur of incomprehensible horror. Sharpening the focus, it is possible to pick out themes: the counterinsurgency war, the dirty war, guerrilla violence and 'ordinary' criminal violence.

The armed forces and illegal paramilitaries are waging a brutal counterinsurgency war in the countryside. Paramilitaries terrorise civilians in order to undercut support for leftwing guerrillas, who have been fighting the State since the 1960s. Horrific massacres have been carried out to instil fear in the rural population. This war has created a humanitarian catastrophe. Two million people have fled their homes since 1985 and the rate of international displacement is rising. In the year 2000, 317,000 people abandoned their homes.

A military-paramilitary alliance of forces is also waging a related 'dirty war' in towns and cities. Civilians who criticise the authorities – community leaders, trade unionists, human rights workers, investigative journalists, councillors, mayors – are viewed as 'subversive' and therefore legitimate targets. 'Social undesirables' (such as the homeless, prostitutes, gays) are also being killed.

The other main source of political violence are the leftwing guerrillas. Guerrillas are responsible for less than a quarter of political killings in Colombia, but are responsible for more than half of all kidnappings. To fund their war against the state, they routinely kidnap civilians for ransom. In the year 2001 the two main guerrilla groups, the *Fuerzas*

Armadas Revolucionarias de Colombia (FARC) and the *Ejército de Liberación Nacional* (ELN) abducted 1,589 people.[3]

Responsibility for political killings

Determining responsibility for political killings is difficult and no figures are entirely reliable. Many crimes are witnessed only by the victims and even in cases where there are surviving eyewitnesses, they are often too scared to talk. Political killings frequently occur in remote areas, making it difficult to establish the facts.

The perpetrators of more than a quarter of political killings remain unidentified. It makes a significant difference to the share of responsibility if unidentified perpetrators are included (see below).

Socio-political homicides, (which comprise political killings and murders of the 'socially marginalized' such as prostitutes, drug addicts, the homeless), extrajudicial executions & forced disappearances.

October 1995-June 2001, where presumed perpetrators were identified.

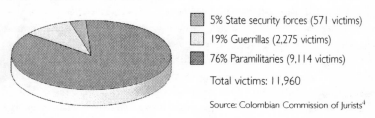

■ 5% State security forces (571 victims)

□ 19% Guerrillas (2,275 victims)

■ 76% Paramilitaries (9,114 victims)

Total victims: 11,960

Source: Colombian Commission of Jurists[4]

Political homicides and extrajudicial executions October 1995-June 2001, unidentified perpetrators included.

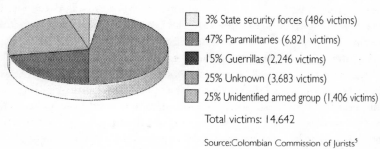

□ 3% State security forces (486 victims)

■ 47% Paramilitaries (6,821 victims)

■ 15% Guerrillas (2,246 victims)

■ 25% Unknown (3,683 victims)

▨ 25% Unidentified armed group (1,406 victims)

Total victims: 14,642

Source:Colombian Commission of Jurists[5]

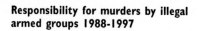

Responsibility for murders by illegal armed groups 1988-1997

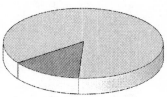

■ 18% Guerrillas (3,532 victims)

□ 82% Other Illegal Armed Groups* (19,652 victims)

Total victims: 23,184

*Paramilitaries, social-cleansing, private justice squads, drugs cartels

Source: Departamento Administrativo de Seguridad (DAS)[6]

It is important to note that most violence in Colombia does not have an explicit political motive. In 2001, 9% of the 26,540 homicides were clearly political assassinations and less than 7% of the people who died violent deaths in that year were killed in combat (on all sides).[7] Colombia has one of the highest murder rates in the world: nine times greater than the United States and 28 times greater than the United Kingdom. In 1991 murder became the main cause of unnatural death. There are many reasons for the high level of violence and Colombia has created a special type of social scientist – the violentologist – to analyse them. Poverty and inequality play a part, but cannot be the only explanation as Colombia is not the poorest country in Latin America nor the most unequal. Colombia's history of recurrent civil wars and resulting enmities are important factors; but it is only in recent years that the level of violence has climbed to such heights: in the 1970s Colombia had a similar murder rate to Brazil, by the 1990s it was three times higher.

Colombia is suffering a crisis of the State that encompasses the political crisis but is broader than it. For political and historical reasons examined in the next chapter, the elite no longer has confidence in the State security forces. Landowners, businesses and local politicians have resorted to hiring private gunmen to defend their interests. The general population has little faith in the justice system, correctly perceiving that there is little chance of any criminal being caught. Only 5% of crimes in the 1990s were investigated and just 1% resulted in convictions, according to government figures; this compares with a conviction rate of 5% in the 1970s and 20% in the 1960s.[8] Drugs are not the cause of this crisis, but have exacerbated it. During the 1970s and 1980s, the establishment turned a blind eye to – or shared in the profits of – the drugs trade, enabling the cartels gradually to undermine the judiciary and penetrate the state apparatus. The cartels followed a policy of *plata o plomo* [silver or lead] to cow the legal profession. Forty judges and lawyers were killed each year between 1979 and 1991, and many more fled the country, left their jobs, kept quiet or accepted bribes. Similarly many police officers were corrupted or killed. This has fatally undermined the rule of law in Colombia. It has also led to a proliferation of armed criminal gangs and professional hitmen known as *sicarios*.

Comparative murder rates 1995	
	Murders per 100,000
Britain	1.4*
France	4.6
USA	8.0
Peru	11.5
Mexico	20.0
Brazil	24.6
Colombia	72.0

*1998
Sources: National governments[9]

Homicides in Colombia 1982-2000	
	Murders
1982	10,580
1990	24,279
1992 (highest)	28,260
1998	23,133
1999	24,621
2000	26,540

Source: Colombian National Police.[10]

The counterinsurgency war

As dawn broke on July 15, 1997, two hundred paramilitary gunmen occupied the small town of Mapiripán, in eastern Colombia. They rounded up the town's leaders and began to search for peasants who they believed had taken part in recent protests against coca eradication. A number of residents, as well as people arriving on a river-boat, were detained. They were taken to the local slaughterhouse, where they were bound and tortured, before having their throats slit. The first man to be killed, Antonio María Herrera, was hung from a hook, while the assailants chopped up his body and threw the pieces into the Guaviare River.[11] Sinaí Blanco, a boatman, and Ronald Valencia, the local airstrip manager, were decapitated.[12] At least 22 people were killed.[13] Most of the bodies were thrown into the river and were disembowelled so that they would not float.

Judge Leonardo Iván Cortés reported hearing the screams from the slaughterhouse for five days while paramilitaries tortured and interrogated their victims. He sent five written pleas for help and made eight telephone calls to the regional authorities. In one letter he wrote:

'Each night they kill groups of five to six defenceless people, who are cruelly and monstrously massacred after being tortured. The screams of humble people are audible, begging for mercy and asking for help.'[14]

But neither the police nor the local army unit – the Joaquín Paris Battalion – responded until the paramilitaries had left the town five days later.

The two hundred gunmen had arrived at San José del Guaviare airport days before the massacre, but the army made no attempt to apprehend the men. General Jaime Humberto Uscátgui, commander of the Seventh Brigade, the regional army division, later tried to falsify documents relating to the massacre.[15] Judge Cortés and his family subsequently left Colombia after receiving death threats.

Carlos Castaño, the leader of the paramilitary group responsible, the *Autodefensas Campesinas de Córdoba y Urabá* (ACCU), told reporters there would be 'many more Mapiripáns'. He was right. The number of massacres rose from 286 in 1997, to 403 in 1999.[16] In the first six months of 2000, there were 235 massacres, in which 1,073 people died.

Massacres 1991-1999

	1991	1992	1993	1994	1995	1996	1997	1998	1999
Victims	929	922	783	448	607	821	1428	1366	1865
Massacres	166	184	151	86	139	188	286	235	403

Source: Colombian Ombudsman's Office & UNHCR[17]

Paramilitary groups, linked to the armed forces, were formed in the 1980s ostensibly to fight guerrillas. A United Nations report for the year 2000 stated:

> 'The paramilitaries claim to be a counterinsurgency force. In practice they almost exclusively attack defenceless civilians in operations of deliberate and surprising cruelty involving large deployments of armed men for purely punitive ends.'[18]

They carry out massacres as part of a strategy to eliminate real or perceived support for guerrillas among the rural population. It is a tactic known as 'leaving the fish without water'. AUC leader Carlos Castaño told one reporter: 'We realised that we could isolate [the guerrillas] and saw that this was a strategy that had very good results'.[19] Methods such as sawing off limbs and throwing acid in victims' faces have been used to terrorise. The UN report stated:

'The majority of the massacres were committed during violent paramilitary raids...The common characteristic of these massacres was the deliberate and extreme cruelty involved, including utter atrocities inflicted on those accused of sympathising with the insurgents. They caused unease and terror among the civilian population.'[20]

Responsibility for massacres in 1998

	Paramilitary	Others	Guerrillas	Armed Forces
Victims	52%	23%	21%	4%
Massacres	48%	28%	20%	4%

*Others include individuals, gangs, common criminals, social-cleansing squads, privately-hired gunmen, drug traffickers and unknown.

Source: Colombian Ombudsman's Office and UNHCR

One instance of terror in recent Colombian history led the Colombian ombudsman to say 'the chainsaw massacre is not a movie in Colombia'.[21] On April 12, 2001, during Easter week, five hundred AUC paramilitaries descended on Alto Naya, a remote mountainous region in southern Colombia inhabited by indigenous communities. The paramilitaries trekked from village to village, murdering inhabitants with chainsaws. 'Dead bodies were left strewn in the road'[22] reported the ombudsman. 'A 17-year-old girl had her throat cut and both hands also amputated,' he said. 'The remains of a woman were exhumed. Her abdomen was cut open with a chainsaw.'[23] The exact number of victims is unknown. The ombudsman's office confirmed the existence of 22 corpses, but since many bodies were thrown into gorges and rivers, it is estimated that the death toll was closer to 40. The Spanish human rights group Equipo Nizkor reported that more than 100 people were killed.

Like Mapiripán, there is strong evidence that the military colluded with the paramilitaries in Alto Naya. The ombudsman's report into the massacre concluded:

'It is inexplicable how approximately 500 paramilitaries could carry out an operation of this type without being challenged in any way, especially since the area that these men entered is only twenty minutes from the village of

Timba, where a base operated by the Colombian Army is located and has been staffed since March 30 of this year.'[24]

The dirty war

The same paramilitary-military alliance is waging a dirty war in towns and cities. The first targets of this systematic killing campaign were leftwingers, trade unionists and grassroots community activists. In the 1990s it was extended to anyone who criticised the military: human rights workers, employees of the ombudsman's office, journalists, local state officials, mayors, councillors and even national congressmen. All fell under the category of 'subversive'. 'Anti-social elements' (prostitutes, drug-addicts, gays, homeless) were also targeted. The United Nations report states:

> 'As regards "selective" killings, during the period covered by this report [year 2000] municipal officials, candidates for a variety of popularly elected posts, demobilized servicemen, indigenous persons, academics, students, trade unionists and human rights defenders, among others, met violent deaths at the hands of paramilitaries.'[25]

Attacks on trade unionists

1996	1997	1998	1999
253 assassinations	156 assassinations	91 assassinations	69 assassinations
101 deaths in 14 massacres	9 kidnappings	319 death threats	4 disappearances
16 disappearances	342 displaced	3 disappearances	676 death threats
5 attacks on union offices	278 death threats	9 kidnappings	6 attacks on union
	10 disappearances	530 displaced	headquarters

Source: Escuela Nacional Sindical[26] & CUT

On average three trade unionists were killed each week during the year 2001. The Colombian trade union congress, *Confederación Unitaria de Trabajadores* (CUT), estimates that since 1986, 3,800 union leaders and activists have been assassinated. Many others have fled their homes following death threats. Teachers are one of the most targeted groups: in the department of Antioquia, 32 teachers were killed between January 2000 and March 2001.[27] They are chosen because of their perceived position of 'influence' in the community and because the teachers' union, Fecode, has a record of militancy. A young teacher (28) and trainee teacher (26), who were both too scared to have their names published, described how working in Antioquia left them with a constant feeling of fear and unease. 'I don't talk to members of any armed group,' one said, 'not even the police.'

Oil workers are another heavily repressed sector. At least 125 members of the oil workers' union, *Unión Sindical Obrera de la Industria del Petroleo* (USO) have been killed in the last decade. At the time of writing in 2002, the most recent murder was that of Aury Sará, president of the Cartagena branch of USO. He was kidnapped by gunmen on November 30, 2001. His body and that of his bodyguard were found on wasteland on 5 December. Many other public sector workers have also been attacked. In December 2000, Wilson Borja Díaz, the president of Colombia's public sector union, Fenaltrase, and a leading member of the CUT, was shot by gunmen who, following judicial investigations, were found likely to have been active and retired military and police officers.[28] Borja survived and after temporarily fleeing the country, returned and was elected to Congress.

Killings of state officials 1996-99

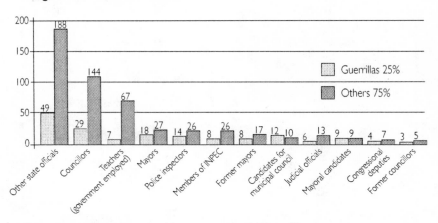

* Others are paramilitaries, privately hired gunmen, armed gangs, drug traffickers

Source: Colombian intelligence service, DAS. Published by Vice President's Office

Human rights workers

Human rights workers are viewed as a threat because they document abuses committed by the military and the paramilitary.[29] They have been victims of selected assassinations for two decades, but in the late 1990s the AUC made them a priority target. Carlos Castaño said:

> '[This] marks the beginning of a regrettable, but inevitable stage in the conflict...We do not want to create panic in the non-governmental organisations, but we do call for a purge of guerrillas from said organisations, a call we extend to the human rights department of the Attorney General's office'.[30]

One group which came under particular attack was the Association of Family Members of the Detained and Disappeared (Asfaddes). Asfaddes member Elizabeth Cañas Cano was shot dead on June 11, 2000 near her office. Two other members, Angel Quintero and Claudia Patricia Monsalves, were disappeared in Medellín, Antioquia, on October 6, 2000. After this date, the group received constant death threats, including one in which a woman could be heard crying and begging for

---

Mirabel López Aros is 43, a single mother with six children. In December 2000, she fled from 'armed groups' in Guaviare, eastern Colombia. She came to the city of Villavicencio, but found it hard to make ends meet. 'I'm the head of the family, I have to earn my money to feed my children, but I couldn't find a job.'

She built her family a makeshift house in a shantytown. Three and a half thousand families who had fled the war in the countryside live there. 'The conditions are inhuman, corrugated iron and plastic sheeting. All we want is a dignified life'.

The city's mayor tried to evict the families and twice sent in armed police, who used tear gas and dogs. But the families, who had been forced to abandon their homes once before and had nowhere to go, formed a community association to campaign for the right to stay. Mirabel was elected vice-president of the association.

On August 20, 2001 the families of the community held a bingo night to raise funds. Gunmen burst into the community hall and started shooting. A community teacher, Pau Pinto, was killed. Mirabel was shot and injured.[31]

> **Luisa Cristina Puig Jiménez** is 40. 'My husband works in a dental factory. A month ago, he went fishing with two friends. They all disappeared. I think they were kidnapped by the FARC. I haven't heard anything and they have not asked for a ransom. Not knowing is unbearable. The pain is indescribable.
>
> Every week, I take a photograph of him and stand with other wives and mothers in the central plaza in Medellín. Some have had their loved ones taken by the FARC and some by the paramilitaries. We are all suffering.'

mercy as though she were being tortured. The group temporarily stopped its activities in December 2000 to protect the lives of its members.

The regional human rights corporation in northeastern Colombia, Credhos, was another victim of the paramilitary onslaught. Seven Credhos members have been shot dead and twelve have had to flee the region since 1992.

Collusion, lies and impunity

The government of Andrés Pastrana (1998-2002) claimed that the human rights situation in Colombia was improving. It admitted that there had been 'isolated' cases of collusion between the military and paramilitaries in the past, but asserted that the government was doing all it could to crack down on them. Nobody else agreed. In 2000, a United Nations report stated:

> 'Paramilitary operations against the civilian population have been stepped up in intensity and frequency; far from diminishing, they have increased; but they have not encountered any governmental action aimed at stopping them.'[32]

Furthermore, the Colombian Office of the UN Human Rights Commission said that the government had hindered its work:

> 'The [UN] Office has also experienced some difficulties in dealing with the Government. Bodies through which, since starting up operations in Colombia, it has been providing the State with support and advice...have been dismantled, sidelined by key Government policies...the overwhelming

> ▓ **José** is a mechanical engineer who worked as a handyman in a small town in Chocó, northern Colombia. He was a community activist, who helped to set up a local health centre. He and others launched a campaign for a pipeline to bring clean running water to the community. 'The pipeline was never built and after we denounced the corruption of the municipal councillors, death threats were pushed under our doors...Two of my cousins were killed ...We had no electricity in our houses, and a few years later, I took part in a community strike demanding that the council give us electricity... My friends told me to watch out because the police had taken my photo. I started sleeping in different houses. In August 2000, four paramilitaries came to where I was staying, they beat me up and fractured one of my bones... I went to the police, but they said they couldn't do anything... Then one policeman, who was a friend, told me that the paras were planning to kill me. I left town early in the morning on August 16, 2000. I lost everything I had built in ten years and I lost my four-year-old daughter [who stayed with her mother]. I went to Bogotá and stayed in a cheap hostel, but I couldn't find work. It's hard to find a job when you are 42. I used to weigh 97 kg and now I weigh just 82 kg. I feel like the state has abandoned us.'

majority of Governmental responses to Office communications about specific cases and situations (such as early warnings) have been unsatisfactory, inoperative and purely bureaucratic.'[33]

Over 80% of arrest warrants issued by the Attorney General's office against alleged paramilitaries, including 22 warrants against Carlos Castaño, have not been carried out. The number of arrests of alleged paramilitaries fell from 120 in 1998 to just 65 in 2000. Government officials told Human Rights Watch that the military either refused to send forces to make the arrests or gave paramilitaries prior warning.

The Pastrana government devoted more energy to an international whitewashing campaign. The Human Rights Watch investigation concluded:

> 'The Pastrana administration has spent a great deal of energy, money and time on a public relations campaign designed to show that it has made significant progress in improving human rights protections. That campaign generates a blizzard of reports, statements, graphs, tables, press releases, and pamphlets asserting that notable gains have been achieved. Yet after a review of many of these materials, Human Rights Watch concluded that they are notoriously unreliable, occasionally contradictory, often fictitious, sloppy and frequently plain wrong.'[34]

The PR drive was particularly important because President Pastrana was trying to persuade foreign governments to contribute to Plan Colombia. One element of this propaganda campaign was to highlight the fact that abuses by military officers had fallen. Figures from the Colombian Commission of Jurists show that between 1993 and 2000 the armed forces' responsibility for human rights violations fell from 54% to 4% and one explanation for this could indeed be that the armed forces had cleaned up their act.[35] However there is a another possible explanation: that in order to improve the military's image and to prevent it from being directly implicated in human rights abuses, the job of physically carrying out the atrocities was passed to the paramilitaries while the army's role shifted to providing 'logistical' support.

Given the abundant evidence presented by the United Nations, the Colombian ombudsman's office, the Attorney General's office and human rights groups, that collusion between paramilitaries and the military is more widespread and more brazen than ever before, the latter argument is more convincing.

A 2001 Human Rights Watch report stated:

'Human Rights Watch has documented abundant, detailed and compelling evidence that certain Colombian army brigades and police detachments continue to promote, work with, support, profit from and tolerate paramilitary groups, treating them as a force allied to and compatible with their own.

At their most brazen, the relationships described in this report involve active co-ordination during military operations between government and paramilitary units; communication via radios, cellular telephones, and beepers; the sharing of intelligence, including the names of suspected guerrilla collaborators; the sharing of fighters, including active-duty soldiers serving in paramilitary units and paramilitary commanders lodging on military bases; the share of vehicles, including army trucks used to transport paramilitary fighters; co-ordination of army roadblocks, which routinely let heavily-armed paramilitary fighters pass; and payments made from paramilitaries to military officers for their support.'[36]

A United Nations report published in February 2001 repeated:

'The Office has seen for itself the alarming consolidation and spread of the

> ▨ **Alberto Rodríguez** is 67 years old and has five children and one granddaugher. 'I used to have a little farm and a pharmacy in Vichada. The FARC ordered me and my family to leave. They burned the pharmacy shop to the ground. I don't know why. Maybe it's because I didn't want to get involved with any armed group or maybe it's because I am an evangelical Christian.
>
> I came to Villavicencio with two months' rent, but then I couldn't find any work and the money ran out. I started selling bits and pieces – tissues, fruit – at traffic lights. I helped to set up an association of *micro-empresas* (small businesses). There are now 73 families in it, we sell fruit, sweets, knicknacks, on the street. Times are very hard: some families daughters' have taken to prostitution. We don't want charity, we want loans.'
>
> [There have been numerous cases of harassment of evangelicals in guerrilla-held areas. The FARC say they represent US interests.]

paramilitaries and their growing operational capacity...In its constant visits to rural areas the Office kept being told of and witnessing many signs of negligent attitudes and persistent close ties between some members of the security forces and paramilitary groups.'[37]

The UN stated that it informed the government of numerous paramilitary bases, but no action was taken:

'As long ago as 24 March [2000] the Office told the authorities of a paramilitary base on "La Iberia" farm, municipality of Tuluá (Valle del Cauca); by the time this report was completed, however, it had not been notified of any action taken in response. In "El Guamo", in the Montes de María (Bolívar) region, there is a paramilitary base whose location has even been acknowledged to this Office by the Brigade I authorities in Sicelejo (Sucre). Apparently, it was from this base that the Ovejas and El Saldo massacres were ordered. In San Blas (Bolívar), there is another paramilitary base that controls access to Santa Rosa and Simití. In May, the Office informed the authorities of another paramilitary base in "El Jordán", municipality of San Carlos (Antioquia). Counter-guerrilla Battalions No. 14, "Granaderos", and No. 42, "Héroes de Barbacoas", are stationed 20 minutes away. The paramilitaries have remained at all the sites observed all year, committing killings and massacres in the towns and countryside nearby.'[38]

The armed forces have integrated the paramilitaries into their counterinsurgency strategy; numerous witnesses have told human rights investigators that army units have driven through their villages warning that if they don't co-operate 'the men who chop people up' will follow.

The military can commit these crimes knowing there is very little chance of being prosecuted. Only one general has ever been convicted for crimes relating to paramilitary violence – General Uscategui who 'turned a blind eye' to the massacre of Mapiripán, in which 22 people died. In February 2001 Uscategui was convicted, not of collusion, but of 'omission' and sentenced to 40 months' prison by a military tribunal. This short sentence was hailed as a great step towards improving human rights in Colombia. According to the Ombudsman's office, though, one year on he had still not served his sentence, but was a free man waiting for his appeal.[39]

In November 2001 the special representative of the Secretary General of the United Nations complained that the problem of impunity was worse than ever. She criticised the Colombian government and, in particular, the prosecutor's office (*fisacalía*) for failing to crack down on members of the military who had violated human rights. She cited the example of the retired General Rito Alejo del Río who had collaborated repeatedly with Carlos Castaño's paramilitaries in Urabá and who the government had failed to prosecute. She stated that his was not an isolated case. Far from a cracking down on collusion, she said, the Colombian prosecutor's offices action against human rights abusers was 'diminishing'.[40]

Barrancabermeja: the next step?

Barrancabermeja is an oil port in northern Colombia. Oil workers had a well-organised union in the refineries and the town contained a wide array of community and civic groups. Due to its strategic importance, it attracted leftwing guerrillas – both the FARC and the ELN – who maintained a presence in the area.

Events in Barrancabermeja not only provide a clear example of paramilitary-military collaboration, but also give a chilling indication of where the dirty war may be heading. Paramilitaries have taken control of Barrancabermeja, the first time they have managed to take over a city of this size.

The operation has taken over two years. On May 16, 1998, a heavily-armed unit of the AUC paramilitary group drove into working-class districts of the town – undisturbed by nearby army units – and proceeded to round up residents. Eleven people were killed and 25 were abducted. They have never been seen since.

In 1999 paramilitary forces began to take control of surrounding municipalities including San Pablo, Yondó, Cantagallo and Puerto Wilches. Paramilitaries maintained a base just outside San Pablo throughout the year 2000, even though the United Nations Commission for Human Rights informed the government of its existence.

In August, the armed forces announced they could not guarantee the security of international monitoring groups in the region of Bolívar. In September, the regional human rights corporation, Credhos, received this letter:

FOR A COLOMBIA FOR ALL, FREE COUNTRY

BARRANCABERMEJA, SEPTEMBER 28, 2000

PRESS RELEASE, WARNING...

THE AUC IDENTIFIES THE HUMAN RIGHTS WORKERS AND ESPECIALLY MEMBERS OF CREDHOS AS GUERRILLA SYMPATHIZERS, AND FOR THIS REASON FROM THIS MOMENT FORWARD WE CONSIDER THEM MILITARY TARGETS OF OUR ORGANIZATION. IT IS IMPORTANT TO SAY THAT ALL OF THIS CRAP THAT THEY ARE DOING IS THE POLICY OF THE FARC AND ELN GUERRILLAS, SINCE WE KNOW WHO YOU REPORT TO AT THE END OF THE DAY.

THE AUC IS AN ANTISUBVERSIVE ORGANIZATION AND WE ARE GOING TO CARRY OUT A SOCIAL CLEANSING IN BARRANCABERMEJA AND ALL OF COLOMBIA, TO CREATE A COUNTRY FREE OF KIDNAPPING, EXTORTION AND TRICKERY.

WE HAVE IDENTIFIED THE MEMBERS OF CREDHOS AS WORKING FOR THE POLITICAL WING OF THE FARC AND ELN GUERRILLAS. THESE INDIVIDUALS ARE WELL KNOWN TO US AND WE KNOW WHERE TO FIND THEM, THEY DO NOTHING MORE THAN DENOUNCE CRIMES COMMITTED BY THE AUC AND ATTACK US CONSTANTLY AS ENEMIES OF PEACE AND NEVERTHELESS THEY DO NOT PUBLICLY DENOUNCE THE CRIMES COMMITTED BY GUERRILLAS.

WE CARRY OUT THIS CLEANSING FOR THE FUTURE OF COLOMBIA BECAUSE IF WE ELIMINATE THEM WE WILL BE CONSTRUCTING THE COUNTRY WE DESIRE.

WE HAVE IN OUR POWER A CLEANSING LIST AND WE ARE GOING TO GIVE SOME STATISTICS TO THESE S.O.B.S. IF THEY DON'T CLEAR OUT, WE WILL KILL THEM...

CREDHOS...............TWENTY-SOMETHING MEMBERS, GET LOST S.O.B.S
ASFADDES...............3, AND YOU S.O.B.S KNOW WHO YOU ARE [41]

During the year 2000, 569 people were killed in Barrancabermeja, the majority of them left-wingers, trade unionists or community activists. Human rights groups wrote to the police, army and national government warning that a paramilitary incursion was imminent.

On December 22, 2000, paramilitaries entered the working class districts in northeastern Barrancabermeja and, began a house-to-house campaign of intimidation. Families were forced to feed, clothe and accommodate paramilitary fighters under threat of death.[42] Neither the police nor the army took action during this onslaught; on the contrary a military helicopter reportedly hovered over the besieged neighbourhood. Paramilitary roadblocks were established, manned by men who held lists of names, which were checked off before people were allowed to pass. According to one source, the paramilitaries demanded 'safe-conduct passes' which had been distributed to residents by police officers a week earlier.[43] At one roadblock a taxi driver was dragged from his cab and beaten in front of two manned police tanks.[44] At least 12 people were killed during the Christmas period.[45]

In the first two months of 2001, 111 people were killed by paramilitaries or unknown assailants in Barrancabermeja and surrounding areas, according to police figures.[46] Another source, *Medicina Legal*, reported that 200 people died in January alone. In February, the women's group, *Organizición Feminina Popular* and the human rights monitoring group, Peace Brigades International, were declared 'military targets' by the paramilitaries. The killings continued in the following months. According to the police, in March 61 people were killed, in April 29, in May 39, in June 14, in July 37 and in August 28. Bit by bit the paramilitaries established their control over Barrancabermeja.

The bishop of Barrancabermeja described the situation in July 2001:

'During the current year AUC presence has increased in the urban area of Barrancabermeja. These units have placed themselves strategically at various points in the town, even used family homes as camouflage, or occupied houses, so that people have been forced to leave their homes. Their penetration strategy includes selective assassinations for 'social cleansing', threats and intimidation, and disruption of communications by destroying telephone exchanges, leaving large areas of the population with no service.

The AUC have organised their own night-watch networks. They call meetings of the population to impose their own rules of civic life. They publicly judge and punish people, impose social tasks on those whom they consider guilty, or point them out to the community.

In addition they have struck hard at organisations which defend Human Rights and popular social organisations, stigmatising their leaders and hindering their social action, as happened with the Women's Popular Organisation (OFP). They have taken control over the so-called 'Petrol Cartels', whose quotas enable them to finance themselves amply.'

The police and the local brigade of the army (the fifth brigade) did nothing to stop this paramilitary takeover. On the contrary, residents reported that paramilitaries openly talked to police and military officers on street corners. It defies belief that the national government did nothing to stop paramilitaries taking over a town of 250,000 inhabitants. The interior ministry claimed that 150 troops were sent to Barrancabermeja in January 2001, but even these minuscule numbers appear to be false: the military authorities in Barrancabermeja told Human Rights Watch that just 45 special forces soldiers had been sent.

According to the Jesuit priest Francisco de Roux, paramilitaries represent a sizeable section of the Colombian elite, who now believe that only a Pinochet-style 'solution' will be adequate to defeat the guerrillas. They think it is necessary to eliminate any possible breeding ground for subversion, whether it be trade unions, community or human rights groups, and think that only a totalitarian dictatorship, lasting for at least two generations, will achieve this. In Father De Roux's view, Barrancabermeja is the first step along this path.

Guerrilla violence

There are two main guerrilla groups in Colombia, the FARC and the ELN. The FARC, which has links to the Communist party, has up to 18,000 fighters and controls about a third of the country. It is fundamentally a peasant army which was formed by poor settler-farmers in the 1960s. Stark inequality in the countryside continues to be its main reason for existence today. The ELN is much smaller, it controls no territory and has about 3,500 fighters. It was formed in the 1960s by middle class intellectuals, inspired by the Cuban revolution, but today its recruits are drawn mainly from the rural poor and urban unemployed.

Organización Feminina Popular (OFP)

Gloria Amparo Suárez and Edilsa Beltran work for the women's group OFP.
The group trains women in skills such as dress-making, ceramics, cooking. It also runs
workshops on health and provides emotional support for women who have lost
relatives in the conflict. It has set up a library on human rights issues and runs cheap
'popular cafes'. It was established in 1972 by the Catholic Church but has since become
autonomous.

On 27 January 2001, paramilitaries came to the OFP centre in Barrancabermeja and
demanded the keys. Gloria was there: 'My immediate reaction was anger and indignation
and I refused. The men left, but said they would be back soon and ordered us 'to get the
hell out' of Barrancabermeja. Only afterwards did I feel scared. We had a discussion and
we decided that we would not let fear defeat us and we decided to stay.'

'We appealed to all peaceful groups to support us and on 8 March 2001,
International Women's Day – which is not widely celebrated in Colombia – more than
1,000 people marched through Barranca with us, despite the danger, to show their
solidarity.'

Edilsa says: 'The paramilitaries are trying to create a climate of fear and intimidation.
Women have been forced to let paramilitaries stay in their houses and cook and wash
for them. One woman was forced to walk round the city with a sign saying 'I am a
prostitute' to humiliate her. Barranca used to be a lively town, with a nightlife and people
sitting out in the streets. Now people are scared, they go straight home from work, and
stay in their houses in the evenings. People are scared about who they can talk to.
We are determined to overcome this fear. These are our slogans:

'Women don't give birth or nurture life for war'

'It's better to live with fear than let fear stop you living'

Gloria is 33 and has two children aged 6 and 7. Edilsa is 38 and has three children,
aged 21, 17 and 7.

Membership of the guerrilla groups soared in the 1980s and 1990s, in response to state repression and economic crisis. Their behaviour deteriorated dramatically during the same period. The guerrillas have always used kidnapping as a form of extortion, but since the 1990s abductions have risen to an unprecedented level. As the territorial war intensifies, the guerrillas have also committed massacres of rural civilians and prompted thousands of families to flee their homes in fear.

In recent years the guerrillas have chosen to prioritise military objectives above any other consideration. This is perhaps a natural tendency for any armed group, but it has strengthened since the 1980s. In that decade the FARC agreed to a truce and formed a broad political coalition, the Unión Patriótica (UP) to stand in elections. Three thousand UP candidates and supporters were killed by death squads, including two UP presidential candidates. The fate of the UP not only made the FARC extremely cynical about the Colombian state, but weakened its faith in any type of civil political action. The rise of the paramilitaries in the 1990s simply confirmed their view that the elite were not to be trusted and strengthened the position of military hardliners within the guerrillas. They now have a jaded view of politics and dismiss all political activity as worthless unless it furthers their own military objectives, while civilians are regarded simply as potential recruits or enemies. Their narrow and rigid war-strategy has led them to massacre rural civilians on the grounds that they are paramilitary 'sympathizers' and it has led them to kidnap more and more civilians.

Kidnapping

The guerrillas were responsible for 58% of the 13,364 kidnappings in Colombia during 1997-2001. The FARC abducted 3,343 civilians and the ELN abducted 3,412 civilians in that period. Sometimes the guerrillas kidnap politicians or diplomats for propaganda purposes, but in the vast majority of cases the motive is purely monetary. Kidnapping

Outcomes of kidnappings in 2001*

Outcome	Number
Freed	1021
Still captive	956
Rescued	662
Freed Under Pressure	102
Died in Captivity	79
Escaped	36
Total	**2,856**

*to mid December 2001

Source: País Libre (police figures)[47]

is the second-largest source of income for the FARC and the largest source for the ELN.

Children are frequently abducted: of the 1,195 kidnappings carried out in the first five months of 2001, 243 (20%) of the victims were below the age of 18. In the year 2000, a three-year-old boy, Andrés Felipe Navas Suárez, and a five-year-old girl, Clara Olivia Pantoja, were kidnapped by the FARC in Bogotá and taken to the guerrilla-controlled zone in the Amazon until their parents paid a ransom, according to the United Nations.[19] Old people are not spared either: 129 (11%) of those currently kidnapped were above the age of sixty.

The guerrillas are notorious for carrying out mass kidnappings or *pescas milagrosas* [miracle catches] as they describe them. In July 2001, the FARC stormed a residential apartment block in Neiva and abducted 15 people, seven of whom were under the age of 18. The ELN, which is militarily weaker on the FARC, relies more on mass kidnappings in order to strengthen its negotiating hand with the government. On May 30, 2000 the ELN kidnapped an entire church congregation in Cali – 143 men, women and children – and in September 2000, the group abducted 53 people who were having Sunday lunch with their families in restaurants in Cali.

Massacres and threats

The guerrillas' strategy differs from the paramilitaries, in that they do not regard civilians as their primary targets. The FARC, in particular, frequently engage in combat with the armed forces and also attack police

Massacres

	1998		1999	
	Massacres	Victims	Massacres	Victims
FARC	31	161	47	219
ELN	13	112	13	44
Joint FARC-ELN	31	161	47	219
Other guerrillas	1	3	3	16
Total	46	287	65	285

Source: Colombian ombudsman & UNHCR[18]

stations (which they regard as military targets). However, with the intensification of the war, the practice of the guerrillas is beginning to resemble the paramilitaries in one way – that of murdering villagers suspected of sympathising with the other side. In 1999 the FARC carried out 47 massacres in which they killed 219 civilians, according to the United Nations. The ELN carried out 13 massacres killing 44 civilians. In joint FARC-ELN operations, they massacred another 219 people.

The guerrillas have prompted thousands more to flee their homes in fear. Although the guerrillas are responsible for just 30% of displacement cases, this nevertheless means that they caused 74,530 people to abandon their homes in 1997, 107,800 to flee in 1998, and 80,640 to flee in 1999. These figures are based on the testimony of displaced families and compiled by the charity Codhes.[50]

Abuses in the demilitarised zone

In December 1998, the government, implicitly recognising that the FARC controlled great swathes of southern Colombia, agreed to withdraw troops from 16,000 square miles in the departments of Caquetá and Meta, in order to create a neutral zone in which to hold peace talks. This demilitarised zone, known as *el despeje,* existed until February 2002, when the peace process collapsed and government troops were ordered to 're-take' the area.

The level of violence in the demilitarized zone is a sensitive subject: one of the reasons the government gave for ending the peace process was the FARC's abuse of human rights within the zone. Given the controversy, it should be noted that the level of violence (as reported by human rights groups) was lower than the national average.[51] This is unsurprising because it was the only place in country where there were no opposing armed groups fighting each other – the FARC was the only military force. It is very hard to ascertain how far the FARC abused its authority because there was no official or independent monitoring. According to Human Rights Watch, the FARC 'established a pattern of abducting civilians suspected of supporting paramilitaries groups, many of whom are later killed'.[52] The group directly investigated three such killings during a two-month visit and was informed of 20 more cases. According to the Colombian Ombudsman, there were 23 extra judicial killings and 22 abductions in the first 20 months of the zone's existence, although it could not confirm that the crimes had been perpetrated by the FARC.

What is known is that thousands of people fled the zone after receiving direct threats or in fear. The author spoke to numerous displaced people living in the shantytowns of Villavicencio, Meta, who had left after receiving threats from the guerrillas. According to the charity Codhes, 3,700 people left in 1999.

One crucial point about the zone – which in the press was frequently referred to as a 'guerrilla safe haven' or 'guerrilla enclave' – was that some 100,000 civilians lived there. These residents were never asked if they wanted the zone to be established and were given no warning of its disappearance. Now many risk being targeted as 'guerrilla sympathisers'.

Guerrilla violations of humanitarian law

Human Rights Watch has criticised the FARC for its use of indiscriminate weapons that frequently kill civilians and violate international humanitarian law. One of the most common is the gas-cylinder bomb: domestic gas containers normally used to power household stoves are loaded with fuel and shrapnel, then placed in a tube packed with dynamite. The bombs, which are normally fired from the back of a pick-up truck, are impossible to aim accurately and have exploded in residential homes, shops and health centres. In one terrible case in May 2002, a gas-cylinder bomb hit a church in Chocó, killing at least 60 people, mainly women and children, who had sought refuge there.[53]

The FARC, like the paramilitaries, refuse to respect the Red Cross and medical aid workers. After attacks on ambulances by both groups in October 2000, the Red Cross pulled out of medical rescue operations in Colombia for three months. The FARC also threatened to bomb the San Juan de Dios Hopsital, in Antioquia, after staff allegedly treated wounded paramilitaries.[54]

The FARC have also been widely criticised for their use of child soldiers – some as young as ten. Children are not forced to join the FARC, but once they become members, it is very hard for them to obtain permission to leave. Children who desert are subject to the same punishment as adults: the firing squad. The FARC has promised to demobilise all combatants under the age of 15 and in February 2001 freed 62 children.

Journalists

Journalists have long been the victims of intolerance in Colombia. Ninety-three were killed and 74 kidnapped between 1988 and 2000.[55] In the first seven months of 2001, nine were killed, at least 13 received death threats and 17 were kidnapped.[56]

In the 1980s, journalists were the target of Pablo Escobar and the *extraditables* – drug barons fighting extradition to the US. Guillermo Cano, editor of Colombia's oldest newspaper, *El Espectador*, was shot dead on December 17 1986. The editor of Colombia's other respected broadsheet, *El Tiempo*, was kidnapped by the *extraditables* in 1990. Having survived the ordeal of eight months' captivity, Pacho Santos was forced to flee Colombia in 2000, after receiving death threats from guerrillas.

Death squads are frequently hired to kill journalists who offend powerful interests; Oscar García Calderón, an *El Espectador* journalist, was shot dead in Bogotá in February 1998, after covering corruption in bullfights. Juan Camilo Restrepo, the director of a community radio station in Aragón, was killed in October 2000 after reporting several cases of alleged corruption by local officials, and reporter Gustavo Rafael Ruiz, who worked for a radio station in Pivijay, Magdalena, was shot dead in November 2000 by 'a gang of hired gunmen financed by the rich people in the area,' according to his colleagues. He had received threats from people warning him 'to stop reporting bad news about Pivijay'.[57]

Other killings by paramilitaries are more overtly political. Jaime Garzón, a journalist and satirist who worked for Caracol Television, was shot dead by two men on a motorcycle on August 13, 1999. Garzón, a well-known and popular figure, had previously tried to secure the release of people kidnapped by guerrillas. Because of this work, the government asked him to act as a mediator while it set up peace talks with the country's second-largest rebel group, the ELN. Garzón was threatened by Carlos Castaño a few days before he was killed, according to colleagues. His death horrified the public, who attended mourning marches in their thousands; it seemed to demonstrate that the armed groups were leading the country into the abyss of totalitarianism, where not even the jokes of a comedian would be tolerated.

Another shocking case was that of Jineth Bedoya, a woman reporter for *El Espectador*, who was investigating paramilitary violence in Bogotá's Modelo prison. When she arrived at the jail for a prearranged interview with an inmate on May 25, 2000, she was met by armed men who in front of the prison guard, put a hood over her head and forced her into a waiting car. She was beaten and raped, before being found unconscious on the roadside by a taxi driver the following day.

Leftwing guerrilla groups also attack journalists. Of the 12 journalists killed in 2000, three were killed by the FARC.[58] In the first seven months of 2001, the FARC killed three more reporters. Pablo Emilo Parara, a reporter for a local radio station in Tolima, and also the head of a regional Red Cross office, was dragged from his home and shot twice in the head, by suspected guerrillas in June 2001. His body was found dumped on a dirt track with a sign which read 'For Snitching'. Three thousand people attended his funeral in the small southern town of Planadas. Three reporters for the *Voz de La Selva* radio station based in Florencia, Caquetá were killed by the FARC in 2000-2001. The station – an affiliate of the national Caracol network – is owned by the Turbay family which has been declared a 'military target'.[59]

The FARC's press spokesman, Raul Reyes, has been quoted as saying: 'The media have no commitment to the peace process because they make irresponsible accusations, misinform and create scepticism.' He added: 'They are a business sector that is doing nothing for peace... they back the system and are against dialogue'. He defended the practice of kidnapping reporters, stating that 'if a journalist has money, he should pay a levy'.[60]

Source: InterAmerican Press Association & International Press Institute

Humanitarian crisis

The war has caused a human catastrophe: more than two million Colombians have fled their homes since 1985 and thousands continue to leave each month, according to the United Nations. The number of 'internally displaced persons' has risen dramatically: from 27,000 in 1985 to 257,000 in 1997 to 317,175 in the year 2000.

Internal displacement 1985-2000							
Year	1985	1990	1995	1996	1997	1998	1999	2000
Displaced	27,000	77,000	89,000	181,000	257,000	308,000	288,000	317,175

Source: Codhes[61]

In 1999, paramilitaries were responsible for 49% of displacement cases, guerrillas 29%; unidentified armed groups, 17%, and the armed forces, 5%.[62]

Death threats, fear and selected assassinations are the three most common reasons prompting families to abandon their homes. More than three quarters of the displaced come from rural areas, although the proportion from cities is rising, as armed groups make inroads into urban areas. The poor are the main victims of displacement; 54% of those fleeing from rural areas owned no land, and of those who did, 47% had farms of less than ten hectares.[63]

Responsibility for displacement					
	1995	1996	1997	1998	1999
Paramilitaries	35	33	54	47	49
Military	18	16	6	8	5
Guerrillas	26	29	29	35	29
Others	21	22	11	16	17
Military and paramilitary combined	53	49	60	55	54

Source: Codhes and Unicef [64]

Reason for fleeing	%
Threats	34
Fear	18
Assassinations	14
Military conflict	10
Massacres	9
Disappearances	6
Assassination attempts	3
Torture	2
Other	2
Aerial attacks	2

Source: Codhes[65]

Children suffer disproportionately: 70% of the displaced are below the age of 19 and 42% are younger than 14. In total, 1.1 million children were forced to abandon their homes between 1985 and 1999. One young girl describes her experience:

'We used to live in the Valle del Cauca, from where my family was forced to leave because of my parents' troubles. They were threatened and that is why we had to come to Bogotá. We used to live in a village with mountains, trees and animals. It was like being in the countryside. I liked living there because I had friends, I played a lot, I used to run down the mountain and I had five little birds that my father had given me as a present. We arrived here and it was very hard because we were used to our home. I don't know why they detained my father, I just know that he is a good man and he helps other people...I am living with a family who are friends of mine. I feel very sad because I miss my family. I don't say anything about these problems, I feel so lonely, living in a neighbourhood where I don't know anybody and I suffer.'[66]

Hundreds of thousands of families now live in grim poverty in the cities, in shantytowns and slums, having lost their homes and possessions. The displaced receive three months' rent from the government on arrival in the city, but after that have to make their own way. Many squat vacant plots of land and build houses out of tarpaulin and corrugated iron. Most don't have access to basic services; only 32% have a clean water supply, 43% have electricity and 34% access to health services. Seventy-seven percent of children and young people who were receiving formal education before being displaced, did not continue their studies after resettlement.[67]

As well as being uprooted from their homes, the displaced have to live with the trauma caused by the violence they have witnessed and the death of loved ones. Family members are frequently split up and have to bear the agony of uncertainty about each other's fate. Once in the cities, they are looked down on for being poor and for coming from rural backwaters. Perversely, they are often stigmatised as being supporters of one or other of the armed groups.

A displaced girl from Chocó said:

'My father tells me that I can't say in school that I am displaced because people look down on you, but he had to tell the truth to get a place for me in the school...what is happening here is that people look down on you for being poor, for being black and worse still if you are displaced person.'[68]

A bleak picture. But many Colombians do speak out against injustice: Across the country, organisations of the displaced, trade unionists,

His Excellency Álvaro Uribe
President of the Republic of Colombia
Palacio de Nariño
Santa Fe de Bogotá
Republic of Colombia

August 26 2002

Your Excellency

I have the honour to address you to reiterate my concern about the deterioration in the humanitarian situation and human rights in Colombia, which constitutes the main challenge for the future of the Rule of Law.

At the same time, by virtue of my office, I wish to express my anxiety about some of the measures recently announced by the Colombian Government in the matter of public order and civil security, as these could be incompatible with the international standard of human rights and humanitarian law. Measures such as the setting up of networks of informers and the domestic use of weapons by peasant recruits may, within the context of generalised violence and worsening of the conflict, contribute to the civil population becoming involved in the development of military operations, or exposed to risk caused by the obscuring of the principle of distinction.

As I have already expressed to you recently, measures adopted by states to maintain or re-establish public order in exceptional conditions must conform to commitments arising from international conventions. These standards regulate the limits to how the public authority may act when it imposes restrictions on fundamental rights and freedoms.

I am also concerned that the strengthening of military power may contribute to the deterioration of civil institutions or bring about the subjection of civil authority to military power, which would weaken the Rule of Law and increase the rate of violations of human rights.

My concerns also include the constant expansion and consolidation of paramilitary groups and their persistent links with public servants. It is important to fulfil international recommendations on the dismantling of paramilitarism and the removal of those State agents who support or encourage it.
[extract].

Mary Robinson
UN High Commissioner for Human Rights[69]

human rights activists, peace campaigners and relatives of the victims stand up for their rights and the rights of others, despite the fear of reprisals. The words one most commonly hears when talking to these people are 'respect' and 'dignity' – the right to have a voice and be treated as a human being.

It is hard to believe that most of the violence described in this chapter occurred while a peace process was underway (1998-2002). These peace talks collapsed in February 2002 and in May the hardliner Alvaro Uribe was elected on a promise to crack down on illegal armed groups and restore order.

Uribe first came to public attention when, as a state governor in the 1990s, he promoted armed 'private justice and vigilance' groups (Convivir) to combat the guerrillas. So many of these armed civilians' groups evolved into paramilitary death squads that they were outlawed by the national government in 1999. In his 2002 presidential election campaign, Uribe tried to shed his extremist image but paramilitaries still claimed him as 'their man'.

Uribe was inaugurated in August 2002 and a number of his initial measures drew criticism from the United Nations and human rights groups. He immediately gave the military emergency powers by declaring a state of 'internal disturbance' for 90 days, renewable for two additional 90-day periods. His interior minister also announced plans to restore the right to call an indefinite state of siege, which was outlawed by the 1991 constitution. Other proposed constitutional reforms may make it harder to monitor human rights abuses. The government plans to downsize the most important independent human rights monitoring body in Colombia, the national ombudsman's office (*defensoría del pueblo*), by merging it with the attorney general's office.[70] Local ombudsmen (*personerías*), who catalogue abuses at a municipal and state level, are to be abolished altogether.

But Uribe's most controversial measures were a drive to recruit one million informants to work alongside the armed forces and a plan to recruit 20,000 part-time peasant soldiers. These part-timers were to guard their village by day and return home, unarmed, at night. Both could further embroil civilians in the war and exacerbate the proliferation of illegal armed groups.

Massacres 1998-1999

	1998		1999	
	Massacres	Victims	Massacres	Victims
Autodefensas				
and/or paramilitaries	113	716	155	902
Guerrillas				
ELN	13	112	13	44
EPL	1	3	2	12
ERP			1	4
Joint FARC-ELN	1	11	2	6
FARC	31	161	47	219
Sub Total	**46**	**287**	**65**	**285**
Other armed groups				
Unknown armed groups	21	91	70	258
Militias	1	4	1	3
Sub Total	**22**	**95**	**71**	**261**
Armed forces	9	55	6	20
Others				
Individuals	1	4	11	37
Gangs			12	48
Common criminals			7	24
Unknown	29	140	53	203
Social cleansing death squads	15	69	16	60
Drug traffickers			7	25
Sub Total	**45**	**213**	**106**	**397**
Total	**235**	**1,366**	**403**	**1,865**

Source: Colombian ombudsman and UNHCR[71]

Responsibility for violations of human rights and infractions of international humanitarian law 1995-2000 (%)

	1995-2000	2000
Autodefensas	18.96	33.74
Subversion [Guerrillas]	79.39	65.49
Armed forces	1.65	0.77

Source: Armed forces[72]

2 History

The Colombian State has never had control over all of its territory. Since independence there have been local armies, guerrillas, bandits, armed peasants and landowners controlling parts of the country. A glance at the map of Colombia will help to show why. It is a vast and diverse country, sliced by three Andean mountain ranges that historically have been the most populated areas. To the south is the Amazon rainforest and to the east are barren plains: these two lowland regions account for 56% of national territory, but contain less than 5% of the population. To the north is the Caribbean coast, with its own distinctive history. The size and topography of Colombia form the backdrop for the succession of regionalist wars that wracked the country in the nineteenth century, as well as the endurance of armed conflict in the twentieth century and beyond.

The weakness of the State and lack of national cohesion has historical roots which predate the current territorial make-up of Colombia established in 1903. During colonial times what is now Colombia was part of the Viceroyalty of Peru and later Nueva Granada (made up of present-day Colombia, Panama, Venezuela and Ecuador). Colombian territory was split up into three main regions: Cartagena, a bustling Caribbean port and an important colonial military and ecclesiastical centre; the eastern Andes, centred around Santafé de Bogotá, a densely-populated area with large estates worked by indigenous labour; and the western Andes and Pacific coast, where gold mines, worked by African slaves, were the mainstay of the economy.[1]

Along with most of Latin America, colonialism left a legacy of a wealthy, land-owning elite who feared and despised the poor non-white majority. In Colombia, it would be more accurate to say there were a variety of regional elites to whom local power was more important than the abstract concept of a nation.

Part of the Spanish Empire

Before Estimated indigenous population of 3 to 4 million. By 1800 had fallen
1530 to 130,000 due to repression, forced labour and disease.

1533 Cartagena, the first permanent Spanish settlement, founded

1538 Santafé de Bogotá founded

1563 Santafé de Bogotá becomes a Captaincy General within the Viceroyalty of
Perú. The six regions of the Captaincy General were: Cartagena, Santa Marta,
Riohacha, Antioquia, Popayán and Panamá.

1739 Viceroyalty of Nueva Granada is founded (present-day Colombia, Panama,
Venezuela and Ecuador). Santafé de Bogotá becomes the capital of Nueva
Granada.

Independence

These competing regional elites made it virtually impossible to forge a
unified state, and some historians believe the task has barely been
completed today. Cartagena declared independence in May 1810,
followed by Bogotá in July. The subsequent period is known as the *Patria
Boba* [Foolish Country], because the rulers of different regions found it
impossible to unite, making it easy for the Spanish to reconquer the
territory in 1815-1816.

Independence finally came from outside, when the great Venezuelan
military leader Simón Bolívar defeated the Spanish at the battle of
Boyacá in 1819. Bolívar dreamed of uniting South America into one
unified state, but was unable to overcome powerful local interests. In
1821, the new nation of Gran Colombia (now Venezuela, Colombia, and
Panama) was proclaimed in the Constitution of Cucutá, but while
Bolívar travelled south to liberate Ecuador and Peru, the nation began to
disintegrate. He returned to Bogotá and declared himself dictator in
1828, but found it impossible to hold the country together. He resigned
in March 1830 and died in November. On his deathbed he lamented:
'America is ungovernable. Those who have served the revolution have
ploughed the sea.'

Colombia has had fewer military regimes than other Latin American
countries and some historians believe it is because the military forces
which led the independence struggle were not Colombian, but

Venezuelan. In addition, the civilian elite in Colombia was less affected by the independence wars.[2]

Although the independence struggle was led by men inspired by the French and American revolutions, who fought under the banner of the Enlightenment and universal citizenship, the old colonial social structure of vast estates with a backward system of agriculture continued to exist, and the dominant class remained landowners.[3]

The torturous birth of Colombia

1832   Republic of New Granada (present-day Colombia and Panama)
1858-1861 Granadine Confederation
1861-1863 United States of New Granada
1863-1886* United States of Colombia
1886   The unitary Republic of Colombia declared (includes Panama)

*Between 1863 and 1885, there were 50 insurrections and 42 constitutions promulgated in nine different states.

The formation of the Liberal and Conservative Parties

The Conservative Party was founded in 1848 and the Liberal Party a year later. Their main differences hinged on religion (the Conservatives were closely identified with the Catholic Church, the Liberals espoused a secular state) and the constitution. Conservatives supported the centralising ideas of Bolívar and Liberals advocated a federal state.

Traditional Latin American historiography has portrayed Conservatives as great landowners and military leaders, while Liberals were thought to be merchants or professionals. It is not immediately clear that this is accurate in the Colombian case since merchants tended to invest their earnings in great estates and become landowners themselves. It is suggestive that the first Liberal president, General José Hilario López (1849-1853), implemented many reforms that would create the basis for capitalist agriculture (eliminating the state's monopoly on tobacco, abolishing indigenous reserves, emancipating the remaining slaves and introducing direct taxation).[4] In any case, it is clear that within a few generations the merchant-landowner oligarchy was represented in both parties.

Party loyalty and bi-partisan wars

The parties were the first truly *national* organisations in Colombia, at a time when the nation state had yet to take root. Although founded and led by the upper classes, the parties soon developed a mass following and people felt a greater loyalty to their party than to any distant national government. As Gabriel García Márquez notes, Colombians felt they were 'born' Liberal or Conservative.

These loyalties were cemented during successive bi-partisan wars. In the nineteenth century there were eight civil wars, six of which involved the parties. As Liberal and Conservative peasant armies swept through villages committing atrocities, each generation vowed to avenge the last attack and a dynamic of violence followed by reprisals emerged. While party divisions grew deep and bitter between the lower classes, the elite managed to overcome its differences and repeatedly formed coalition governments from 1857 onwards.

The longest and bloodiest of the bipartisan wars was the War of a Thousand Days (1899-1902) in which an estimated 100,000 people died. Liberals lost the war and Conservative presidents ruled the country until 1930. In keeping with an established tradition, Liberals were given cabinet seats in all of these administrations.

The early twentieth century: economy and development 1870-1930

Landowners began to plant coffee as early as 1850, but sales took off in the twentieth century. By 1920 coffee accounted for 70% of exports and Colombia was the world's second-largest supplier. Antioquian gold merchants were the richest in the country and they invested their money in coffee *haciendas*. The north-western region also had a substantial number of smallholders, poorer Spaniards who had been originally attracted by the prospect of gold-panning. The traditional coffee zones of Antioquia and Caldas were distinctive for having a high number of small and medium-sized farms, dotted among the great estates.

The emergence of a class of small coffee growers is central to Colombian history, but another agrarian development, which occurred in tandem, is also vital. In the late nineteenth century, public lands were privatised and the beneficiaries in most of Colombia were the big landlords, who increased the size of their estates. Waves of poor peasants and penniless farmhands, squeezed out by the great landowners in central Colombia, migrated to the lowlands. They expanded the agricultural frontier, in places where the state was barely present; these were the sites of recurring agrarian conflict throughout the twentieth century.[5]

The cities of Bogotá, Medellín and the Caribbean port of Barranquilla grew, while the old colonial centres of Cartagena and Popayán declined. From the 1920s, some textiles and food-processing industries grew up and with them a small urban working class. Like its neighbours, Colombia relied mainly on imported industrial goods which were paid for by exporting primary products (coffee, in this case).

The emergence of a coffee market meant Colombia's insertion into the world economy. Foreign banks provided loans to build railway lines to the ports. During the same period, the US-owned United Fruit Company established large banana plantations on the Caribbean coast. The 1920s are known as a 'Dance of the Millions' as foreign money poured in. US investment rose from US$4 million in 1913 to US$173 million by 1929.

US dominance and the loss of Panama

In 1899-1900 the United States decided to build a canal in the then Colombian state of Panama, the thinnest point of the Central American isthmus and the best place for a trade route linking the Pacific and Atlantic oceans.[6] The Colombian senate refused on the grounds that the terms offered would violate national sovereignty. President Theodore Roosevelt then provoked a rebellion in Panama, sent US marines to 'protect it' and recognised it as a new country in 1903. Construction of the US-owned Panama Canal began in 1904.

Divisions within the elite 1900-1950

As the cities grew and industry developed, a minority nationalist current emerged within the Colombian elite, which broadly speaking represented the interests of urban industrialists, bankers and professionals. They wanted to stimulate the growth of domestic industry by imposing protective tariffs and favoured greater state intervention. This nationalist strategy was advocated by the Radical Liberals, although it won broader support after the Great Depression caused a slump in world trade and the growth of protectionism across the world.

The Radical Liberals wanted to harness the support of the growing labour movement and urban poor, but remained hostile to militant leftwing groups. They were reformers who wanted to improve the lot of the poor, but who felt threatened when the poor organised themselves. This tension between wanting lower-class support, but fearing independent mass action, led the Radical Liberals to oscillate between bursts of radicalism, followed by backtracking or repression.

The majority of the Colombian elite, however, continued to earn its wealth from growing produce for export on large commercial estates and favoured the existing policy of free trade and a small state. From the 1940s onwards they began to accept that the state could play a role in fostering economic development, but remained resolutely opposed to strengthening social and labour legislation (and were certainly not in favour of mobilising the masses). These views were espoused by Moderate Conservatives and Moderate Liberals.

Finally, an ultra-rightwing faction emerged in the Conservative party, which was called 'Historic' or 'Independent' Conservatism. They were ardent Catholics who sympathised with the Falange in Spain, and looked back to the golden days of the Spanish Empire. They won the support of landowners and other members of the upper classes who were horrified by the growth of the cities and the urban 'mob'.

The revolution on its way

In 1930 the Liberals returned to power after over half a century of Conservative rule. Enrique Olaya Herrera (1930-34) headed a mildly reformist government which imposed import restrictions and recognised trade unions. He was followed by the Radical Liberal Alfonso López Pumarejo (1934-38) whose administration was known as 'the revolution on its way' (*la revolución en marcha*). He introduced universal male suffrage, increased state intervention in and protection of domestic industry, restricted the role of the Church, reformed the law to allow expropriation of property, levied taxes on profits and legalised strikes. His term was the highpoint of Radical Liberalism in power and subsequent governments were more cautious.

President Eduardo Santos (1938-42), a moderate Liberal, did not implement many of his predecessor's reforms, although he did not rescind them either. He strengthened Colombia's ties to the United States and backed the Allies in the Second World War. López Pumarejo's second administration (1942-45) was known as the 'reform of the reformer', since it was much less radical. Nevertheless trade unions demonstrated in his defence when he was seized by military officers in an abortive coup attempt in 1944. The Liberal Party's final break with organised labour came under the interim President (Radical-turned-Moderate) Alberto Lleras Camargo in 1945. By ordering troops to repress a Communist-organised strike by dockers and transport workers – the strongest union in the country – on the Magdalena River he effectively broke the strength of the labour movement, ensuring that it was not central to the explosive urban revolt which broke out two years later.

The *Bogotazo* of 1948

There was one Radical Liberal who strayed too far from paternalism and in doing so terrified the elite. Jorge Eliécer Gaitán was a lawyer, from a modest Bogotá family. He was a *mestizo* (mixed race), unlike most traditional politicians who were *criollos* (of Spanish descent). He was an inspiring orator and, in the 1930s, as a congressman and mayor of Bogotá, he lambasted the oligarchy and foreign capitalists, defended peasants expelled by landowners and spoke up for the urban poor.

His radical rhetoric divided the Liberal Party and in the 1946 it chose two presidential candidates, Gaitán and the moderate Gabriel Turbay. During Gaitán's campaign thousands of people gathered to hear him condemn the *país político* – the country of the rich elite – and speak up for the *país nacional* – the real country of the poor. His audience was made up of artisans, shopkeepers, the unemployed and workers. He was a social reformer, not a revolutionary, but the sight of thousands of poor people flooding the streets unnerved the elite. As González Sánchez notes, the moderate themes of economic redistribution and political participation 'were backed by a social mobilisation of such magnitude as to seem to transform their reformist content, leading the forces of the status quo to perceive a threat to the entire social edifice.'

The Conservatives won the 1946 election because the Liberal vote was split, but Gaitán, who was elected Liberal leader in 1947, continued to hold mass rallies in Bogotá. On April 9, 1948, Gaitán was shot dead by an assassin who was immediately lynched by the crowd. A wave of angry protest and mass rioting shook Bogotá. The revolt – known as the *Bogotazo* or *el 9 de Abril* – was in part a frustrated revolution; it failed due to lack of co-ordination, strategy or leadership. *El Bogotazo* was also a spontaneous eruption of impotent rage by the urban poor who attacked and looted government buildings, offices, shops, churches and grand-looking houses.

Immediately after Gaitán's murder, the crowd rushed to the presidential palace. It was invaded and ransacked, but the protestors were later ejected by the military. Many police officers joined in the uprising and handed out guns to the crowds but in the chaos, no one was sure who to attack. A group of university professors, writers and intellectuals formed a 'revolutionary junta' and radical students took over the radio stations. Revolutionary proclamations were broadcast to the nation and in towns and villages across the country, people revolted against the oligarchy. In Barrancabermeja, workers took over the oil refineries and a 'revolutionary council' held power in the town for 14 days, while in many regions peasants occupied their landlords' estates. In Bogotá the junta did not try to seize power, but instead allowed a 'committee of notables', led by the Liberal politician Carlos Lleras Restrepo, to negotiate a deal with the Conservative government. Liberals were invited back into the cabinet and the revolution petered out.

The *Bogotazo* was one element in a longer period of upheaval known as *la Violencia* (the Violence). Historians disagree about the dates: some argue it started in 1946 when the Conservatives came back into government, because at a local level the leadership of the police forces and town councils changed hands, encouraging Conservative peasants to seize land from Liberal peasants and setting off a new wave of bi-partisan violence in the countryside. Traditionally, historians have dated the start of *la Violencia* from the *Bogotazo* in 1948. The first phase of *la Violencia* ended in 1953, with a military coup, although bandits, guerrillas and rural 'resistance communities' continued to fight well into the 1960s.

The barbarity of *la Violencia* was one of its most salient characteristics. Between 1948-53, 200,000 people were killed, 50,000 in 1950 alone. Victims were tortured and mutilated. Gruesome killing methods were invented such as the *corte de corbata* [necktie], which left the victim's tongue hanging from a slit in his throat. Villages were burnt. Women were raped in front their families. Each act of violence sowed the seeds for a reprisal.

La Violencia defies simple explanation. It was partly a civil war between Liberals and Conservatives, in which – like the nineteenth century bi-partisan wars – peasants killed other peasants. In some areas it was a spontaneous social uprising against the landlords and village notables, and in other areas there were conscious attempts to carry out a revolution.[8] In 1950 the ultra-right Conservative Laureano Gómez became President and unleashed a wave of counter-revolutionary repression. The army and police force were politicised to an ever greater degree and terrorised Liberals and other rebellious rural communities. The most notorious police force was known as the *Chulavitas*, famed for their atrocious killing methods.

'Hurricane' 'whirlwind' 'maelstrom' 'cyclone' are the words traditionally used to describe *la Violencia* – the only words adequate to describe what was a complete breakdown of the social order. Bi-partisan war had become a conduit for a host of other conflicts: social and economic, local and personal, which, when taken together, threatened the cohesion of the country. *La Violencia* represented, in however inchoate and anarchic a way, an explosion of repressed fury by the poor against the rich. This social revolt was successfully defeated and, following a period of mediation by the military, the landowning and business classes continued to dominate the country.[9]

Origins of the FARC

La Violencia continued in the form of banditry after the 1953 coup. Most Liberal guerrillas accepted the military's amnesty, but a minority continued to live as outlaws in the countryside. Some were simply intent on revenge and determined to exact reprisals on Conservative villagers, but others had a broader political vision.

Since the 1930s, Communists had been organising with peasants in southern Tolima and south-western Cundinamarca, areas dominated by large coffee estates. They developed a tactic known as armed self-defence, in which groups of peasant families would occupy public lands or an absentee landowner's *hacienda* and set up militia to defend themselves from eviction. During the Conservative onslaught of 1950-53, Communist and Liberal guerrilla-militias were once again formed to defend the villages in this region. Many Liberal peasants from other areas migrated to these 'resistance communities' after their villages were terrorised by Conservative police and army squads. When they were offered an amnesty by the dictator General Rojas Pinilla in 1953, the guerrillas in these areas refused to lay down their arms.

In 1955, Rojas launched a military offensive against the communities – known as the

War of Villarica – which prompted the families to march south in two long columns, defended by the guerrillas. They set up new self-sufficient farming communities in southern Tolima, Meta and Caquetá. In 1964, the government declared these areas 'independent republics' and under the aegis of the US-sponsored Alliance for Progress, launched a new military offensive on one of the communities – Marquetalia. The rebels were eventually forced to flee, but over the next two years, meetings were held with guerrillas across the southwest and in 1966, the FARC was formed. The long history of armed peasant struggle that preceded the formation of the FARC explains the deep-rooted support it has in some rural communities and why it has managed to survive so long.

The National Front

In 1953, at the height of the anarchy and terror of *la Violencia*, when the nation appeared to be disintegrating, General Gustavo Rojas Pinilla led a coup against the ultra-right Conservative government. Under the banners 'Country above the Parties' and 'Peace, Justice and Liberty' he professed to rule in the name of all Colombians and rise above partisan divisions. As well as pacifying most areas of the country by offering all warring groups an amnesty, he introduced many nationalist reforms. He nationalised the oil industry and created the state oil company Ecopetrol. He poured money into public works, building irrigation systems, hydroelectric plants, an Atlantic railway network and a national television centre. He also extended suffrage to women (although there were no elections) and was conciliatory to the trade unions, despite remaining a firm anti-Communist. As support for the regime ebbed, however, it became increasingly repressive.

The traditional parties at first supported Rojas, but grew wary when he began to discuss the creation of a permanent 'Third Force' in politics. Liberal leader Alberto Lleras Camargo began negotiating with the Historic Conservatives and later the Moderate Conservatives (who were reluctant to withdraw their support for Rojas) and the parties agreed to a power-sharing deal. In May 1957, the commanders of the armed forces asked Rojas to step down and in December a national referendum was held in which the voters, exhausted by violence and dictatorship, overwhelmingly endorsed the traditional parties' power-sharing scheme – the National Front. In August 1958, Alberto Lleras Camargo took office as the first of four National Front presidents.

Under the terms of the National Front agreement, the Liberal and Conservatives agreed to alternate the presidency every four years and to divide equally the seats in all legislative bodies (congress, regional assemblies and municipal councils). Mayoralties, governorships and cabinet posts would also be shared out between the parties. All legislation had to be passed by a two-thirds majority of congress and the vote was given to women.

The political system now formally became the exclusive property of the elite. Ministerial posts and other positions of power were seen as prizes to be shared out among a select few. Backroom deals became normal political practice. The lubricant of the system was clientelism: Liberal and Conservative regional bosses maintained their prestige by doling out favours, from large contracts for businessmen to new roads for shantytown dwellers. Their ability to do this depended on their proximity to power and so they were willing participants in the incessant game of political push-and-shove.

The USA's favourite

Its was during the National Front years that the United States began to promote Colombia strongly as the region's model democracy. From the 1950s, Latin America was plagued by military dictatorships (often supported by the United States). However, these were not the ideal regimes to substantiate Washington's claim that the Cold War was an epic struggle between the 'free world' and 'Communist tyranny'. Colombia, with its regularly-alternating civilian governments, was feted by the Eisenhower administration and chosen as the showcase for Kennedy's Alliance for Progress.

This idyllic democracy was, of course, a mirage. Conflict continued in rural areas, and it was during the years of the National Front that Colombia's four main guerrilla groups were founded. These years also saw the increase in size and professionalism of the armed forces – between 1964 and 1968 for example, the number of troops increased from 22,800 to 64,000. US military aid also rose and in 1964 it helped to draw up a comprehensive counterinsurgency plan, the Latin American Security Operation (LASO).

The failure of agrarian reform

With the backing of the Alliance for Progress, President Lleras Camargo established an agrarian reform institute in 1961 aimed at distributing public lands in colonisation zones, as well as idle land on private estates. Even these modest ambitions were blocked by landowners and very little land was given out. Agrarian reform ground to a halt during the administration of Conservative Guillermo León Valencia (1962-66), an ultra-right sympathiser of the Spanish Falange. The Radical Liberal President Carlos Lleras Restrepo (1966-70) tried to overcome the intransigence of the landowners by establishing a grassroots peasant movement, the *Asociación Nacional de Usarios Campesinos* (ANUC), in 1967 to pressure for reform from below. ANUC gradually became independent from the government and increasingly radical, but it became bogged down by internal divisions after attracting many different leftwing groups, particularly Maoists.[10]

The failure to push through an agrarian reform was also due to a change in strategy on the part of the elite. Initially it was thought that agrarian reform was necessary to modernise agriculture because large estates were intrinsically 'backward' and unproductive. ANUC was therefore an attempt to unite the peasants with 'progressive' sectors of the elite against the 'anachronistic *latifundistas*'. However, as large landowners responded well to government incentives offered throughout the 1960s, it became increasingly clear that big estates could be modernised and turned into efficient capitalist enterprises. Misael Pastrana's administration (1970-1974) therefore abandoned agrarian reform, and focused on improving the efficiency and technical proficiency of agribusiness.

Despite all the rhetoric of agrarian reform during the period of the National Front, land ownership became more concentrated, a tendency which accelerated from the 1970s onwards. In 1960, farms of over 500 hectares accounted for 29% of cultivated land; by 1996 they accounted for 60.5%. The effect was to speed up peasant migration to the lowlands, creating a class of poverty-stricken farmers in isolated regions with little infrastructure or state authority.

Political exclusion and the rise of guerrilla groups

Rural poverty was not the only stimulus for the rise of armed insurgency; the rigidity of the National Front system was also a factor. This was a period of rapid population growth and migration to the cities. Bogotá's population, for example, rose from 1.7 million in 1964 to 4.2 million in 1985 and that of Medellín, Cali and Baranquilla also grew. Domestic industry, banking, communications, transport, utilities and public services grew rapidly. A much larger middle class and working class emerged, and with them new political demands that could not be adequately articulated by the two old parties of the traditional elite. Although the FARC was fundamentally a peasant army, other guerrilla groups were formed by frustrated urban middle class radicals who were inspired by the Cuban revolution and impatient at the slow pace of change at home.

The appeal of voluntarism was particularly strong because of the fragility of the civic left. The trade unions came out of *la Violencia* weakened by repression and party rivalries. Peasant organisations had, meanwhile, been decimated by *la Violencia*. Although there were bursts of student protest (particularly in the late 1960s), isolated strikes and a plethora of small leftwing groups, it was not until the late 1970s that combative, independent unions and a popular radical civic movement came together.

Some historians believe that there were longer-term structural reasons for the weakness of the labour movement. Charles Bergquist argues that because Colombia's most important export crop, coffee, was grown by small peasants and not on large plantations (like sugar in Cuba for example), the working class were absent from a key sector of the economy.[11] Traditionally, the best-organised unions were dockers and boatmen (in the Magadelena Medio), oil workers and banana plantation workers, but these were geographically diverse. As the state grew in the 1960s and 1970s, public sector employees (teachers, health workers, civil servants) and transport workers (railways, ports, airports) became important in the labour movement.

FARC

The Fuerzas Armadas Revolucionarias de Colombia (FARC) were formed in 1966 by Communist and dissident Liberal guerrillas, after the government attacked peasant communities in newly-colonised regions of southern Colombia. The defensive tactic of 'armed resistance communities', was replaced by an offensive strategy, in which peasant self-defence groups were turned into mobile fighting units and sent across the country.

The guerrillas found it easiest to expand in colonised regions such as the eastern foothills and plains of Meta, Caquetá, Guaviare, and the lowlands of the Magdalena valley. In these regions, the state was barely present and the FARC were welcomed – even by large landowners in some cases – as forces of law and order. The FARC taxed large landowners and in return ensured that their property was not attacked. In some regions, the FARC encouraged poor colonisers to work communally, pooling their resources, and setting up rudimentary health and education services. They set up local 'courts' which would arbitrate in cases such as neighbour disputes, and mete out punishments such as mending holes in the road. The FARC were popular because they stopped the advance of the property speculators and ranchers, who would buy up the settlers' land when they could no longer make ends meet.[12]

Although the FARC had strong links to the Communist Party and took a pro-Soviet line, it was not synonymous with the Party, which, in 1966, did not think that the armed struggle was a priority. The FARC expanded rapidly because it received strong support from peasant settlers and the Party trailed in its wake. The FARC's nature as a grassroots peasant army prevented it from becoming an ideologically 'pure' Marxist group, and its activities have always been marked by a high degree of pragmatism. Its philosophy is a mixture of radical agrarianism and anti-imperialism, rather than Communism, and many of its members probably did not have a global – or even national – political vision, but joined to defend or improve conditions in their immediate locality.

ELN

The *Ejército de Liberación Nacional* (ELN) was founded in 1964 by middle class students and intellectuals from Santander who were inspired by Che Guevara's *foquista* theory in which a small group of dedicated men creates the conditions for revolution. One of the founding members was Fabio Vásquez Castaño, who had been part of a group of scholarship students in revolutionary Cuba in 1962, and who asked for and received military training there. The ELN was formally founded by 18 men on July 4, 1964 on a ranch in Santander.[13]

Initially the ELN made rapid headway in northeastern Colombia, winning support from displaced peasants and oil workers. Their most famous recruit was the Catholic priest Camilo Torres, who was well known locally for his work with the poor. He was killed in action within four months of joining. The ELN guerrillas never managed to implant themselves in rural communities in the same way as the FARC, and this made it easier for the military to defeat them. By the end of the 1960s, the ELN had been virtually wiped out, only to re-emerge in the 1980s after a wave of popular civic struggle had been met with state repression.

EPL

The *Ejército Popular de Liberación* (EPL) was formed in 1967 as the armed wing of the Maoist Communist breakaway party, the *Partido Comunista Marxista Leninista* (PCML). It was dominated by urban middle-class intellectuals who advocated Mao's theory of 'prolonged popular war' in the countryside. It launched operations in Valle del Cauca and Antioquia, but was easily curtailed by the military. Its strength was also sapped by a series of internal splits which resulted in new factions such as the Marxist-Leninist League, the Marxist Leninist Tendency and the Pedro León Arboleda (PLA) group. By the end of 1960s, it too faced extinction, but re-appeared in the 1980s.

M19

There were other small guerrilla groups which by the end of the 1960s had been militarily defeated or subsumed by other organisations. These included the *Movimiento Obrero Estudiantil Campesino* (MOEC); the *Fuerzas Armadas de Liberacíon* (FAL) and the *Ejército Revolucionario de Colombia* (ERC).

A new force was the M19 guerrilla group which was formed by a later generation of city radicals but was less ideological and had a broader base than the ELN or EPL. It grew out of the populist movement *Alianza Nacional Popular* (Anapo) which was widely believed to have lost the 1970 presidential elections as a result of government fraud.

Anapo was founded by former dictator General Rojas Pinilla in 1961 and became the most important political challenge to the traditional parties during the National Front years. It was an alliance of those excluded by the political system: the lower middle class, the young, shantytown dwellers and migrants from the countryside. It also won support from landowners in regions outside of the dominant Antioquia-Cundinamarca axis.[14] Under the rules of the National Front, no other parties could stand in elections, but Anapo got round this by presenting its candidates as dissident Liberals or Conservatives. In 1966, a little-known Anapo presidential candidate won 28% of the vote. In 1970, Rojas himself stood for the presidency. On the night of the election, radio stations broadcasting live results declared Anapo the victors soon after the polls closed. Street parties were already underway, when the government ordered transmissions to stop. The next morning it was announced that the Conservative candidate Misael Pastrana had won the election by 40.3% to Rojas' 38.7%. After the elections, Rojas soon fell ill and handed the leadership of Anapo to his daughter María Eugenia, under whom it fell into decline.

The *Movimiento Diecinueve de Abril* (M19) was named after the date of the 'stolen' 1970 elections. It was founded in 1972 by leftwing Anapo intellectuals and FARC dissidents who had been expelled from the Communist Party. It had a populist nationalist philosophy and its first act was to steal the sword of independence leader Simón Bolívar. It specialised in daring actions such as stealing 5,000 guns from the military's central arsenal outside Bogotá (1979) and holding diplomats hostage in the embassy of the Dominican Republic (1980). It also carried out 'redistributive actions' such as holding up milk or food trucks, and giving the contents to shantytown residents. It was most popular in Cali and the department of Cauca, but also had a strong following among the poor in Bogotá and other cities. M19 had the same sort of broad-based populist platform as the Sandinistas in Nicaragua and were greatly encouraged when the FSLN successfully toppled the Somoza dictatorship in 1979.

The end of the National Front

The farcical 1970 election marked the end of the National Front. Even government supporters believed the results had been fixed and the system lost legitimacy. Yet the National Front was not completely dismantled: competitive presidential elections were introduced in 1974, but parity in the cabinet and the civil service was maintained until 1978. From that date onwards, the largest party was required by law to give 'adequate and equitable' representation in the government to the second-largest party.

The election of President Alfonso López Michelson in 1974 raised cautious hopes among reformers. As a young man, López Michelson had founded the radical dissident Liberal group, *Movimiento Revolucionario Liberal*, which frightened older politicians with slogans like: 'Passengers for the Revolution, jump aboard!' However, he disappointed his supporters by returning to the Liberal fold and negotiating with the old-style politician Julio César Turbay Ayala to win the presidential ticket. Once in office, he not only failed to introduce redistributive reforms, but he also implemented a severe austerity plan to contain inflationary pressure caused by the rise in international price for coffee and oil (and the first effects of the drugs' money boom).

The rise of the popular movement

The heightened political expectations which followed the dismantling of the National Front rapidly turned into frustration. Throughout the 1970s, trade union militancy grew: in 1975, 197,000 workers went on strike for 1.7 million hours; by 1979 this had risen to 210,000 workers and 4.6 million hours. Community groups sprang up in shantytowns and working class districts demanding access to public services. To pressure the government, they used a new tactic – the 'civic strike' – which combined labour stoppages with community marches, protests or roadblocks to bring a particular neighbourhood, city or region to a halt. In 1977 the first national civic strike, backed by all four trade union federations, was organised.

On September 14, 1977 factories, public services and the transport system were paralysed by strikes and military police were sent into slums to break up mass protests, sparking riots and long-running battles. Despite increased repression, the protest movement grew: between September 1977 and May 1978, there were 50 civic strikes and in 1982-83 there were 78 civic strikes involving five million people. A network of grassroots community campaigners grew up which culminated in the foundation of the National Co-ordinating Committee of the Civic

Movement, CNMC, in October 1983.[15]

Trade union activists also began to overcome the old partisan divisions. The existing confederations were Liberal, Conservative and Communist respectively, with a newly-created Christian Democratic federation. In 1981 independent unionists, Communists and dissident members of the partisan unions formed the Committee of Trade Union Unity (CUSI). This was a militant body which helped to organise a second national civic strike in 1981, despite rising government repression and the withdrawal of the other union confederations. In 1985, a third civic strike was held, and in 1986, the independent *Confederación Unitaria de Trabajadores* (CUT) was formed, which attracted the majority of unionised workers.

The late 1970s and early 1980s were periods of hope and optimism for the Left in Latin America. In 1979 the Sandinistas had led a popular insurrection against the Somoza dictatorship in Nicaragua. Guerrilla wars were raging in El Salvador and Guatemala. In Brazil there was a huge upsurge of strikes and popular protest, led by the Sao Paulo metalworkers; in Argentina a wave of powerful strikes rattled the junta and in Peru mass mobilisations brought down a military government. To the Left (and the frightened elites), it appeared as though popular revolutions could sweep the continent.

Despite the upsurge of activism in Colombia, the popular movement did not create an autonomous party or organisation that could articulate its political demands. This was mainly because the armed groups, particularly M19 and FARC, assumed the political voice of the opposition. The Sandinista victory underlined the possibilities of guerrilla strategies, and many leftwing militants thought that mass action should be subordinate to the armed struggle.

Turbay Ayala and the backlash

The Colombian state treated the mass movement as just as great a threat as the guerrillas. The government of President Turbay Ayala (1978-82) was the most repressive government since *la Violencia*. He advocated a doctrine of 'national security' (developed by the Argentine and Chilean military to justify their dictatorships), which viewed all opposition to the government as 'subversive'. A new security statute gave the armed forces a much greater role in civilian life, allowing them to arrest and prosecute people for 'political crimes' in military courts. A semi-permanent state of siege was enforced and numerous trade union militants, peasants and community campaigners were arrested and tortured. This convinced many on the Left that the armed struggle was the only option and guerrilla activity intensified from the 1980s onwards.

The coca boom

Another reason for the growing strength of the insurgency – at least in the case of the FARC – was land concentration, which led to a wave of rural migrants setting up farms in outlying areas, where they found that the only forces of law and order were the guerrillas. The large number of poor peasant settlers living in areas where the state was virtually absent, also explains the boom in the cultivation of marijuana, coca and opium poppies from the late 1970s. Coca and other illicit crops gave poor farmers the chance, for the first time, to accumulate capital to invest in buying cattle, or expanding and improving their farms. Until that point, the poverty-stricken *colonos* lived a precarious life growing yucca, maize and plantain which did not provide sufficient returns to build up any savings. The *colonos* were always one harvest away from destitution. The guerrillas were initially opposed to the introduction of illegal crops both for moral reasons and because they thought it would create a class of rich farmers who would no longer support their political project. However, they did not want to be seen to be denying peasants a chance of a higher standard of living and, in any case, were powerless to stop the rapid spread of the illicit crops. Pragmatic as ever, the guerrillas learnt to co-exist with the drug traffickers and eventually turned the coca boom to their advantage. They began to tax the trade, but did not traffic drugs themselves, which, by and large, remains the case today.

Rise of the death squads

Private security squads had been legal since 1968 when legislation was passed to allow the military to arm civilians as part of the counterinsurgency effort. They grew into an ever more powerful force from the 1980s onwards. Private militia were most frequently found in areas rich in resources or near businesses in need of protection. One of the most conflict-ridden regions of Colombia is the Magadelena Medio, the country's economic hub, which contains the most fertile lands, oil and natural gas reserves to the east, and coal mines to the north.[16]

In the 1960s and 1970s, landowners and ranchers increasingly resorted to using private militia to protect themselves from guerrillas who were demanding irksome 'protection taxes' and rustling cattle. These private militia, often including off-duty soldiers and police officers, frequently worked with the knowledge of the army, who welcomed their help in their war against subversion. Private security squads existed before the rise of the drug traffickers and their existence cannot be attributed to the cartels.

Drug trafficking entrepreneurs not only shared a hatred of guerrillas with the traditional landowning oligarchy, but they soon became powerful landowners themselves. Traffickers invested in ranches, partly to launder their money, but also because in Colombia land ownership is a status symbol. Of the US$4 billion drug traffickers invested in Colombia in the 1980s, 45% went into land. They acquired between 7.5 million and 11 million acres – some 10% of Colombia's most fertile lands.[17] Rapidly, then, an alliance grew up between the traditional landowners, the narco-bourgeoisie and the military.

In 1982 in Puerto Boyacá, army captain Oscar Echandía and other officers, representatives of the Texaco Petroleum Company, the local ranchers' association and traders, shopkeepers and local politicians met and agreed to fund a death squad which would work with the army.[18] This squad was called *Muerte a Sequestradores*, MAS (Death to Kidnappers) and drug traffickers who owned land locally contributed generously to it. After wiping out opposition in Puerto Boyacá, MAS expanded to become a nationwide force.

Two minor members of MAS, brothers Fidel and Carlos Castaño, went on to form another powerful paramilitary force based on the same alliance of traffickers-ranchers-military, the *Autodefensas Campesinas de Córdoba y Urabá* (ACCU). The brothers were sons of a rancher who had been kidnapped and killed by the FARC. Fidel was also heavily involved in drug trafficking, the proceeds of which he had invested in large tracts of land in northern Colombia. After carrying out a murderous campaign against the Left in Urabá – in which the tactic of the civilian massacre first emerged – the Castaños expanded their activities to other regions. In 1997 the various regional *autodefensas* were united under the umbrella of *Autodefensas Unidas de Colombia* (AUC), which was headed by Carlos

Castaño, and is the most powerful paramilitary group in Colombia.

Paramilitary groups saw their greatest period of expansion after 1984, when the government of Belisario Betancur tried to make peace with the guerrillas. The armed forces were enraged at having to abide by a ceasefire and increasingly turned to paramilitaries to continue the war in a covert manner.

Peace processes 1982-1991

Conservative President Belisario Betancur recognised that the hardline stance adopted by his predecessor, Turbay Ayala, had simply resulted in a resurgence of guerrilla activity. On taking office in 1982, he immediately announced an amnesty before the guerrillas had even agreed to talks. A year and a half later the FARC agreed to call a ceasefire and in August 1984, M19 followed suit. However, within a few months the truce was being broken by both the military and the guerrillas. The peace process with M19 finally collapsed when they seized the Palace of Justice in November 1985. War Minister General Miguel Vega Uribe ordered tanks to attack the building and in the ensuing bloodbath over 100 people died, including all the rebels and 12 of Colombia's 25 Supreme Court judges. Although Betancur took responsibility for the attack, it is probable that the army under General Vega acted of its own accord.

The FARC nevertheless decided to participate in the 1986 presidential elections. The *Unión Patriótica* (UP) was formed by the FARC and the Communist Party, but its appeal and its membership was far broader, as it was a pole of attraction for all sorts of non-aligned activists. In 1986, the UP candidate Jaime Pardo Leal won 312,000 votes (4.4%). However, in the next few years, during the administration of President Virgilio Barco, the 'dirty war' began in earnest. Between 1985 and 1989 some 3,000 UP candidates and supporters were shot dead including Pardo Leal and the 1989 presidential candidate Bernado Jaramillo. This murderous campaign helps to explain the FARC's current scepticism about the possibilities for democratic due process in Colombia.

The M19 continued fighting until 1989, when it signed a peace accord with President Barco, which was carried into effect by his successor President César Augusto Gaviria (1990-94). The EPL, the

The Constitution of 1991[19]

The make-up of the constituent assembly was extraordinary by Colombian standards; more than half the seats went to non-traditional parties. The abstention rate to elect the assembly, however, was extremely high at 74%.

Seats

Liberals (24)
Alizanza Democrática-M19 (19)
Movimiento de Salvación Nacional (MSN) (11)
Conservatives (5)
Independent Conservatives (4)
Unión Patriotica (2)
Indigenous groups (2)
Christian Union (2).

Three smaller demobilised guerrilla groups were granted seats with a voice, but no vote, EPL (2), Quintín Lame (1), PRT (1).

The Constitution of 1991 became law on July 4, 1991 replacing the 1886 constitution. It has 380 articles, making it one of the longest constitutions in the world. It:

* established a unitary democratic republic, with greater autonomy given to the regions.
* introduced directly elected mayors and governors[20]
* created the post of ombudsman to provide independent monitoring of citizens' civil, economic and human rights (*Defensoría del Pueblo*)
* created a public prosecutor's office (*Fiscalía*)
* defined more clearly the role of the Attorney General (*Procuradoría*) - to investigate charges against public officials
* gave citizens the right to take legal action against public officials for violation of their constitutional rights (*acción de tutela*)
* made it easier to reform the constitution (through referendum)
* granted indigenous communities greater self-government
* granted indigenous communities two permanent seats in the senate
* abolished the right of the president to call an indefinite state of siege
* outlawed the death penalty and life imprisonment
* outlawed extradition
* gave Colombians the right to minimum standards of housing, education, work and wages.

The 1991 constitution lacks support in the Colombian political establishment: hardliners think the constitution is excessively liberal and hinders the fight against the insurgency. The guerrillas, on the other hand, think of it as mere window dressing. Since the main party that promoted the process, Alianza Democrática-M19, has been dissolved, the constitution does not have the enthusiastic backing of any major party in congress.[21] It continues to be strongly defended by human rights and civil society groups.

indigenous guerrilla group Quintín Lame, and the small *Partido Revolucionario de los Trabajadores* (PRT) also demobilised. As part of the peace deal, a constituent assembly was elected in 1991 to draw up a new constitution.

M19's party, Alianza Democrática-M19, won the second-largest number of seats in the constituent assembly (and 27% of the popular vote). President Gaviria appointed former guerrilla Antonio Navarro Wolff health minister in his first cabinet. However, the party was unable to capitalise on its popularity and rapidly lost influence.[22] Why did M19 lay down their arms in 1989? Its leaders argued that the armed struggle had not only failed to achieve its objective of bringing down the oligarchy, but it was also contributing to the cataclysm of violence in which the country was engulfed. Narco-terrorism had been growing through the 1980s and by the end of the decade, it was no longer the guerrillas that posed the greatest threat to the establishment but the drugs barons whose power had swelled to unimaginable proportions.

The drug cartels

Pablo Escobar was the son of a schoolteacher, born in 1949 in the village of Ríonegro, just outside Medellín. As a teenager he sold fake lottery tickets and stole cars, and by his early twenties he was a small-time gangster, known locally for killing and kidnapping those who crossed him. He was quick to see the opportunities that the rapidly burgeoning cocaine trade offered and in the mid-1970s he muscled in on the trade run by the Ochoa brothers, Jorge Luis, Juan David and Fabio. Together with José Rodríguez Gacha and Carlos Lehder, they became known as the Medellín Cartel, the richest and most powerful criminal business in Colombia's history. Escobar's success stemmed from his ability to concentrate all aspects of the business (buying coca paste, refining the paste in laboratories in Colombia, storage and shipment, and sales in America) under his control. The Cali Cartel was a smaller organisation in these years, and only rose to prominence in the 1990s after it had helped the state defeat Escobar.

Early on Escobar began to use a policy of *plata o plomo* [silver or lead], bribing and terrorizing the police, the local judiciary and politicians. He was able to offer bribes of hundreds of thousands of dollars to police chiefs, and made million dollar donations to both major parties. In

Medellín he became a celebrity, building a housing estate for the poor, a soccer stadium, a skating rink and other attractions. His poverty relief programmes were backed by the local Catholic Church and he published a newspaper called 'Medellín without slums'. In 1978 he was voted a 'stand in' member of Medellín City Council and in 1982 he was elected to the national Congress, again as a stand in member.

Drugs money corrupted all sections of society. The media wrote fawning biographies of Escobar, legitimate businesses welcomed the flood of contracts that the new wealth brought and the even the Central Bank sought to benefit by opening a *ventanilla siniestra* [left-handed window] in which anyone could exchange dollars for pesos with no questions asked. Eighty percent of the Medellín police force was said to be on the payroll of the cartel and drugs-related money flooded the armed forces. Three ministers of defence have been linked to drugs scandals. Both major parties accepted money from the cartels and it is estimated that during the 1980s at least a third of congressmen had links to drug traffickers.

The politics of extradition

As the influence of drug traffickers grew in the 1980s, some members of the government recognised the danger and sought to confront the cartels. When it became clear that the Colombian judiciary and state security forces had become so corrupted and cowed that they could not defeat the cartels alone, extradition became a key issue, albeit a highly controversial one, as the country with most requests for extraditions was the United States.

Many Colombians resented US grandiloquence and its interference in Colombia's domestic affairs. Conservative Belisario Betancur, who came to office in 1982, was keen to follow an autonomous foreign policy and keep his distance from the hardline Reagan administration. He took Colombia into the non-aligned movement and played a leading role in the Contadora peace process in Central America. He also opposed extradition. However, in 1984 his justice minister, Rodrigo Lara Bonilla, an outspoken critic of the cartels who had pursued them relentlessly with very little government support, was gunned down. At Lara's funeral Betancur reversed his opposition to extradition and also launched a series of raids on laboratories and warehouses, although no major drug traffickers were arrested.

The Medellín cartel began to call itself 'The Extraditables' and launched an offensive against the judiciary. Between 1979 and 1991, 40 judges and lawyers were killed each year. Anyone who spoke out against the traffickers was targeted: Guillermo Caño, the editor of Colombia's oldest newspaper, *El Espectador*, was shot dead and the judge investigating the case received this note:

> We are friends of Pablo Escobar's and we are ready to do anything for him ....We are capable of executing you at any place on this planet ... in the meantime, all the members of your family will fall, one by one ... For calling Mr Escobar to trial you will remain without forebears or descendants in your genealogical tree.[23]

President Virgilo Barco came to office in 1986 promising to implement the extradition treaty, but within months the supreme court ruled that extradition was unconstitutional, raising suspicions that the judges had been bought off.

The real turnaround in Colombian government policy came in 1989, after the cartel killed the Liberal presidential candidate, Luis Galán. President Barco approved extradition using an 'administrative procedure' and set up a special SAS-trained elite corps to combat the cartels while he accepted more US overt and covert military help.

War against the state: 1989-93

The traffickers declared 'war' on the state, precipitating the biggest wave of urban terrorism the country had ever experienced. In November 1989 a bomb exploded on a commercial Avianca flight killing all 110 passengers, including two US citizens. In 1990 six notables (relatives of top politicians and journalists, including Francisco (Pacho) Santos, editor of the best-selling newspaper, *El Tiempo*) were kidnapped. Two of the hostages – Marina Montoya and Diana Turbay, the daughter of former President Turbay, were killed. Escobar offered US$2,000 for every policeman killed and car bombs were set off in major cities. The number of homicides soared from 9,721 in 1982 to 28,224 in 1992 – the highest ever level.

In 1990 President César Gaviria took office and followed a dual policy of making peace with M19 guerrillas and the drug traffickers. He offered the traffickers reduced sentences and immunity from extradition (which was in any case outlawed by the new 1991 constitution). Escobar eventually handed himself in 1991, but continued to run his empire from a comfortable 'prison' furnished with plush furniture, a mini-bar and a jacuzzi. He would frequently leave the prison to watch football games and had access to a bank of telephone lines and an arsenal of firearms. In effect, Escobar and his bodyguards ran the prison. The extent of the military's complicity with Escobar was revealed in 1992, when he easily escaped from the prison despite it being surrounded by four hundred troops.

In December 1993 Escobar was tracked down and shot by the Colombian police, with extensive US help. The shine of this victory was rapidly tarnished when the police officer leading the mission, Colonel Hugo Martínez and the chief of police, General Vargas, were accused of accepting money from the Cali Cartel. The extent of the Cali cartel's influence would become clear under President Ernesto Samper.

Samper, the Cali Cartel and the USA

Two days after the election of Liberal Ernesto Samper Pizano in 1994, audiotapes were leaked to the press with evidence that his campaign team had taken money from the Cali Cartel. The controversy dominated his entire presidency and soured relations with the United States.

Samper was cleared by an initial investigation, but the case was re-opened a year later when his party treasurer accused him of personal involvement. On June 12, 1996, the lower house of congress voted 111 to 43 to acquit Samper of charges of having known about the donations from the Cali Cartel. The move did not clear the cloud of suspicion hanging over the president, since it was suspected that many congressmen had themselves accepted drugs-tainted money. Fernando Botero, defence minister and Samper's campaign manager, Santiago Medina, party treasurer, and the Attorney General, Orlando Vásquez Velasquez were later found guilty of accepting drugs money and imprisoned.

Between 1995 and 1996 the leaders of the Cali Cartel – the Rodríguez-Orejuela brothers, José Santacruz Londono, and Helmer "Pacho" Herrera-Buitrago – were all imprisoned or killed. Today Colombia still provides 80% of the world's cocaine, but the drugs trafficking business is more decentralised and not dominated by one major cartel.

Relations with the United States reached their lowest point during the Samper administration. The State Department refused to certify Colombia as co-operating in the war on drugs in 1996 and 1997, and gave it only conditional certification in 1998. Colombia stopped receiving US credit exports and the US voted against loans to Colombia from international banks, damaging its creditworthiness. Anger at US interference in Colombia affairs (particularly its unilateral certification scheme) ensured that Samper's popularity remained reasonably high despite the funding allegations.

The drugs scandal and war of words with the US dominated the headlines, but during Samper's administration, the counterinsurgency war was intensified. The military's direct responsibility for human rights violations fell, but cases of collaboration with the paramilitary rose. Samper's administration made a number of overtures to the guerrilla alliance, *Coordinadora Guerrillera Simón Bolivar*, and, in 1995, offered to establish a demilitarised zone in which to hold the negotiations. However, the military did not support these initiatives and Samper did not have the political legitimacy needed to overcome their resistance. The FARC and the ELN, meanwhile, were reluctant to negotiate with a discredited president. The FARC agreed to talk to his Conservative rival Andrés Pastrana, and the promise of peace talks was the main reason for Pastrana's electoral victory in 1998.

Pastrana, the USA and Plan Colombia

President-elect Andrés Pastrana met the leader of the FARC 'Manuel Marulanda' (known as *Tirofijo* or Sureshot) in July 1998 in the Colombian Amazon rainforest where they pledged to start peace talks. When the video footage of the septuagenarian guerrilla chief in battered army fatigues sitting down with Pastrana under a makeshift jungle canopy was broadcast on TV, war-weary Colombians began to feel a real sense of hope.

Pastrana's election also transformed Colombia's relations with the United States.[21] He met President Bill Clinton in the White House days before his inauguration and two months later made the first official visit to Washington by a Colombian president for 23 years. In 1999 Colombia was given full certification for its anti-drugs effort. In the same year Pastrana unveiled an integrated peace and development plan. Following a year of discussion with US officials, this original 'Plan Colombia', focusing on peace and economic justice, was transformed into a militaristic anti-drugs trafficking plan. The extent of US involvement in designing Plan Colombia is illustrated by the fact that the document was written in English (not Spanish).

Plan Colombia is discussed in more detail in Chapter 5, but, in summary, these were the main effects: thousands of small farms were sprayed with pesticides, harming the health of humans and animals, and poisoning the land. Politically, the armed forces were given a huge boost when they received the biggest US military aid package in Colombia's history and paramilitaries celebrated receiving help in their brutal 'counterinsurgency' war. The guerrillas immediately became suspicious of the government's intentions and achieving peace became an even more remote possibility.

Pastrana turned Colombia from a pariah-state into one with which the US and Europe were delighted to work. Pastrana is an award-winning journalist and, having studied at Harvard, speaks impeccable English. Born into the traditional Colombian elite (he is the son of former President Misael Pastrana), he is comfortable networking with world leaders, but can also justifiably claim to have been personally touched by the violence, having been kidnapped for a week by the Medellín cartel in 1987. Pastrana launched a public relations offensive, touring foreign countries to drum up support for Plan Colombia and advertise his commitment to peace. The Europeans were sceptical about the 'military side' of the Plan, but backed Pastrana's efforts to end the war and improve human rights. The Pastrana roadshow admitted that there had been 'isolated' cases of military collusion with paramilitaries, but emphasised the government's determination to stamp out death squads once and for all. However, as outlined in the previous chapter, collaboration between the military and paramilitaries became more widespread in this period. Paramilitary violence soared and their ranks swelled to 8,000.

In the latter half of his administration Pastrana was the most unpopular President in living memory. It was not his failure to crack down on the death squads that angered most voters. It was the severe economic crisis and his incapacity to stop the guerrillas 'running rings round him'.

Economic crisis

Colombia's economy used to be viewed as one of the most stable in Latin America, apparently immune to the violence in the countryside. It was one of the few regional economies judged by risking-rating agencies as 'investment grade'.

In 1998 Colombia began to feel the impact of the Asian Crisis. Traders panicked and dumped their 'emerging market' shares, bonds and currencies. In an attempt to stop the currency sliding, the Colombian central bank raised interest rates to 50%. Thousands of lenders then defaulted on their debts, plunging the banking sector into crisis. The credit squeeze also tipped Colombia into the worst recession since the 1930s. In 1999, the economy contracted by 4.5% and official unemployment soared to 20%. The government was forced to sign a US$2.7 billion credit deal with the IMF, its first ever formal agreement with the Fund. In the same year, the risk-rating agencies Standard & Poor's and Moody's stripped Colombia of its 'investment grade' rating, citing political violence as a factor. The downgrade was not only deeply resented by the Colombian business community, but increased the cost of servicing the foreign debt (because investors demanded higher rates of interest as compensation for the greater risking involved in lending to Colombia).

The economic crisis hit Pastrana's poll ratings as millions of Colombians lost faith in him. For decades businessmen and government technocrats, in air-conditioned offices in Bogotá or Medellín, went about their day-to-day business of economic management and profit making unaffected by violence in the countryside or urban slums. But now, not only was kidnapping and robbery an increasing threat in even the most well-to-do city suburbs, the conflict had also started to hit profits and the running of the economy. This double blow led to a profound crisis of confidence among the elite, and a growing willingness to support extremist 'solutions' such as paramilitary-led authoritarianism.

The peace processes

During his jungle meeting with the FARC leader, Pastrana agreed to withdraw troops from an area the size of Switzerland (42,000 square kilometres) in the southern departments of Caquetá and Meta, to create a neutral zone in which to carry out peace talks. Although this decision drew criticism from the military – the defence minister and 300 officers, including 16 generals resigned soon after – it was really an admission that the FARC already had *de facto* control over this region. The FARC had expanded its area of operations enormously: in 1985 it was present in 173 of Colombia's 1050 municipalities, in 1985 this rose to 437 and in 1995 to 622 (or 59% of the total). At the beginning of Pastrana's term, the FARC had an estimated 12,000 fighters.

Peace process with the ELN

The peace process with the ELN started on an optimistic note in July 1998 when the guerrillas met Colombian civic groups in Germany and signed the 'Heaven's Gate' agreement. They proposed holding a national convention in Colombia to which all of 'civil society' would be invited to discuss peace and social reform. However, the ELN wanted a second demilitarised zone to be established in north eastern Colombia, in which to hold the convention, and this became the sticking point throughout Pastrana's term.

Creating an ELN demilitarised zone was much more controversial than creating the FARC zone in the south. Firstly, the proposed area for the ELN zone, (Bolívar and Santander) was right in the heart of the country's resource-rich region, the Magdalena Medio. It was close to the country's main oil reserves and refineries, its most important river network and its most fertile lands. By contrast, the FARC's demilitarised zone in the south contained only poor peasant farmers living on logged rainforest land.

Secondly, northeastern Colombia is the most contested area in the country: all leftwing guerrilla groups are present, but it is also a stronghold of paramilitaries who, having made huge territorial advances in the area, were unwilling to give the ELN the advantage of a safe haven. Whereas the FARC already controlled the region before its zone was created, the ELN were in retreat. Furthermore, the ELN had a far weaker base than the FARC, who had the longstanding support of many peasant settlers and were viewed in isolated southern areas as the forces of law and order. The Magdelena Medio is far more integrated into national state structures and its inhabitants did not see the ELN as the natural authority in the region.

Since the ELN were in a far weaker position than the FARC, the government refused to set up a second demilitarised zone as a precondition for talks. The ELN responded in April 1999 by hijacking a commercial Avianca flight, taking all 56 passengers and five crew members hostage. In June 1999, it kidnapped the entire congregation of a church in Cali and a week later the President agreed to talks. The ELN relies on mass civilians kidnappings to increase its bargaining power. In September 1999, to step up the pressure on the government, it abducted 30 people having Sunday lunch in two restaurants in Cali.

In the year 2001 proposals for a second demilitarised zone were drawn up. It was to be a tenth of the size of the FARC zone, just 4,000 square kilometres covering the municipalities of Cantagallo and San Pablo on the border of Bolívar and Santander. It was to have far stricter supervision and was to be policed by international monitors. Even before formal proposals were announced, tens of thousands of locals mounted roadblocks to protest against the zone.

Proposals for a demilitarised zone and international monitors were, however, supported by the local Catholic Church and civic groups. The area had suffered a brutal advance by paramilitaries who were carrying out a systematic assassination campaign against their opponents (community leaders, human rights workers, trade unionists). They viewed the zone, less as an ELN-controlled area, than an internationally monitored space that would provide respite from the killings and show that the government was willing to confront the paramilitaries. After the peace process with the FARC collapsed, the ELN continued to talk to the government, but all hope of creating a second demilitarised zone evaporated.

The historic peace talks with the FARC were scheduled for the first week of January 1999 and anticipation was high. The FARC leader, Marulanda, did not turn up as scheduled, leaving the President humiliated in front of the world's press. Marulanda blamed his absence on a lack of guarantees for his security and appeared a few weeks later, only to announce a three month postponement of the talks. This was a fitting start for a peace process that stalled innumerable times and achieved little. No ceasefire was agreed (apart from a short Christmas truce) and far from reducing violence, the war intensified.

The FARC accused the government of failing to crackdown on paramilitarism and using Plan Colombia as a pretext to launch an US-backed counterinsurgency offensive. It could be argued that some sections of the Colombian military (and their paramilitary allies) were so resolutely opposed to the peace process that it was doomed to fail. The large dose of US military aid made hawkish generals begin to think that the balance had tipped in their favour.

As in the 1980s, when death squads shot dead demobilised guerrillas despite President Betancur's guarantees, Pastrana was not in a position to offer the guerrillas peace because he could, or would, not control the paramilitaries. Neither could he offer sweeping social reform. The FARC, even in its pro-Soviet days, had a radical anti-imperialist rather than communist agenda. Since the fall of the Berlin Wall, it has described its philosophy as Bolivarian (after the independence leader Simon Bolívar). Its manifesto demands are fairly moderate: a mixed economy, wealth redistribution and defence of civil rights. This explains why the FARC are sometimes described as 'Scandinavian Social Democrats in Arms', despite the rather odd picture that conjures up. However, the Colombian government, tied to a cost-cutting agreement with the IMF, could not even offer the smallest rise in the public spending. Pastrana's final problem was a lack of credibility among his own class: in the first few months of his administration he perhaps had enough public backing to make bold moves, but as the 'peace' process dragged on, even maintaining the demilitarised zone was viewed as a foolhardy concession to the guerrillas. And Pastrana did not have the standing to persuade landowners or businesses to accept agrarian reform or other redistributive measures.

Whether the FARC initially believed in the peace process is unclear, but very soon they were accused of bad faith. They appeared to be using the demilitarised zone as a base from which to wage war, attacking army units or kidnapping civilians before fleeing back into the safety of the zone. The FARC refused to agree to a moratorium on kidnapping or other abuses of civil rights; on the contrary the number of FARC abductions rose to 728 in the year 2000. Pastrana, who had staked his personal reputation on the peace process declaring 'Tirofijo is a man who keeps his word,' was repeatedly outfoxed.

The original time limit of the demilitarised zone was extended numerous times and the approach of each deadline turned into a cliffhanger, as the FARC broke off talks or stepped up operations, apparently daring the government to abandon the process. Each time, Pastrana backed down or accepted less than he had demanded at the start. In December 2000, for example, he extended the duration of the zone even though the FARC were refusing to talk to the government. In February 2001, in the face of strong public opposition (a poll suggested 76% were opposed to it), Pastrana agreed to extend the zone for nine months. He failed to persuade the FARC to call a ceasefire or to stop kidnapping civilians. But the two sides did agree to a prisoner exchange and the demobilisation of child soldiers. The FARC's handover of 62 children to Unicef and the release of 329 captured soldiers and policemen were the only concessions made to the government during the entire process.

In the run-up to the October 2001 deadline the FARC appeared to go out of their way to enrage domestic and international opinion. In July, the guerrillas violated United Nations immunity and kidnapped a diplomat travelling in a UN vehicle. Shortly afterwards, they kidnapped three German citizens, a charity worker and two government visitors to an agricultural development project in Cauca. Later that month, the rebels stormed a residential apartment block in the city of Neiva and took 15 hostages, including seven teenagers. In August three Irish men, travelling on false passports, were arrested after leaving the demilitarised zone. They were accused of being members of the Irish Republican Army (IRA) and training the FARC in urban warfare techniques. Days before Pastrana had to decide whether to extend the zone, the FARC killed the wife of the Attorney General, who was also a popular folk singer. Consuela Araújo was found dead on wasteland with two gunshot wounds to the face. Thousands in her hometown came out to the streets to mourn her. On the same weekend, the FARC, in a show of strength, turned back a peace convoy, headed by the leader of the opposition, on its way to the demilitarised zone.

To a clamour of disapproval, Pastrana extended the zone once more in October 2001. This time, however, he announced that security would be stepped up around the zone, creating 'a ring of steel' around it. The airforce was to tighten up control of airspace above the zone, foreigners were banned from entering and the military would step up attacks on armed groups outside of the demilitarised zone. The announcement led the FARC to suspend talks.

It was the beginning of the end of the peace process. One other external factor turned the tide against peace: September 11th 2001. The United States had formally supported the Colombian peace process, but after September 11th, the US stance hardened and they became willing to openly advocate counterinsurgency; the Colombian government was

Presidential Elections 2002*

Candidate	Party	Share of valid votes cast (%)
Alvaro Uribe	Primero Colombia	53.0
Horacio Serpa	Partido Liberal	31.7
Luis Eduardo Garzón	Polo Democrático (leftwing)	6.2
Noemí Sanín	Si Colombia (centre-right)	5.8
Ingrid Betancourt (kidnapped by FARC before elections)	Partido Verde Oxígeno (green)	0.5
Six other candidates		2.8

*Abstention rate: 53%

Source: Registraduría

assured that any offensive against the FARC would have its full support.

Talks remained frozen until January 2002. On 9 January, Pastrana declared that the FARC had 48 hours to leave the demilitarised zone before the armed forces moved back in. At the last moment, Pastrana allowed United Nations special negotiator James Lemoyne to facilitate a compromise. The FARC agreed to draw up the terms of a ceasefire by April. The guerrillas also made an important concession, which was overlooked at the time. They agreed that the demilitarised zone should be independently monitored by the United Nations, the Vatican and the so-called friendly countries (Germany, France, Sweden, Norway, Venezuela, Cuba, Canada, Switzerland, Spain and Japan).

A week after the deal was signed, the FARC began bombing electricity pylons, generation plants and other infrastructure, leaving large parts of the country without power. The idea was to strengthen its hand at the negotiating table by demonstrating its military capacity, in a campaign against 'property' (as opposed to people). However, the offensive simply convinced the government and the non-partisan population that the FARC had no desire for peace. In February an aircraft was hijacked and forced to land near the demilitarised zone. A senator, Jorge Gechem Turbay, was taken hostage. President Pastrana said the FARC were responsible for the kidnapping. In a TV address to the nation that night, he announced the end of the peace process and ordered the armed forces to re-take the demilitarised zone.

At midnight on February 20, 2002 the airforce began to bomb southern Colombia. The 100,000 civilian inhabitants who had never been asked if they wanted the zone to be established were given no warning of its end. In the first two days of the campaign, three civilians, including one child, were killed by airforce bombs, according to the military. In response to the bombardment, the FARC blocked highways leading to major cities and bombed electricity and telephone lines. The combination of army and FARC offensives left civilians in the towns with no power, no external means of communication, no food or medical supplies and in some cases no water. Paramilitaries, who previously had not had the strength to operate in the demilitarised zone, entered in the wake of the armed forces, and threatened to murder 'collaborators'. Military rule was declared in southern Colombia and journalists were banned from the theatre of operations. A silent war had begun.

War once more

In May 2002 hardliner Alvaro Uribe Vélez was elected President, by a population exhausted by interminable violence and disillusioned with a peace process that had achieved nothing. Described as Colombia's Ariel Sharon, Uribe promised to crack down on guerrillas and negotiate only from a position of strength. His campaign pledge to recruit one million civilians to work alongside the armed forces did nothing to allay fears that he would go to any lengths to defeat the insurgency.

3   The Economy

The Colombian economy has not behaved like a 'typical' Latin American economy in the last fifty years. It has not suffered bouts of hyperinflation, dramatic debt crises or cycles of boom and bust but instead grew steadily (on average about 2% per capita per year) from 1950 to 1997. It grew during the 'lost decade' of the 1980s when the rest of region plunged into recession as a result of the debt crisis. It appeared immune to the guerrilla war in the countryside and violence in the cities.

Colombia has always been the darling of foreign bankers and financial leaders. Until recently, it was one of the few Latin American countries regarded as 'investment grade' by risk-rating agencies. It won this accolade because its government never reneged on its foreign debt and kept a tight reign on public spending. It was the first country to receive a World Bank mission (in 1949), and Lauchlin Currie, the mission leader who designed the policies that would be implemented for the next 30 years, wrote, 'Colombia became a favourite country of the Bank throughout the following decades'.[1]

Yet in 1999 the Colombian economy sank into the deepest recession of the century.

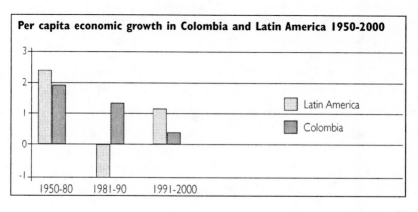

Per capita economic growth in Colombia and Latin America 1950-2000

	1950-80	1981-90	1991-2000
Latin America	2.7	-0.9	1.5
Colombia	2.3	1.6	0.6

Source: United Nations and E Cardoso/A Helwege[2]

Elite consensus

Colombia avoided the 'excesses' of economic populism (high public spending aimed at stimulating economic growth and income distribution)[3] or indeed extreme monetarism[4] because there has been an extraordinary consensus within the Colombian elite to preserve a political system which has excluded the working class and the poor.

This closed, but stable, political system led to a technocratic approach to macroeconomic management and broad agreement that 'prudent' policies should be pursued: balanced budgets, controlled inflation, a carefully managed exchange rate and sustainable levels of debt. (In the late 1970s, when the region was flooded with easy credit and Latin American governments lapped up foreign loans, Colombia reduced its foreign debt).

The consensus extended to Colombian businesses, which set up extremely effective lobbying associations, organised along sectoral lines (Fedecafe for coffee, Andi for industrialists, Anif for banks). In contrast with the exclusion of the trade unions and popular organisations, business leaders have always been closely involved in policy making. The coffee growers' federation, in particular, was influential due to running the national coffee fund (which bought coffee at fixed prices to ensure growers a steady income) and, at times, appeared to be a parallel government.

The harmony between politicians, technocrats, businessmen, newspaper editors, was due, by and large, to the fact that they all come from the same class, were born in the same parts of the country, went to the same universities and moved in the same circles or belonged to the same families.

'Clientelism'

At a national and local level, politicians have contained pressure from below by buying off poor communities or individuals with promises of help (roads, clean water, new houses – or simply a few pesos or a good meal). Miguel Urratia, a Berkeley-educated economist and governor of the central bank (1993-), gives a surprisingly candid defence of this chummy – and corrupt – system of politics known as 'clientelism'.

'Ideologues and intellectuals find clientelistic democracy repugnant, and in Colombia it has a very bad name. It is considered immoral to have a system in which the resources of the state are used in part with the aim of maximising political support... [yet] Japanese democracy, which is very close to the ideal clientelistic regime ... has produced a very egalitarian society, spectacular economy growth and the voters seem satisfied with the system ... In summary, the Colombian political system, very dependent on clientelistic practices, is not admired by national and foreign intellectuals, but it receives support from more than 80% of the voters in election after election. In the last two decades, it has produced economic growth, an improved income distribution and fairly progressive government expenditures.'[5]

There are also longer-term reasons for Colombia's relative economic stability. Coffee plantations, in contrast to other mono-exports in Latin America, were Colombian-owned and mainly cultivated on small and medium-sized farms, which created a reasonably stable class of farmers (in Antioquia, Caldas, Risaralda Quindio, northern Tolima and the northern part of Valle), for the first three quarters of the twentieth century.[6] Secondly, the country had vast tracts of unexploited land, which meant that small farmers squeezed out of the central regions could establish their own plots in outlying territories. The process of 'colonisation' has provided a pressure valve for conflicts in the countryside. Colombia has a much smaller industrial working class than Brazil or Mexico, for example, and the trade unions have less power. Governments have dealt with union pressure with a mixture of repression and favours (granting benefits to well-organised groups such as public sector unions).

The economy of drugs

The impact of drugs trafficking on the Colombian economy has been the subject of many academic studies and much speculation. Given the difficulties of accurately measuring the trade, the estimates of the size of the drugs economy have varied wildly from 50% of GDP (US$25 billion in 1994) to 3% of GDP.[7] In spite of the proportions, the lion's share of earnings are made in the USA. According to one conservative estimate, Colombian total revenues from manufacturing and exporting cocaine in 1994 were less than US$3.5 billion, while North Americans' gross revenues from selling the finished product to consumers were at least US$11 billion.[8]

The drugs boom started in the late 1970s and cannot, therefore, explain Colombia's long-term economic performance. Without doubt, however, drug money helped the country to avoid recession in the 1980s and helped to ameliorate the conditions of the poor. Drug traffickers, needing to launder their dollars, invested heavily in real estate, stimulating a boom in the construction industry, creating thousands of urban jobs. Cultivation of coca, poppies and marijuana also provided poor farmers with a source of income, when the prices of most other agricultural commodities were falling. However, the drug trade also had negative economic effects: the influx of dollars distorted the exchange rate, created inflationary pressures and fed the black market.

From state intervention to neoliberalism

Despite the conservative nature of Colombian economic policy, it was by no means laissez faire. In the late 1940s, 1950s and 1960s, the government sought to stimulate the growth of industry by raising tariff barriers and providing subsidies – the same import substitution policy as was followed in the rest of the region. State-owned monopolies were created in key industries such as oil (Ecopetrol), coal (Carbocol) and electricity (ISA and Isagen). In the 1970s, the authorities sought to diversify exports and reduce dependence on coffee, which still provided the country with over half of its foreign earnings. Foreign investment was welcomed, but was carefully controlled.

Manufacturing's share of GDP rose from 14.8% in 1945 to 22.9% in 1975, while agriculture's contribution fell from 40.5% to 23.4%. Services (including commerce, banking, water, gas, electricity and transport) rose from 38.6% to 49.1%.

Until 1969 over half the population worked in agriculture; by 1980, this had fallen to 33.8%. From the 1960s onwards, as agriculture was modernised and new non-traditional exports such as flowers and bananas were promoted, the ownership of land became increasingly concentrated in the hands of large landowners or agribusiness companies.

Neoliberalism and crisis

In the 1980s governments began to liberalise trade, cutting or abolishing import tariffs, forcing domestic companies to compete with cheap imports. Controls on direct foreign investment were relaxed and foreigners were encouraged to trade on Colombia's stock and bond markets. The foreign debt ballooned from US$6.5 billion (19.3% of GDP) in 1980 to US$16.9 billion (46.9% of GDP) in 1990. The government of Belisario Betancur (1982-86) also introduced a severe adjustment plan, cutting public spending and sacking state employees.

In the 1990s, the neoliberal revolution gathered pace: publicly owned companies were put up for sale; state monopolies dismantled, subsidies eliminated and free competition promoted; the social security system was cut back, private pensions were encouraged and legislation was passed making it easier to hire and fire workers.

In 1997-98, the Asian Crisis spread to Latin America and panic on the stock markets sent interest rates in Colombia soaring. Thousands of lenders defaulted on their debts and the government was forced to spend US$1.8 billion bailing out troubled banks, as the financial system faced near collapse. The crisis also depressed the international price of commodities (including coffee and oil), reducing Colombia's export earnings. The economy imploded, contracting by 4.5% in 1999 – the deepest recession of the century. In 1999, the IMF granted Colombia a US$2.7 billion loan. In return the government agreed to slash public spending and 'deepen structural reforms' (privatise the pension system, and change the constitution in order to cut central government spending in the provinces).

Poverty and inequality

Colombia's development model has been based on inequality and widespread poverty, particularly in countryside. Nevertheless, until the 1980s, defenders of the model could at least point to a gradual improvement in living standards. Since the introduction of neo liberal polices though, and particularly since the recent economic crisis, poverty and unemployment have increased dramatically and the divide between rich and poor has grown.

In 1999, 55% of the population – or 22.8 million people – lived below the national poverty line, a proportion which rises to a staggering 79.7% in rural areas. In addition, 21% of the population nationally, and 46% in rural areas, lived below the 'indigence line' – a level of such extreme poverty that basic subsistence needs are not met. At the beginning of the decade, national poverty and indigence rates were 53% and 20%.

The rise in rural poverty has been bleak. Between 1991 and 1999, the proportion living in poverty rose from 68.4% to 79.7%, and the proportion living in extreme poverty rose from 35% to 46%.[9] Living conditions in rural areas, on average, are far below those in the cities: only 44% of households have a clean water supply and only 16% are connected to the sewerage system. Twenty-three percent of rural households are without electricity and 96% don't have a telephone.[10] The child infant mortality rate is 54% in the countryside compared with 27% in urban areas and a third of children over the age of 12 do not go to school.[11]

Poverty rates also vary across the country: in some departments over two thirds of the population live below the poverty line: Cauca (68%); Córdoba (69%); Nariño (71%) and Chocó (75%).[12] The proportion of under-fives suffering from chronic malnutrition in Colombia is 15% – a terrible figure which in some rural areas rises to almost a quarter of the population: Casanare (22%); Amazonas (23%); Nariño (26%). While the national infant mortality rate is 34 per 1,000, in some rural areas it is over 80: Putumayo: (86.7); Vichada (82) and Chocó (125). This means that for every 1,000 babies born in Chocó, 125 will die before they reach the age of one.[13]

The growth of the informal sector

At almost every set of traffic lights in Bogotá, there are two or three people, often children, selling fruit, newspapers, knick-knacks or offering to wash car windscreens. Away from the centre, the streets are dusty, full of potholes and heavy smog fills the air. It is a 21st century city, but there are men, and women, pushing wooden carts filled with

---

Ciudad Bolívar

A sprawling shantytown has appeared on the mountains to the east of Bogotá in the past twenty years, as rural poverty and violence has prompted families to seek a new life in the city. 'Bolívar's City' is home to 1.5 million people.

Lower down the mountain, older residents have had time to build small brick houses with corrugated iron roofs and have persuaded the authorities to pave the streets. Further up, newcomers live in shacks made of plastic sheeting and bits of wood; the paths are mud and rubble and the land is vulnerable to erosion and mudslides.

Fifteen-year-old Sandra Sánchez has lived in 'El Paraiso' (Paradise) district of Ciudad Bolívar for eight years. Her mother and father moved from the countryside because there was no longer room in her grandparents' house for the growing family and there was no work in the area. Her father is an electrician, but has not been able to find a job in Bogotá either and the family (Sandra, her 12-year old sister, Alejandra, and her eight-year-old brother) are surviving on the odd jobs he can find.

Like all families arriving in Ciudad Bolívar, they built their own house, first with pieces of tarpaulin and wood, then later with bricks and mortar. For six years the little hut had no water, and they had to walk down the steep mountain to fill urns from a tap and then carry them up again. Two years ago, the council connected their house to the water supply.

Although only fifteen, Sandra has years of activism behind her. Aged ten she launched a campaign to get chairs, books and a computer for her overcrowded school. She is worryingly mature, often sounding more like a middle aged woman than a teenager. Last year, she persuaded the municipal government and charities to provide enough funds to build a small community centre: a 12 by 10 foot brick building, with corrugated iron roof and no water, which is used by youth groups and 'grandparents'.

---

potatoes or yucca alongside the buses or wheeling steel contraptions held together with string and wire, in which they will cook *empanadas*. Cigarettes, sweets, Colombian flags, dollars, lottery tickets, fake watches; anything you care to buy is sold on the streets by this army of wandering salesmen and women.

In 1997, 56% of the urban population worked in the 'informal sector', that is, outside the official tax and social security system; 22.9% worked in 'commerce and services' as street hawkers, screen wipers (or prostitutes), 7.1% were unskilled construction workers and a further 20.6% worked in small, unregistered companies with more than five employees, according to a United Nations report. The size of the informal sector almost certainly grew during the economic crisis of 1998-99. In 1998 alone, 200,000 jobs were lost and 185,000 gave up trying to find employment in the formal sector. The official unemployment rate soared from 8% in 1990 to 20.5% in 2000.

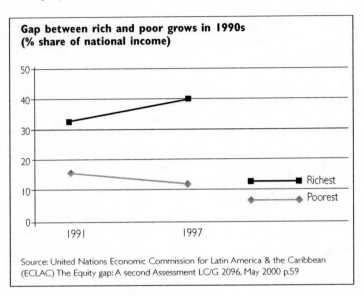

Gap between rich and poor grows in 1990s
(% share of national income)

Source: United Nations Economic Commission for Latin America & the Caribbean (ECLAC) The Equity gap: A second Assessment LC/G 2096, May 2000 p.59

Income inequality

The rise in poverty was not just caused by economic recession, but was the result of a clear transfer of the nation's wealth from the poor to the rich. Income inequality grew steadily in the 1990s. In 1991, the poorest 40% of the population owned 16% of national income; by 1997, their share had fallen to 13%. The richest 10% of the population, meanwhile, saw their share of national income rise from 32% to 39.5%.

By the year 2000, the richest 10% owned 42.7% of national income, according to the United Nations Human Development Report.[14] Colombia's ranking in the UN's gini index, which measures the gap between rich and poor, rose from an average of 45.0 in 1975-88, to 57.1 in 2000, the ninth most unequal division of wealth in the world.[15]

Coffee

Historically, coffee has been Colombia's most important export. Although reliance on a single, primary export made the Colombian economy vulnerable to swings in world demand and prices, it had advantages in relation to the other Latin American mono-exports (bananas, copper, sugar): it was Colombian owned, it was mainly cultivated on small and medium-sized farms, its harvesting was labour intensive (providing many jobs) and it provided some value added processing work (drying, grinding).

The price of coffee has been falling since the 1980s as world production increases, although there was a short-lived boom in the late 1980s. In 1989, the International Coffee Pricing Agreement was abandoned, under pressure from rich countries, and the price plummeted to unprecedented lows. During the 'emerging markets crisis', the international coffee price slumped further, from 168 cents per pound in 1997 to 67 cents in the year 2000.[16]

World prices have had a devastating impact on Colombia's coffee sector: between 1990 and 2000 output fell 25% and export earnings halved. Coffee's share of the country's total export earnings fell from 33% in 1988 to 8% in 2000. In the same year, Vietnam overtook Colombia as the world's second-largest coffee supplier (after Brazil). Nevertheless, at the end of the century, the sector accounted for 35% of agricultural jobs and 8% of total employment, while four million people (10% of the population) remained economically dependent on it.

The slump in world coffee prices in the 1990s has caused misery not just in Colombia, but across the developing world where peasants have been left on the brink of destitution. In the same period, coffee bar chains have sprung up across the US and Britain. The number of Starbucks stores in the US grew from 275 to 2,500 between 1993 and 2001. In Britain, coffee is the fastest growing market after mobile phones. Costa Coffee, the largest chain in the UK, opened one store a week in 1998-99 and Starbucks, the second biggest, opened six a month. Even McDonalds is cashing in on the coffee craze, buying the Aroma coffee chain in Britain and launching McCafé in the US.[17]

Colombia's exports (% share of total)		
	1995	2000
Oil and derivatives	21.4	34.8
Coffee	18.0	8.1
Coal	5.8	6.6
Flowers	4.7	4.4
Bananas	3.9	3.3
Emeralds	4.4	0.7
Ferronickel	1.8	1.6
Subtotal	**60.0**	**59.6**
Other agricultural goods	3.3	2.5
Other mining products	2.6	2.7
Industrial goods (including agro-industry)	34.1	35.1

Source: Colombian foreign trade ministry

How important are Colombian exports to the world?	
Export	World Ranking
Cocaine	Largest supplier
Emeralds	Largest supplier
Coffee	2nd/3rd largest
Flowers	2nd largest
Bananas	3rd largest
Coal	4th largest

Oil rush

Oil has overtaken coffee as Colombia's largest export earner and, in 2000, accounted for 35% of the country's export earnings. However, known reserves of oil are rapidly running out, and Colombia will become a net oil importer by 2005, if new deposits are not found.

The Colombian government is therefore desperate to find new oil. In 1999, it eased the conditions for foreign oil companies to search for oil in Colombia and in the following two years 47 exploration contracts were signed. At a London conference for foreign investors in 2001, mines and energy minister Ramiro Valencia Cossio assured the audience 'there's going to be a lot of drilling'. He urged companies to 'come to Colombia – a country of opportunities', adding 'we're not here to talk about Mother Teresa, we're here to talk business'.[18]

It is almost certain that there is oil to be found. Although Colombia's known reserves total about 2.6 billion barrels of oil, or 0.2% of the world total, geologists' studies show that more than two thirds of Colombian territory lies on potentially oil-bearing sedimentary basins, which are likely to contain the equivalent of anything up to 37 billion barrels of oil.

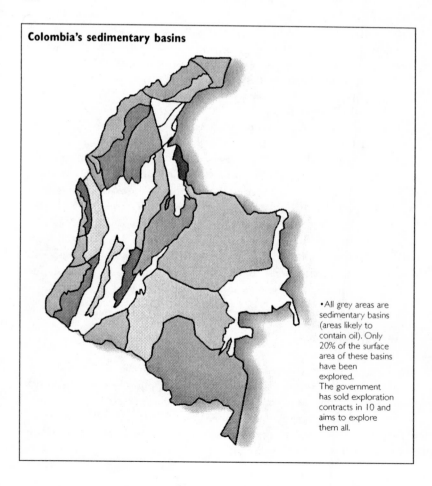

Colombia's sedimentary basins

•All grey areas are sedimentary basins (areas likely to contain oil). Only 20% of the surface area of these basins have been explored. The government has sold exploration contracts in 10 and aims to explore them all.

If the Colombian government wishes to fully explore and exploit its oil and mineral wealth, it will have to wrest control of much of its territory from armed groups. Those seeking an alternative explanation for Plan Colombia's overwhelming military focus might note that the new export model, based on oil and minerals, requires the Colombian state to have control over all of its national territory; whereas the coffee-economy was concentrated in the densely-populated western mountain ranges and could coexist with guerrilla control of outlying regions.

One of the richest seams of oil is in the foothills of the eastern Cordillera and the eastern plains or *llanos*. This is where Colombia's largest oil fields, Cusiana and Cupiagua, (operated by BP) and second largest, Caño Limón (operated by Occidental Petroleum, in association with Shell) are located. The government has sold an additional 26 exploration contracts in the *llanos* to transnational consortia. The armed forces fight a constant battle with guerrillas for control of the area and paramilitaries also operate freely. The further east one goes in this sparsely populated, barren land, prone to flooding, the weaker the government's presence becomes.

The need to reassert government control is even clearer in Putumayo, which until recently was a stronghold of the FARC. The state oil company Ecopetrol extracts here and six other companies are prospecting. The trans-Andean pipeline which runs through this area, pumping oil to Ecuador and the Pacific port of Tumaco, is regularly bombed by the guerrillas. Putumayo was the first target area of Plan Colombia.

The Amazonian departments of Caquetá, Vaupés and Amazonas are also believed to contain oil, but the authorities have had little chance to test this because the region is under the *de facto* control of the FARC. No exploration contracts in these regions have yet been sold.

The fuel guzzlers

The United States (which consumes a quarter of the world's oil) also needs to find new sources of crude; its own supplies will dry up in the first quarter of the twenty-first century at its current rate of production. In 2000, Colombia was the sixth-largest supplier of oil to the US, but it has the potential to be as important as neighbouring Venezuela, which has 65 more years of oil to exploit.

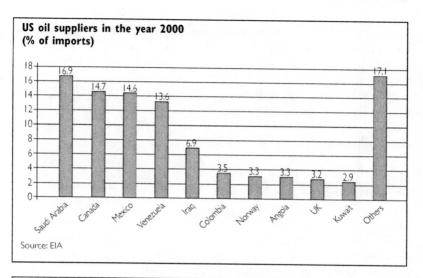

US oil suppliers in the year 2000 (% of imports)

Supplier	%
Saudi Arabia	16.9
Canada	14.7
Mexico	14.6
Venezuela	13.6
Iraq	6.9
Colombia	3.5
Norway	3.3
Angola	3.3
UK	3.2
Kuwait	2.9
Others	17.1

Source: EIA

Proven oil reserves in the Americas

	Billion barrels	Share of world reserves	Years left
USA	28.6	2.8%	10.0
Canada	6.8	0.7%	9.3
Mexico	28.4	2.7%	24.5
Total North America	**63.7**	**6.2%**	**13.8**
Argentina	2.7	0.3%	9.1
Brazil	7.3	0.7%	18.1
Colombia	2.6	0.2%	8.5
Ecuador	2.1	0.2%	15.3
Peru	0.4	†*	8.9
Trinidad & Tobago	0.6	0.1%	12.9
Venezuela	72.6	7.0%	65.2
Other S. & Cent. America	1.2	0.1%	25.0
Total South & Central America	**89.5**	**8.6%**	**37.7**

*less than 0.05%

Source: BP World Energy Review 2000

North Sea oil has made Britain the largest oil producer in the European Union (Norway is larger, but is not in the EU). The world's second and third largest oil companies are British: Shell (owned jointly with the Dutch) and BP.

North Sea oil is running out though, so British oil companies will have to seek more sources abroad if they want to retain their pre-eminence. At present Britain is a net oil exporter, but exports top-quality crude and imports low-grade oil mainly from the Middle East.

Oil companies

Many multinationals have been attracted by Colombia's promise of oil. British Petroleum is the largest foreign investor in Colombia. Other oil companies operating there include: Occidental Petroleum, Triton, Shell, Chevron, Exxon, Elf Aquitaine and Total.

Oil companies often operate in conflict zones. They are also targeted by guerrillas who accuse them of stealing the country's natural resources. Colombia's second-largest rebel group, the ELN, has a history of bombing oil pipelines; they dynamited the Caño Limon-Covenas line, for example, a record 127 times in 2001. Foreign oil workers have also been kidnapped by rebels.

One of the key concerns of the companies, therefore, is security. They have cooperated with military battalions with appalling human rights

---

Pipeline attacks

• Attacks on oil pipelines between 1992-2002 spilt the equivalent of 1.9 million barrels of oil, eight times more than the Exxon Valdez disaster. The government estimates 2,600km of rivers have been polluted.[20]

• All armed groups attack oil infrastructure, but the tactic is most commonly used by the ELN.

• These attacks can have tragic consequences. The most horrific incident occurred on October 18, 1998, when an ELN pipeline bomb caused a fireball to engulf the village of Machuca in Antioquia. Seventy-three people were burned alive.[21]

records and which are known to have collaborated with paramilitary death squads. In Arauca and Casanare, the army has dedicated entire brigades (the eighteenth and sixteenth respectively) to defending oil production. Both of these brigades have been accused of extrajudicial killings.[19]

The oil industry's entanglement in the counterinsurgency war became even more explicit in the year 2002, when the Bush administration asked Congress to approve US$98 million in military aid to defend oil infrastructure from rebel attacks in Arauca, the region in which US-company Occidental Petroleum operates. This was the first explicit US counterinsurgency aid for Colombia since the end of the Cold War.

British Petroleum

In the mid 1990s, people living near BP's oil fields in Casanare, eastern Colombia, complained of repeated harassment from the military after they protested against oil spills on roads and farmland. Their complaints included death notices being posted on walls and inclusion of their names in a military list of 'guerrilla' targets. The complaints were catalogued in a joint report by the Colombian attorney general's office, the state prosecutor's office, the ombudsman's office, the President's human rights advisor and two human rights groups.[22]

The report named numerous peasant activists who had been threatened by the security forces and named seven who had been killed by either paramilitaries or the military in Casanare between 1991 and 1995. Carlos Mesias Arrigui Cerquera, who was assassinated on April 13, 1995, was the leader of the local peasants' association (ANUC) and had led a civic strike against BP in January 1994.

In this period BP paid the Defence Ministry for protection and worked closely with the armed forces on security issues. In 1995, for example, BP signed a three-year agreement with the Defence Ministry, in which it agreed to make cash and in-kind payments worth US$11 million to the army. The contract stated that the army would provide a presence throughout Casanare's petroleum zones and BP would, in turn, provide security and communications equipment, administration materials, 'information', engineering and health services, helicopter time and land transport to the armed forces.[23]

Local people believed that BP were collaborating with the armed forces' dirty war. In particular they alleged that BP gave the military photographs of activists taken at community meetings. These claims were apparently corroborated by the Commander of the B-2 unit of the Army's XVI Brigade. The Attorney General et al's report stated:

> 'The Commander of the B-2 unit of the XVI brigade said that the oil companies have very valuable information because their own security systems are quite sophisticated. For this reason the army tries to get access to it. For example, the photographic archives of the Brigade contain a number of photos supplied by the companies, taken at meetings that they have held in the local community; these meetings are recorded on video and this filmed material is used in intelligence work. The commission records the fact that during this meeting, its members were photographed and filmed by the brigade'.[24] [Note he did not specify 'BP', although BP was the major oil company operating in Casanare, the XVI brigade's area of responsibility].

BP admitted taking photos of local people, but denied handing them over to the armed forces.[25]

BP asked the State Prosecutor's Office to investigate the allegations, which reported its findings in January 1998. It concluded that the armed forces were probably responsible for the murder of Carlos Arrigui. However, it could find no evidence that BP was involved in this murder or any of the other killings it investigated. It stated that it was 'no secret' that paramilitaries had committed 'barbarous and inhuman' killings but that it was 'a big step, that judicially would have to be substantiated with evidence and not mere speculation' to link these events to BP. It concluded that there was not sufficient evidence to open a full inquiry into BP, but said it would re-open the investigation if new evidence came to light.[26]

BP says this report clears it of all charges. However, the public prosecutor's investigation has been questioned. A confidential study commissioned by a group of British NGOs (Oxfam, Christian Aid, Cafod, Save the Children and Caritas) noted that the prosecutor's office:

• did not interview the original team of investigators who had written the first report for the Attorney General's Office *et al* (1995).

• did not interview the Commander of the B2 unit of the XVI brigade who alleged that oil companies had given photographs to the military

- did not investigate the matter [of photographs] very thoroughly at all. It merely visited BP's community relations department and reported that the department's photo archive did not contain photos of people in meetings or demonstrations of the type BP had been accused of handing over to army intelligence.[27]

BP no longer has a direct agreement with the Defence Ministry, instead its partner, the state-owned oil company Ecopetrol, negotiates all security deals with the armed forces. The situation in Casanare has also changed: paramilitaries have made great advances and control most rural areas. The peasant movement, which organised civic strikes in the early 1990s, has been subdued and there is virtually no social protest in this region. The oil workers' trade union, USO, cannot operate in most of Casanare due to the strength of the paramilitaries. BP will not talk to the union and will not allow union members to enter its drilling sites. Trade unionists who have tried to approach BP employees have been threatened.

'After the union tried to visit BP sites we began to receive death threats'

'BP's oil drilling sites are entirely militarised; trade unionists cannot enter these areas without risk of being killed by paramilitaries.

Most of BP's workers are sub-contracted, this means that BP can give them very short-term contracts, for instance 3-months long, and can avoid paying social security or health insurance – which is vital in an industry as dangerous as ours.

We [the Colombian oil workers' union] have tried to talk to BP about conditions on their sites, but they refuse to meet with us. We have also attempted to visit BP's drilling sites in Casanare three times to talk to workers there. We were refused entry and after the visits the union began to receive death threats. I cannot prove that BP was directly involved in this, I can only say that threats against union members increased after we visited the sites.

Last year, the union organised a forum on national oil policy in Yopal, the capital of Casanare [the region where BP operates]. Outside the meeting, I got chatting to a sub-contractor for BP, who was telling me how bad his conditions were and how he

> was unhappy with his contract. In the middle of our conversation, a man came up and starting asking me who I was, what my name was and told the other man not to talk to me. He eventually hustled him away. I believe he was a paramilitary.
>
> **Interview with a leader of USO, February 2002**[28]

Pipeline dispute

BP's pipeline company, Ocensa, is refusing to pay adequate compensation to more than 1,000 peasants whose land was ruined by a pipeline built in Antioquia, according to two lawyers bringing a civil suit against the company.[29] The peasants claim that they have lost their livelihoods as a result of the large-scale disturbance of the land, which contaminated water supplies and eroded the soil on their farms. Unable to make a living from the land, some of the families have moved to the shantytowns of Medellín, where they survive by foraging rubbish tips. Ocensa is a joint venture of the state oil company Ecopetrol and five foreign companies; BP has a 15.2% stake in it. However, BP played a key role in the planning of the pipeline, applying for the environmental licence, negotiating right-of-way contracts with peasant families and signing cheques for right-of-way payments to a minority of the families.

Gilberto Torres[30]

Gilberto Torres worked on an Ocensa oil pumping station in Porvenir, Casanare. He was abducted by the Autodefensas Unidas de Colombia (AUC) on February 26, 2002 and was handed over to the Red Cross on 7 April. His kidnapping prompted international condemnation and a 26-day strike by oil workers in Colombia.

Torres, who has since sought temporary exile in Spain, says that he believes he was kidnapped due to his trade union activity for the oil workers' union, USO. 'I was a stone in the shoe of the multinationals,' he says. Paramilitary threats against him increased after he participated in two national oil strikes, in 1998 and 2000, he says. He alleges that while he was held captive, a paramilitary commander told him that the AUC had infiltrated Ocensa by getting jobs as security guards and drivers.

'I was travelling home from work in the Ecopetrol car when the paramilitaries intercepted our path. They called me a 'guerrilla son of a bitch' and ordered me to get into their car. How did I feel? Well, *hombre*, I was sure they were going to kill me…

The first night we stayed in a farmhouse. I was tied up and all my personal things were taken from me, my watch, my glasses, my rosary, my papers …

A few days later we were taken to another farm, where the guards dug a hole in the ground in a patch of woodland. My arms and legs were shackled and I was lassooed to a tree. I was then ordered to get into the hole. I didn't know if it was to become my grave …. Barbed wire was put over the hole. That was when the infestation started. Ants and other insects began to bite me, but I couldn't move because I was chained. They started to eat into my flesh where the shackles had broken the skin ….The next day it started to rain and the hole filled with water. The commander decided that every day at 6pm I was to be brought into the farmhouse, still shackled, to sleep and every morning I was ordered back into the hole. They called me a 'trussed up pig'. After a few days of this the commander came to interrogate me … he wanted information about the guerrillas, but I am trade unionist, not a guerrilla and had nothing to tell him ….

I spent ten days in the hole. Then Easter week began and lots of people started arriving at the farmhouse. It became embarrassing to keep me there … I was taken to another house. When I arrived the old lady who lived there saw me shackled and covered in insect bites and tried to talk to me, but the commander wouldn't let her. They chained me to a hammock with my arms tied to the beam of the porch …One day the old lady approached me with her grandson. She gave the little boy a rosary and told him to give it to me, but he was too scared …So she came and handed me the rosary. A wave of homesickness and emotion swept over me and I began to cry...

We moved on to another house days later. Each time we travelled to a new place, I thought it would be my last journey. I thought they would take me to wasteland and shoot me like they have so many of my colleagues … One morning, after 42 days in captivity, the commander told the guards to get the 'prize cow ready for market'. They took me to a river, washed me and gave me new clothes …. Later that morning I was handed over to the Red Cross.'

Defence Systems Limited

BP uses the services of the Defence Systems Limted (DSL),[31] a London based company set up by former SAS men. It was investigated by the Colombian public prosecutor for allegedly providing local army units with 'lethal' counterinsurgency training to the Colombian army. When the prosecutor's office reported its findings in 1998, it said it could 'not confirm or discard' the allegations. It added:

> '[DSL's] reticence to provide precise information at the time and to hide any relationship between the police and DSL in these activities, leaves a glimmer of doubt over the issue, making one think that something illicit or irregular may have happened in the circumstances in which the training was given.'[32]

The prosecutor decided to continue investigating DSL to establish whether its police training had involved full counterinsurgency methods or whether it was confined to defensive tactics to defend BP's oil installations.[33] The prosecutor's office subsequently put the case in abeyance, pending new evidence.[34]

DSL was also accused of illegally supplying military equipment to an army brigade protecting the Ocensa pipeline in Segovia (Antioquia). This brigade (XIV) has been implicated in numerous extrajudicial killings, most notoriously the massacre of 43 people in Segovia in 1998. The equipment was allegedly procured from the Israeli security company Silver Shadow. The allegations were made in *The Guardian* newspaper by journalists Michael Gillard, Melissa Jones and Ignacio Gómez in 1998. The report was based on correspondence between Silver Shadow and Ocensa.[35]

Oxy and the U'wa

Occidental Petroleum (Oxy), won a contract to drill on the ancestral lands of the U'wa indigenous people in Santander, northern Colombia. The U'wa fought an eight year legal battle to prevent the work going ahead and threatened mass suicide if the 'blood of mother earth' was extracted.

Oxy was granted the licence to explore the area in 1992. The U'wa launched a campaign and in 1995 Colombia's constitutional court revoked the company's licence on the grounds that the government had failed to consult with local people, as required by the constitution. The government then extended the U'wa territory from 61,000 hectares to 221,000 hectares and granted Oxy a new oil exploration licence, 5km outside the U'wa reserve.

As the company prepared to drill, the area was increasingly militarised and the U'wa's attempts to peacefully block entry to their homeland were violently put down. In early 2000, three children drowned when military police armed with batons and tear gas charged a line of families forcing them to jump into a fast-flowing river.[36]

The so-called Samoré site is thought to contain the equivalent of 2.5 billion barrels of oil – an amount which would almost double Colombia's reserves – hence the government's backing to Oxy. Exploratory drilling began in September 2000. However, in May 2002, Oxy abruptly pulled out of the contract. It denied the campaign by the U'wa and international environmentalists had anything to do with the decision, saying simply that it had drilled a 'dry hole'. It is unusual, however, for a company to pull out of such a potentially lucrative site after drilling just one well.

Minerals

Colombia also has great mineral wealth; it is the world's largest emerald producer and a major supplier of coal and nickel. Its lands also contain gold, copper, silver, marble, zinc, lead, garnets, sapphires, diamonds, platinum, iron, gypsum and manganese.

The government is keen to encourage private companies to explore and exploit this underground treasure. A CD-rom produced for foreign investors states: 'Colombia has a variety of favourable geological environments and attractive mineral potential similar to other countries in Latin America, where mining has become the object of the development of major deposits ... There is no reason why the mineral potential of Colombia, which is so evident in countries such as Chile, Bolivia, Peru and Mexico, should stop at our frontiers. Modern techniques for a detailed exploration of potential mining areas have identified targets with a high probabilities [sic] of producing projects of great economic importance. This means the future development of mining in Colombia will be based on the consolidation of large scale projects.'[37]

Just as the terms for foreign oil companies were improved, the government is also pushing a new mining code through congress which offers mining firms tax breaks and concession contracts of up to 75 years.

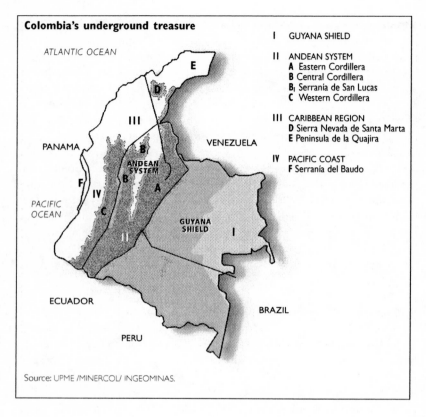

Colombia's underground treasure

ATLANTIC OCEAN

PANAMA

PACIFIC OCEAN

ECUADOR

PERU

VENEZUELA

BRAZIL

E

D

III

B

ANDEAN
SYSTEM

B

F

IV

A

C

II

GUYANA
SHIELD

I

I   GUYANA SHIELD

II ANDEAN SYSTEM
    A Eastern Cordillera
    B Central Cordillera
    B₁ Serranía de San Lucas
    C Western Cordillera

III CARIBBEAN REGION
    D Sierra Nevada de Santa Marta
    E Peninsula de la Quajira

IV PACIFIC COAST
    F Serranía del Baudo

Source: UPME /MINERCOL/ INGEOMINAS.

Coal

Colombia is the fourth largest coal exporter in the world and production has increased by 700% since 1980. The industry is based in the Guajira pensinsula on the Caribbean coast and it is here that Latin America's largest open-cast coal mine – Cerrejón Norte – is found. Fifty percent of the mine is owned by the US energy company ExxonMobil and the remaining 50% was sold to a multinational consortium comprised of Billiton (UK), Anglo-American (South Africa) and Glencore (Switzerland) as part of the privatisation of the state-owned coal company, Carbocol, in 2000. Colombia's second largest mine, La Loma, is owned by the US company Drummond. In March 2001, the president and vice president of the trade union at the Drummond mine were shot dead by paramilitaries.

Violence against energy workers

Oil workers and miners are often targeted by rightwing death squads and have suffered one of the highest assassination rates among Colombian trade unionists.

• In the past 10 years, at least 125 leaders and activists of the oil workers' union, *Unión Sindical Obrera* (USO) have been killed by death squads. At the time of writing, the most recent murder was that of Aury Sará, president of the Cartagena branch of USO. He was kidnapped by the AUC on November 30, 2001 and his dead body, and that of his bodyguard, were found on wasteland on 5 December.

• In March 2001 Valmore Locarno Rodríguez and Victor Hugo Orcasita, President and Vice-President of the mine workers' local union at La Loma mine, owned by the US company Drummond, were pulled from a company-chartered bus while on their way to work. They were shot dead by gunmen, some of them dressed in military uniforms. In October 2001, just four months after he took the post, the new president of the union, Gustavo Soler Mora, was killed by suspected paramilitaries. Another Drummond union official, Cándido José Méndez, was also killed in 2001.

• During 1998-2000 19 members of the electricity workers' union, Sintraelcol, were assassinated. The vice-president of the Colombian union confederation, CUT, and member of Sintraelecol, Jorge Ortega, were murdered in 1998

• In 1998, 17 oil trade unionists were charged with terrorism (after the military erroneously accused of them of being guerrillas). The lawyer representing them, Dr Eduardo Umana Mendoza, was shot dead.

• In October 2001 five USO leaders and one retired leader of Fedepetrol were arrested and charged with rebellion. The arrests occurred after workers at the state oil company Ecopetrol went on strike to protest at the lack of government action on paramilitary violence.

Sources: CUT, USO, Sintraelecol, International Federation of Chemical, Energy, Mine and General Workers' Unions (ICEM)

Green fire

Colombia supplies 60% of the world's high-quality emeralds, known as 'green fire' to collectors and 'green gold' to miners. All of the country's emerald deposits are located in Boyacá, in the eastern Andes mountain range. Unlike oil and coal, the emerald industry is not dominated by foreign multinationals, but is a maze of small shafts or *cortes* exploited by firms using a relatively low level of technology or by poor self-employed prospectors known as *quaqueros*.

There are two major emerald mines: the privately owned El Chivor (controlled by the Chivor Emerald Metal Mining Corp) and El Muzo, which the government leases to the Sociedad de Mineros Boyancences. Chivor and Muzo are internationally sought after emeralds, but the names now usually refer to their colour rather than their origin. Chivor emeralds are deep pine green with a blue-ish tinge; while Muzo emeralds are a warm grassy green with a yellow tone.

The mining firms use bulldozers, hydraulic jacks and explosives to loosen the layer of rock, then pump jets of water at it to wash away the debris. Once a calcite vein is exposed, the machinery is turned off and miners use picks and shovels to dig out the emeralds – often under the watch of armed guards. Further down the mountains, hundreds of *quaqueros* wait for the slurry which they pan for low-grade emeralds. It is a very dangerous occupation and *quaqueros* are often killed by mudslides.

Historically, the province has been one of the most violent in Colombia. Rivalry between the Conservative and Liberal parties was intense and it was from the Boyacá town of Boavita that the infamous *chulavita* police force, which massacred Liberals during *La Violencia*, got its name. Emeralds fuelled the violence. During the 1940s, the state attempted to gain a monopoly on emerald mining, but its control was tenuous and a parallel illegal industry grew. Local emerald traders, *planteros*, bought the stones from the poor prospectors, which they smuggled abroad. As the *planteros* became richer, they set up their own private armies, and began to feud with each other – rivalries that culminated in the 'Emerald Wars' of the 1960s and 1970s.[38]

Today, the government wants foreign mining companies to introduce modern mining techniques to the emerald industry. It wants to eliminate smuggling and small scale, semi-legal (and dangerous) emerald prospecting. It aims to bring the emerald trade into the formal sector so that it can be taxed. At present, given that Colombia is the world's leading supplier, export earnings from emeralds are very low – US$108 million in 1998. This is not only due to smuggling but also because uncut emeralds are cheaper than those embedded in jewellery and it is in the setting process that the profits are made.

Mines, megaprojects and murders

Some of the most intense areas of paramilitary activity coincide with those that contain coal, oil, precious metals, valuable agricultural land or big industrial 'megaprojects'.

Some view this as a concerted strategy on the part of the Colombian elite to implement a strategy of 'development without people', replacing small scale agriculture with ranches and large extractive industries. The miners' union Sintraminercol, for example, argues that 'the most serious human rights violations are intimately linked to the implementation of economic models and the development of megaprojcets which brutally marginalise peasants, indigenous people, miners, workers and the poor civilian population...'[39] Alternatively it may simply reflect the willingness of businesses and landowners to resort to using private security forces – or death squads – in a situation where the state does not have a monopoly on the use of force and does not have the ability (or will) to assert the rule of law.

Non-traditional exports

In the 1960s and 1970s, the Colombian government began an export-diversification drive aimed at reducing dependence on coffee. The most important of these non-traditional exports are flowers.

Colombia is the second-largest flower exporter in the world (after The Netherlands). Eighty-two percent of its flowers are bought by the United States and 10% by the European Union. Within Europe, Britain is the most important market: half the carnations sold in the UK come from Colombia. Most flower plantations are situated in the cool temperatures of the Bogotá savannah, 2,600 metres above sea level. Roses and carnations are the most important exports, but over forty other types of flower including chrysanthemums and lilies are also grown.

The industry employs about 70,000 people, mainly women. Child labour was widespread in the early 1990s, but a government campaign has helped to reduce the problem, according to the ILO.[40] The main complaint of the workforce is the heavy use of pesticides. Two thirds of employees have suffered headaches, rashes, nausea, impaired vision or asthma, according to the Pesticide Action Network. Flower companies could use concentrations of chemicals of just 10% of the current strength, if other pest-control measures were put in place, the Food and Agriculture Organisations (FAO) estimates.[41] The Colombian growers' association, Asocolflores, has launched a campaign to encourage companies to reduce pesticide use and encourage organic production.

Foreign investment

Despite Colombia's moderate economic policies and increasingly investor-friendly legislation, the country attracted just 2% of the US$74 billion direct foreign investment in Latin America and the Caribbean in the year 2000. In 1990-94, Colombia's share was 5.9%, but it has lost out as neighbouring countries also embraced globalisation and competed to attract dollars, pounds, deutchmarks and yen. Latin America, as a whole, only attracted 6.7% of world investment flows in 2000, as trade and investment remained overwhelmingly concentrated in rich countries.

Maria Pérez* is forty years old and has worked on flower plantations in Cundinamarca for 12 years. She has worked for four companies, but was sacked from three after campaigning for better conditions. She has five children aged 24 to six years old.

'The flowers are sprayed with pesticides in covered greenhouses while we are working; only those who are doing the spraying are given gloves and protective clothing. Many of the employees have suffered headaches, dizzy spells and sores on our skin. We are worried that the chemicals could also cause cancers and scleroses but we don't have the funds to carry out a proper scientific study. Two years ago, a woman I know developed sclerosis of the liver, she was 45 and didn't drink or smoke, but we couldn't prove the pesticides were responsible ... We are supposed to work shifts of just eight hours, but the companies make us work 12-14 hour shifts. Trade unions are not tolerated and if the manager finds out you are an activist, you will be sacked. We don't want the flower plantations closed - we want the jobs - but we think we have a right to work in safe conditions.'[42]

*Maria Pérez is a pseudonym
Interviewed July 2001

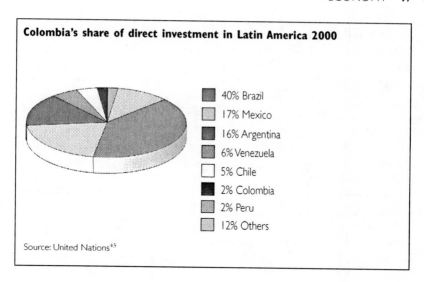

Colombia's share of direct investment in Latin America 2000

- 40% Brazil
- 17% Mexico
- 16% Argentina
- 6% Venezuela
- 5% Chile
- 2% Colombia
- 2% Peru
- 12% Others

Source: United Nations[45]

Ten largest transnational corporations in Colombia, by consolidated sales* US$m

Company	Country of Origin	Sector	Sales
Exxon Mobil Corporation	US	Petroleum	948
BP Amoco Plc (British Petroleum)	UK	Petroleum	451
Endesa España	Spain	Electricity	294
Colgate-Palmolive	US	Hygiene/Cleaning	287
Casino Guichard Perrachon	France	Commerce	259
BellSouth Corporation	US	Telecoms	183
General Motors Corporation (GM)	US	Motor Vehicle	181
Unilever	UK/Netherlands	Foodstuffs	170
Novartis	Switzerland	Chemicals	135
Procter & Gamble	US	Hygiene/Cleaning	122

Source: United Nations[46]

*There are many ways of measuring the scale of corporate foreign investment, for example by domestic sales, exports and direct inward investment. BP is largest in terms of direct foreign investment (DFI), according to the British Foreign and Commonwealth Office. BP exports most of the oil it extracts, so has lower sales in Colombia than Exxon.

Direct foreign investment in Colombia has grown from US$271 million in 1980 to US$5.3 billion in 1997. Since the emerging markets crisis (1997-99), investment has fallen, and in 2000 totalled US$1.3 billion. Oil is by far the most attractive sector for foreign investors; between 1980 and 1998, it accounted for 45% of all investment in the country.

Although governments in the 1990s were keen to privatise state-owned enterprises, they found it hard to attract buyers, except in the extractive industries. The privatisation of the electricity, telecoms and water companies have been delayed due to investors' concerns about the economic crisis and guerrilla violence, as well as political opposition at home.

The United States is the largest foreign investor in Colombia, followed by the United Kingdom. The net book valuation of UK investment in Colombia in 1999 was US$1.5 billion, (including oil).[44] British-owned BP is the largest foreign corporate investor in Colombia and has ploughed more than US$3 billion into the country.[45]

Colombian-British trade 1999

Top British exports to Colombia
1. Pharmaceuticals
2. Organic chemicals
3. Telecoms and sound equipment
4. Power generating machinery

Top Colombian exports to UK
1. Oil
2. Coal
3. Crude animal & vegetable materials
4. Coffee, tea, cocoa, spices

Source: Trade Partners UK[47]

4 Drugs

Sara Restrepo* is a small wiry woman with a huge smile. She is 48 years old and lives with her husband, Alberto, and five children in a wooden hut, three hours' walking distance from a settler-town on the edge of the Colombian Amazon. When she was sixteen, she and Alberto left their homes in Tolima in central Colombia, in search of land. After working for a few years, they saved enough to buy a small plot, but soon found that the only crop that they could make a living from in this remote, inaccessible region was coca.

Coca cultivation has expanded enormously in Colombia during the past decade; in 1989 it covered 42,400 hectares of land, by the year 2000, this had risen to 122,000 – a rise of 187%.[1] Colombia now produces 70% of the world's coca and around 300,000 people make a living from cultivating it. The majority of Colombia's *cocaleros* are like Sara, migrants from other parts of the country, fleeing violence or seeking land.

Civilians in rural areas have borne the brunt of the Colombian conflict and are caught in the middle as guerrillas, paramilitaries and the armed forces fight a vicious territorial war. In the year 2000 317,000 people were forced to flee their homes and since 1985, two million people have been internally displaced.[2] Others have been expelled from their land by gunmen hired by large landowners seeking to expand their holdings.

The families flocking to the coca areas are also trying to escape poverty. Colombian agriculture has undergone a rapid transformation since the 1960s; and one of the most notable features has been a steady concentration of land. In 1960, farms of over 500 hectares accounted for 29% of cultivated land, but by 1996 they accounted for 60.5%. Just 0.4% of Colombian landowners controlled these giant estates in both 1960 and 1996. At the other end of the scale, the share of the poorest 67% of proprietors fell from 6% of the total cultivated land to just 3%.[3] In other words, in 1996, 2.2 million poor farmers tried to scrape a living on farms of less than one hectare while 12,000 big landowners (or companies) owned estates averaging 3,661 hectares each, which covered almost two thirds of the country's farmland. The most effective way to stop people migrating to the coca-growing backwaters would be to carry out agrarian reform in the more fertile lands of northern and central Colombia.

Colombian farmers are finding it difficult to compete in an increasingly globalised economy; agricultural output fell 6.7% per capita in the 1990s,[4] and the value of Colombia's agricultural crops fell 1.5%.[5] By the end of the decade, 79.7% of people in the countryside lived below the poverty line, according to the government.[6]

The collapse of international coffee pricing agreement in 1989 had a devastating impact on the Colombian coffee industry (the country's greatest export earner after oil). Between 1990 and 2000 output fell 25% and export earnings halved.[7] A direct relation between the agrarian crisis and illicit cultivation can be seen: after 1989 thousands of small coffee farmers switched to growing opium poppies which, like coffee bushes, grow at high altitudes.[8] Poppy cultivation soared from 1,344 hectares in 1991 to 20,000 hectares the following year.[9]

Coca boom in the Amazon

Over 60% of Colombian coca is grown in three Amazonian states: Putumayo, Caquetá and Guaviare.[10] The armed forces are fighting an ongoing battle with leftwing guerrillas for control of these regions. In some areas the government rules only in name and in others official state structures are entirely absent. There are few roads or bridges. Away from the towns, many farms don't have electricity and the people here are unlikely to have access to state social security provision, health care or schools. Reliable statistics are hard to come by – the government's 1997 Standard of Living Survey did not include rural Amazonia because there were no civil servants there to distribute census forms.[11]

Unlike neighbouring Bolivia and Peru, most coca growers are not of indigenous origin. Indigenous people make up less than 2% of the total Colombian population. The vast majority of people in the Amazonian region are migrants from other parts of Colombia known as *colonos*. There have been numerous waves of migration since the 1920s, and

Ana is eighteen years old and a *raspachín*, a seasonal coca-picker. She takes her one-year old baby from farm to farm seeking work. If there's no harvest, she'll cook or clean. Her parents' farm near is not big enough to support her and her son, and besides, she says, she prefers to earn her own money.

On Saturday nights, if she can get a baby sitter, she likes to meet friends in town and have a beer or just 'hang out' . She has never taken cocaine and when asked about teenagers in the US or Europe taking drugs, she shrugs and says she cannot imagine what their lives are like.

Some raspachines work until they have saved enough money to buy their own plot of land, but Ana does not have a plan. She simply hopes that by the time her son is grown up, her family will have enough money for him to go to university.

each new group of settlers has travelled deeper into the Amazon rainforest, cutting down trees to make way for farmland. The coca booms have accelerated the process: during 1973-85, the first wave, the population of Amazonia rose by 90%, while national population growth was just 22%.[12] Indigenous people are now a minority in all Amazonian departments except Vaupés.

Indigenous communities have grown coca for hundreds of years for their own consumption (chewing the leaves to relieve exhaustion and distract hunger). Indigenous agriculture is traditionally a subsistence system in which the community grows, gathers or hunts the food they need to survive. In contrast, the *colonos* are peasants who want to be integrated into the market economy; they aim to cultivate a product — any product — which they can sell for money in order to buy food, clothes, sanitary products, household utensils, building materials, seeds, fertiliser and livestock. In theory, they also aim to save so they can expand their holdings and provide for their children.

'Don't tell us to grow bloody yucca!'

At a meeting between coca growers from Putumayo and a government minister, a grizzled man in his forties with rolled-up shirtsleeves roared: 'Don't come and tell us to grow bloody yucca!' Why his anger? In these remote, inaccessible Amazonian regions, where the soil is not suited to intensive agriculture, it costs more to transport small yields of vegetables to the cities than the products will sell for.

A study carried out by Cifisam,[13] a Catholic charity helping families to start growing alternatives to coca, found that for farmers provided with technical assistance (training, loan of equipment, technical advice), the net profit margin of traditional products (vegetables, tropical fruit, fish, and poultry) was 4.52%. For each dollar invested, the farmer would get back an additional 4.5 cents, barely enough to buy essentials for the family, let alone re-invest in the farm. Worse than that, however, the study found that without the charity's assistance, legal products made a loss of 49.25% – in other words for each dollar invested, the farmer would lose 49 cents. In contrast coca had a net profit margin of 49.07%.[14] The study was carried out in Caquetá, which is more accessible than Putumayo, Colombia's southernmost department, deep in the Amazonian rainforest.

To get a picture of why it is so costly to transport goods produced in the Amazon to a market, the journey from the capital Bogotá to Sara Restrepo's home is illustrative. First take a 32-seater plane to the nearest big town. Then go to the small port to catch the one boat that travels up the main river each day. After a two-hour journey, during which the boat gets stuck in the mud numerous times because the water is too shallow, you arrive at a smaller town. It is then necessary to take another boat (you must find your own because there is no longer a boat service) along a minor branch of the river for a further two hours (along which FARC guerrilla patrols are a common sight). After mooring the boat, it is then necessary to walk over hills and through forest (sometimes on a footpath and sometimes not) for about four hours. Who on earth would make this journey for a few pounds of yucca or potatoes?

In contrast, coca paste is a relatively light, compact product which has a huge potential for added value and for which demand is always strong. But the coca farmer is by no means rich. For each hectare of coca, the farmer will make an average net annual profit of US$1,060, according to a study by the Colombian government.[15] The paste from this hectare of coca can be refined into approximately 6,400 grammes of cocaine and sold in the United States for about US$512,000. The coca grower's share of the final price of a gramme of cocaine is about 0.2%.[16]

To make the paste, coca leaves are sprinkled with cement, then squeezed through a wooden press. They are then soaked in a barrel with kerosene and water. This liquid is then put in a bucket with sulphuric acid and by slowly adding sodium bicarbonate the 'paste' separates from the solution, is filtered and dried in the sun. The paste will be sold to a middleman who will take it to a more advanced 'jungle laboratory' to be refined.

Prices and yields

The productivity of coca farms varies and depends on their location, the age of the plants, the weather, and farming techniques. The conversion rate from coca to paste to cocaine also varies.

- An average hectare of coca plants produces 800kg of leaves per harvest.[17] The United Nations Drug Control Programme (UNDCP) estimates that this will eventually yield approximately 1.6kg of cocaine.[18]

- The number of harvests varies, in tropical Colombia it is usually between four to six per year.

- Using the UNDCP conversion rate, a hectare of coca therefore provides the raw material for 6.4kg to 9.6kg of cocaine a year. The CIA's range of estimates for one hectare of coca is 4.0kg to 7.4kg of cocaine a year.[19]

- The UNDCP estimates that the amount of coca grown in Colombia in the year 2000 was sufficient to produce 926,770kg of cocaine.[20]

- Two studies funded by the Colombian government's agrarian development agency (Plante) in 1999/2000 found that the coca growers' net earnings were very low.[21]

One of the studies found that the average annual gross income of a coca grower with one hectare was about US$9,750 for six harvests per year. It calculated that average annual costs for the set up and maintenance of one hectare of coca per year (including installation, set up of the 'kitchen', seeds, and chemical precursors) was approximately

US$8,680. This meant that the net annual profit of a campesino was about US$1,060, equivalent to a monthly income of US$92.

The other study found similar results: that the net annual earnings of an average coca grower were US$1,792, just above the minimum wage of US$1,419.

• The United Nations global illicit drugs trend survey estimated the average price of cocaine in the year 2000 was:[22]

wholesale (per kg): Europe US$38,000 / United States US$ 20,500 retail (per gram): Europe US$70 / United States US$80 (These are average prices. Prices are lower in some major cities. The purity of the drug will also affect the price.)

A farmer cultivating a hectare of coca earns between 0.1% to 0.3% of the street price of a gramme of cocaine sold in the United States (using the above figures).

Drug traffic

The drug trafficking chain starts from the poor coca farmer who sells the paste to an intermediary – it is then refined in jungle laboratories by hired employees, who are also normally recruited from the ranks of the rural unemployed. The refined cocaine is then shipped or flown to the States, often via Mexico or the Caribbean.

Drug traffickers have re-invested some of their earnings into buying vast tracts of land across Colombia, some of which, for example in Guaviare and Putumayo, are turned into large coca plantations. These estates are run by hired labourers or tenants and are situated in between numerous smaller peasant-owned plots.

The structure of the Colombian drugs trade has changed over the last decade; in the 1980s it was controlled by a few powerful cartels – most notoriously those of Medellín and Cali. These were broken up and the trade is now more decentralised and controlled by a larger number of smaller groups. Today's drug-trafficking rings are still run by powerful businessmen, who have connections in the Colombian establishment and in the United States which allow them, for example, to buy aeroplanes, bypass customs, launder money and link up with American bulk buyers.

Evidence that drugs money reaches the highest echelons of Colombian society was provided when a congressional inquiry found that narcotraffickers had funded the election campaign of former president Ernesto Samper (1994-98). Photographs and the names of some of Colombia's most notorious 'drug lords' are posted on the web site of the US Drugs Enforcement Administration (DEA).

Rightwing paramilitaries are heavily involved in drug trafficking; many were first mobilised as death squads formed by drug barons. Like the guerrillas, they are also eager to control areas of illicit cultivation because they provide a lucrative source of 'tax' revenue. They control tracts of land in northern and northeastern Colombia, and have recently made inroads in the guerrilla-controlled territory in the south, particularly Putumayo.

Narcoguerrillas?

US politicians and drugs czars frequently fulminate against 'narcoguerrillas' implying that that the Colombian rebels control the drugs trade. The country's largest guerrilla group, the FARC, tax the coca paste trade in the areas they control and this levy has become their most important source of revenue after kidnapping. There are also some reports that the FARC have launched a minor drugs trafficking route with the Russian mafia, although there is little hard evidence to support this. Not even the US Drugs Enforcement Administration (DEA) suggest that the FARC control the bulk of the drugs trade, as they do not have the contacts within the Colombian establishment or in the United States necessary to mastermind the multi-billion dollar trade.

'The most recent DEA reporting indicates that some FARC units in southern Colombia are indeed involved in drug trafficking activities, such as controlling local cocaine base markets. Some insurgent units have assisted drug trafficking groups in transporting and storing cocaine and marijuana within Colombia. In particular, some insurgent units protect clandestine airstrips in southern Colombia. However, despite the fact that uncorroborated information from other law enforcement agencies does indicate a nexus between certain traffickers and the FARC, there is no evidence that any FARC or ELN units have established international transportation, wholesale distribution, or drug money laundering networks in the United States or Europe.'

Statement by Donnie R. Marshall, Head of the United States' Drug Enforcement Administration (DEA), Testimony to Senate Caucus on International Narcotics Control, March 2, 2001

A pragmatic alliance

The expansion of the coca plantations in rural areas produced an ambiguous relationship between the traffickers and the guerrillas. Given the right climatic conditions, the areas most suitable for cultivation were those which were previously deserted but which attracted large numbers of displaced, colonising peasants, and where the state had little presence and capacity. Such areas tended, for the same reasons, to be under guerrilla influence or control. The guerrillas did not openly confront the peasants, but tried to regulate the process by limiting the number of coca plantations and forcing them to continue growing alternative food crops. But they also decided to take advantage of the drug production business: a fixed rate, usually estimated at 10%, was imposed on coca leaf or paste transactions in exchange for protection of the crop.

In this way, the guerrillas and traffickers formed a pragmatic alliance, although their politics were very different. They were united against state control for their mutual economic and military benefit. The guerrillas received resources and access to contacts who provided them with arms while the drug trade gained a means of protecting crops. Occasional disputes over specific issues sometimes aroused tension: the guerrillas tended to insist on maintaining a basic price for the peasants, even at times when market prices fell. Drug traffickers were not prepared to pay fixed rates in areas they could guard themselves, such as airports and laboratories (although sometimes they agreed to contract guerrilla groups to do this). There was also friction between guerrilla groups and individual drug traffickers; neither the guerrillas nor the traffickers are homogenous groups.

In addition to the operational disputes, there were underlying political differences. The entrepreneurial traffickers in their rural strongholds tended to have rightwing and authoritarian opinions. They sought and, in many places, enjoyed the enthusiastic backing of the local army unit when they were prepared to confront certain guerrilla activities. They were also reconstructing a sizeable network of rural properties which, in practice, constituted a profound agrarian counter-reform. Essentially, traffickers and guerrillas represented contradictory political projects, each requiring relatively comprehensive control of their geographical areas of influence.

Reconciling these conflicting aspirations was difficult. At the beginning of the 1980s, the appearance of networks of anti-guerrilla defence organisations, financed in good part by the *narcos* and viewed approvingly and supported by the army, was evidence of the conflicts between these two groups in areas like Magdalena Medio (1982-85). However, from 1986 the leading drug 'baron' of the central eastern part of the country, Rodríguez Gacha, under whom co-operative activities between the guerrillas and the traffickers were carried out, fell out with the guerrillas. The critical moment came in 1987 with the assassination of the presidential candidate supported by the guerrillas in the 1986 elections, the Communist Party militant Jaime Pardo Leal. After that there were disputes over alleged guerrilla actions against the drugs traffickers, which had included military attacks, kidnappings and appropriations of the assets they were supposed to have been protecting. From them on, political groups connected to the guerrillas, especially the *Union Patriótica* movement, were the victims of an intensive campaign of extermination which was largely co-ordinated and promoted by the drugs traffickers, but always counted on the more-or-less secret support of the members of the state security bodies, in particular the army.

Jorge Orlando Melo, 'The Drug Trade, Politics and the Economy: the Colombian Experience' in *Latin America and the Multinational Drugs Trade*, (1998)[23]

The drug trafficking business in Colombia today

'There are several hundred small cartels operating in an atomized fashion'

Prior to 1994, the Cali and Medellín cartels dominated all aspects of the Colombian drug business, which then focused more or less exclusively on cocaine. However, since the death of Medellín kingpin Pablo Escobar in 1993, as well as the capture of leading members of the Cali inner circle, control of the country's drug trade has become dispersed. Newer, less-structured and 'flatter' organisations now appear to be in the ascendancy, most of which operate in small, autonomous cells that are linked via Internet chat rooms and cellular phones protected by the very latest in encryption technology. Unlike the previous cartels, these 'boutique' groups typically contract out the majority of their jobs to specialists who work on a job-to-job basis rather than as part of an integrated structure.

US authorities admit that they only have limited operation intelligence on the groups that now dominate the drug trade in Colombia, attributing this to the groups' less structured nature. Of most concern is the fact that these transient syndicates necessarily lack the operational 'footprints' of the more established organisations, which has made it far harder for law enforcement authorities to build an accurate picture of dimensions, intentions and capabilities. The irony is that changes in this direction have largely been driven by law enforcement success against the larger and more visible Cali and Medellín cartels. As the Paris-based Geopolitical Drug Watch Group observes: 'The immediate effect of [past] repression was to disorganise the networks. But by making a virtue out of necessity, these large organisations quickly realised that decentralised structures are much less vulnerable and began the process of transforming themselves accordingly.'

The clearest window into the changes surrounding the Colombian drug structures came in late 1999 when Operation Millennium, a joint US-Colombian venture, successfully disrupted the activities of the Alejandro Bernal group. During the course of 1999, the DEA estimated the syndicate had been responsible for shipping 20 to 30 metric tones of cocaine to the United States every month, working in conjunction with the Mexican Ciudad Juárez cartel. Following the operation, however, US and Colombian intelligence sources conceded that the Bernal group did not appear to be a single entity but rather an amorphous organisation with several smaller cells which sometimes only collaborated on one-off operations.

The ad hoc quality of the contemporary Colombian drugs trade effectively means that the arrest of Bernal and his associates will not have much impact on the overall flow of cocaine into the United States. As one Colombian counternarcotics official conceded at the conclusion of Millennium following the arrest of Bernal:

'We [now] estimate there are several hundred small cartels operating in an atomized fashion. Several of those groups fed into the organisation we dismantled. But there are several other people out there as big as Bernal, who can put loads together from small organisations and we don't even have them identified.'

A. Rabasa and P. Chalk, *Colombian Labyrinth: The Synergy of Drugs and Insurgency and Its Implications for Regional Stability.* (2001).[24]

Paramilitaries and drug trafficking

Paramilitaries are heavily involved in drugs' trafficking. They not only tax the trade, but process, store and transport cocaine. For political reasons the State Department focus on guerrillas, but the most wanted drugs trafficker on the web site of the Drug Enforcement Administration (DEA) is linked to Carlos Castaño, the founder of Colombia's largest paramilitary group, the AUC. Castaño himself has openly admitted that a large proportion of his funds comes from drugs' trafficking.

It is unsurprising that such a close link exists, since many paramilitary groups were formed by the drug cartels, in alliance with landowners, businesses and sections of the army.

- The Medellín cartel donated generously to Muerte a Sequestradores (MAS) a death squad formed by army officers and ranchers in the Magdelena Medio region. Pablo Escobar, Jorge Luis Ochoa and González Rodríquez Gacha 'The Mexican' were all local landowners.[25]

- Fidel Castaño made his fortune from trafficking drugs and used the proceeds to invest in large tracts of land in northern Colombia. In the early 1990s, the Castaño brothers co-operated with the police, the Cali Cartel and dissidents from the Medellín Cartel (Henao brothers) to defeat Pablo Escobar. They took over his drug routes.[26]

- In March 2002, Castaño illustrated his close links to the drug barons when he attended a 'summit' of fifty leading drug traffickers and offered to co-ordinate their negotiations with the United States government. He made the announcement in a statement on his web site.[27]

- In 2002 the United States requested the extradition of Carlos Castaño, Salvatore Mancuso (the military commander of the AUC) and Hernán Giraldo (an AUC leader in northeastern Colombia) on charges of drug trafficking.

'Drug trafficking finances 70% of our activities'

For the first time, Colombians have seen the face of the man behind the country's feared right-wing militias. Clad in a shirt and tie rather than the customary military fatigues, Carlos Castaño sat down for a rare 90-minute televised interview. As he revealed his face, Castaño said his forces have committed atrocities against civilians and have close ties to drug trafficking. Asked how he bankrolled the force of paramilitary gunmen he commanded, Castaño said, 'drug trafficking and drug traffickers probably finance 70%. The rest comes largely from extortion', he said.

Colombian death squad leader reveals his face', 2 March 2000, CNN Americas. The broadcast was shown on Colombian TV in February, 2000

'The facility sprawled over 4 square miles and could produce 8 tons of cocaine a month'

Paramilitaries have three main ways of getting money and resources. They tax small businesses and multinational corporations whose operations fall within their territorial control. They collect contributions from large landowners and cattle ranchers. And they traffic in illegal drugs. In 1999, the government discovered one of the country's largest cocaine-processing complexes near Puerto Boyacá, a key paramilitary stronghold. Believed to be operated by the AUC, the facility sprawled over almost four square miles and could produce eight tons of cocaine per month. According to police estimates, the plant cost about US$5 million to build, and before it was destroyed employed more than 100 people.

The discovery confirms suspicions that the AUC is involved in processing, packaging and marketing cocaine and other drugs. The AUC controls the strategic region of Santander next to Panama, which allows drugs and contraband to easily cross the Panamanian border. It is thought this is the mere tip of the iceberg of paramilitary-run complexes.

Nazih Richani, The Paramilitary Connection, NACLA Report on the Americas, Oct 2000[28]

United Nations:

'The paramilitaries are involved [in drugs' trafficking], even more than the FARC, to the extent that in some regions it is difficult to distinguish between the drug traffickers and the paramilitaries.

'We don't consider the FARC to be drug traffickers. We consider them to be a guerrilla group with political objectives... However, they finance their war via the drug trade. They have their system of *gramaje* [tax on the trade of coca leaf] in some areas they also control the trade in coca paste.

'The ELN have never been very involved [in drug trafficking]...there are various reason for this, but the main one is that they don't control extensive zones which contain illicit crops.'

Klaus Nyholm, Colombia country representative, United Nations Drugs Control Programme (UNDCP), May 2001. Nyholm updated his remarks on the FARC in November 2002:

'Of course this was 18 months ago. Since then we have seen several cases of international drug trafficking on the part of FARC. Not very sophisticated, though, mainly bartering drugs for arms in neighbouring countries.'[29]

The armed forces and drug trafficking

Three defence ministers have been linked to drugs scandals:

- General Luis Camacho Leiva's brother was found with cocaine on a Ministry of Defence plane.
- Fernano Botero, Samper's defence minister, was forced to resign after admitting he had accepted money from the Cali Cartel.
- In 1983 an elite army squadron transported an entire cocaine-processing laboratory from Colombia to Brazil using airforce planes.[30]
- When an elite anti-narcotics force was established in 1989, it was

created within the police force because the military was so tainted by drugs money. Even so, the commander of this force, Colonel Hugo Martínez, and the head of the national police force, General Vargas, were later accused of accepting money from the Cali Cartel.

• In 1996 Colombian Air Force officers tried to smuggle heroin to the United States aboard the plane used by President Ernesto Samper to fly to the United States.[31]

• In March 1999, the State Department reported that drug-related corruption in all branches of the government continued to undermine Colombia's counternarcotics effectiveness. The report noted, for example, that in November 1998, US Customs and DEA personnel searched a Colombian Air Force aircraft in Florida and found 415kg of cocaine and 6kg of heroin. Several Air Force officers and enlisted personnel were arrested in connection with that incident.'

Source: US congressional report June 1999 (Drug Control: Narcotics Threat from Colombia Continues to Grow, GAO, June 1999)

Fumigation

Instead of confronting the powerful businessmen heading the cartels or attempting to reduce demand in the purchaser countries, the Colombian counternarcotics strategy, created and supported by the United States, has focused on just one element of the drugs trafficking chain: peasant coca farmers.

Since 1978 the Colombian anti-narcotics police, funded and trained by the US, have been spraying herbicides on illicit cultivations of coca, marijuana and opium poppies. These aerial fumigation missions have used various chemicals including Paraquat (1978); Ticlopyr (1985) and Tebuthiuaron (1986). Since 1986 the most commonly used herbicide has been glyphosate.

Glyphosate (N—phosphonomethyl) is a non-selective herbicide. The biggest-selling commercial formulation of glyphosate is *Roundup*, produced by the biotech company Monsanto. At low doses, according to the manufacturer's label, it causes eye and skin irritation. At high doses it is 'corrosive' and causes 'corneal opacity [blindness] for seven days'. Rural workers exposed to glyphosate have reported nausea, dizziness, respiratory problems, stomach ailments and increased blood pressure. Laboratory tests suggest glyphosate may cause lung dysfunction, infertility and cancer.

A US State Department study concluded that glyphosate was no more

---

Effects on health of glyphosate containing herbicides

Roundup is the herbicide that causes most human poisoning incidents.

Cases of accidental poisoning or intentional ingestion as well as occupational exposure of Roundup studied by Japanese doctors and the following symptoms of acute poisoning were reported: gastrointestinal pain, massive loss of gastrointestinal liquid, vomiting, excessive fluid in the lungs, congestion and lung dysfunction, pneumonia, loss of consciousness, destruction of red blood cells, abnormal electro-cardiograms, low blood pressure, and damaged or reduced hepatic function.

The surfactant in Roundup is considered to be the principal cause of the toxicity of the fumigation formulation. In rat and rabbit feeding studies, glyphosate affected semen quality and sperm counts (Cox 1995, Dinham 1998). According to the US Environment Protection Agency (EPA), continual exposure to residue in water in concentrations higher than 0.7 milligrams per litre can cause reproductive problems in humans. Concerns regarding the potential carcinogenicity of glyphosate persist, because of the contaminant N-nitroso-glyphosate (NNG). It is known that the majority of N-nitroso compounds are carcinogenic. And there is no safe dose for carcinogens. Additionally, in the case of Roundup, the surfactant POEA is contaminated with 1-4 dioxane, which has caused cancer in animals, and liver and kidney damage in humans. Formaldehyde, another known carcinogen, is also a breakdown compound of Glyphosate.

'Effects on health and the environment of herbicides which contain glyphosate'
Extracts of a speech by Dr Elisa Nivia. Pesticide Action Network[52]

QUESTION: *Does glyphosate fumigation harm cattle, chickens or other farm animals?*

ANSWER: Hair loss is the most visible symptom in cattle affected by fumigation, especially among calves and breeding cows. Hair loss is caused by moderate exposure and gradually disappears as the cattle are moved to non-fumigated pastures. Abortion is frequent among pregnant cows, possibly affected by the noise of overhead helicopters, which startles them, causing stampedes. Death of fowl affected by spraying or drinking contaminated water has been confirmed, as well as the death of fish in sprayed rivers, and the totality of the pond fish bred by settlers for their own consumption or to supply local inhabitants.

QUESTION: *Does glyphosate destroy the soil and prevent plant growth?*

ANSWER: Information regarding glyphosate mobility and persistence in the soil varies. It is known to be almost static in soils. It remains in the upper soil layers, with little propensity for percolation and a low runoff potential. Other studies, however, conclude that glyphosate can easily be leached from some types of soil; that is, glyphosate particles may be released, thus becoming quite mobile. Sub-lethal glyphosate doses carried by the wind (drift) damage wild flowers and can affect certain species more than 20 meters away from the site fumigated.

Analyzing glyphosate residue is costly and cumbersome. For this reason, the U.S. government does not routinely carry out such studies. Some research does exist, though, demonstrating that glyphosate can be carried by plants to the parts used for food. For example, glyphosate has been found in strawberries, blueberries, raspberries, lettuce, carrots and barley after its application. According to the World Health Organization, using glyphosate to dry the grain before wheat is harvested results in significant residues in the grain.

QUESTION: *Does glyphosate contaminate the water where it is sprayed?*

ANSWER: Glyphosate is highly soluble in water. According to the U.S. Environmental Protection Agency, it can enter aquatic systems through accidental spraying, drift or surface runoff. It is considered to disappear rapidly in water, as a result of adsorption to particles in suspension such as organic and mineral particles, to sediments and probably by microbial decomposition. If we accept that glyphosate is easily adsorbed into soil particles, it will have little potential to contaminate surface and ground waters. But if it is de-adsorbed or easily leached from soil particles, as it has been proven already, the situation changes. What is known is that glyphosate has contaminated ground and surface waters in various countries.

QUESTION: *Is glyphosate dangerous for the environment?*

ANSWER: Glyphosate is toxic for some beneficial organisms such as parasitic wasps and other arthropod predators, and soil arthropods that are important for soil aeration and humus formation. Some fish varieties are susceptible to *Roundup*, which is approximately 30 times more toxic to fish than glyphosate used alone. A study of rainbow trout and tilapia fish found that the chemical caused erratic swimming and respiratory difficulties among them. These behavioural changes altered their feeding, migration and reproduction capacity and they also lost the ability to defend themselves. As to how glyphosate affects birds, a study of exposed bird populations showed that the product is moderately toxic for birds; the changes it causes in plants affect birds, because they depend on such plants for food, protection and nestling. Field studies have demonstrated that some groups of small mammals have also been affected by glyphosate, due to death of the vegetation that either they or their prey use for foodstuff and protection. A study made in New Zealand showed that glyphosate substantially affected the growth and survival of one of the most common worms found in its farming soil.

Fumigation severely affects one of the most vital components of the Amazon ecosystem, known as the *cananguchales*. Clusters of *canangucha* palms form oases in the Amazon, inhabited by a great variety of animals and birds. Water constantly surrounds the palms in each oasis. Many cananguchales have been affected beyond salvation by spraying, when glyphosate has been transported by the wind or through the soil. The cananguchales are found on low terrains, which makes it easier for the water from fields sprayed nearby to reach them.

Acción Andina, Transnational Institute and Rapalmira, Extract from 'The Aerial Eradication of Illicit Crops: A Counter-Fact Sheet', 9 February 2001

toxic than 'baby shampoo'. However, what most official environmental studies have failed to take into account is that glyphosate is usually not sprayed alone, but mixed with other chemicals.[33] Monsanto's Roundup Ultra formula, for example, contains the surfactant polyoxyethylamine (POEA), which gives it very different toxic properties from glyphosate in its pure form.[34] Monsanto has refused to reveal the exact chemical composition of POEA, making it hard for agronomists to predict how it will affect the environment.

Since 1999 two additional chemicals have been added to the spray mixture, Cosmo Flux 411F and Cosmo-In-D. Cosmo Flux has a particularly pernicious effect: it ensures that the corrosive mixture sticks to the surface – leaf or skin – on which it is sprayed. This has resulted in humans and animals suffering serious skin burns. One of the key ingredients in Cosmo Flux was manufactured by the British chemical company ICI. However, when a British journalist exposed how these chemicals were being used in Colombia, ICI pulled out.[35] Other chemicals in the spray mixture are manufactured by Exxon.

In mid 2002 the State Department carried out the first study into the effects of mixing the EPA-registered formulation of glyphosate with Cosmo Flux 411F. In a report to Congress in September 2002, it concluded that 'the chemicals used in the coca spraying, in the manner in which they are applied, do not pose unreasonable risk or adverse effects to humans or the environment'. The report did concede that there was 'the potential for acute eye toxicity, due to an inert ingredient in the particular glyphosate formulation used by the program.'

In addition, the aircraft spray the mixture from above the recommended height of ten metres and use a much more concentrated solution - 23.66 litres per hectare, rather than the 2.5 litres per hectare recommended by the Colombian and US government regulatory bodies.[36]

In 1996, the Colombian authorities launched an intensive spraying campaign in the eastern department of Guaviare, at the time the country's main coca-producing region. A team of observers from the human rights group the Washington Office on Latin America, went to Guaviare in 1997 and reported:

'We received numerous complaints of health-related problems that have occurred after people literally have been sprayed while working in the fields or were nearby. One individual, for example, told of going blind in one eye after the field of banana trees he was working in was fumigated along with a neighbouring field containing coca. Others complained of skin infections, respiratory problems and stomach ailments. Others told of animals dying after drinking water from contaminated streams, or cattle dropping dead shortly after fumigation planes came through. Local communities are worried about contamination of water sources and the long-term impact of herbicide use on agricultural and cattle production.'[37]

The fumigation missions, together with the increased militarization of the region, outraged small farmers' who organised protest marches which attracted 216,000 people. The security forces reacted brutally, killing 12 marchers and, subsequently, seven protest leaders, including trade union

---

Chemical inputs in cocaine processing and the environment

The chemicals used in the production of coca paste and cocaine, as well as the fertilisers used in intensive coca cultivation, also present a risk to the environment. The waste from processing coca paste and cocaine is rarely disposed of safely, more often dumped on land or in rivers. Growers cannot ask for official help with disposal because coca cultivation is illegal.

- 500kg of cement, 500 gallons of gasoline and 12 litres of sulphuric acid are used to produce coca paste each year per hectare of coca.
- In 2001, this would be equivalent to:
  - 72 million kilos of cement
  - 72 million gallons of gasoline
  - 1.7 million litres of sulphuric acid.
- Coca farming uses an estimated 200,000 gallons of herbicides, 16,000 tonnes of fertilisers and 100,000 gallons of insecticides/fungicides per year.

The range of chemicals used in the second stage of processing – from paste to cocaine hydrochloride – is even greater.

They include:

- potassium permanganate
- ethyl alcohol
- hydrochloric acid
- chloroform
- aliphatic solvent
- acetone
- ammonia
- ethyl acetate
- butyl acetate
- methyl isobutyl ketone
- hexane
- toluene

900,000 tonnes of precursor chemicals were used in the production of drugs between 1984 and 1998, the Colombian environment ministry estimates.

Source: Plante and Colombian environment ministry[12]

leader Víctor Julio Garzón. Seven more people were disappeared. In 1998 and 1999 the anti-narcotics squads launched a spraying campaign in Caquetá and in late 2000 intensive fumigation began in Putumayo.

The herbicides do not, of course, only kill coca, but any plants they come into contact with. In all of the fumigation missions, farmers have complained that food crops including maize, yucca, bananas and tropical fruit have been destroyed. In Remolinos del Caguán, spray planes eradicated fields of rubber, cacao and family gardens that had been painstakingly created and tended by farmers as part of a six-year development project launched by the local Catholic parish.[38] Ironically, while it is possible to re-sow coca six months after fumigation, it takes much longer before the poisoned soil is safe to grow food again. According to the parish report:

> 'One of the factors that has encouraged families to withdraw from the [alternative development] project has been the constant fumigations that have...caused greater damage to productive lines, which take longer to recover than the coca plants.'[39]

After successive fumigations families have little choice but to move on, travelling further into the Amazon and clearing more virgin rainforest. The poorest, who have nothing to eat while waiting for new crops to grow, may join the ranks of the FARC, who will give them food and shelter.

The chemicals are being sprayed in one of the most complex and fragile ecosystems in the world, the Amazon rainforest. There is pressure from Washington to introduce new chemicals such as Imazapyr, Hexaxinon and Tebuthiuron, which would have an even more serious impact on the rainforest because of their low degree of dissolution in water. Colombian policymakers have also considered using a biological agent, the poisonous fungus *fusarium oxsyporum*.

The biological war on drugs

The United States has long been interested in engineering biological agents to eradicate illicit crops and has been investigating the use of the fungus *fusarium oxsyporum* – since the 1980s.

The State Department did not, however, want to be perceived as the main promoter of biological agents and in 1999 persuaded the United Nations International Drug Control Programme (UNDCP) to head the research. The Colombian government and the UNDCP were planning to start testing fusarium oxysporum ready for aerial application in Colombia in 2002.

However, following widespread protest, the UN pulled out of the project in November 2000.[10] In January 2001 the Colombian environment ministry also confirmed that it would not continue with the testing programme.[11] US funds for Plan Colombia were originally tied to the use of biological agents, but, once again, environmentalist campaigns forced President Clinton to back down.

'The balloon effect'

Aside from the health and environmental risks of fumigation, it has also been a singularly ineffective policy. During the 1990s, the Colombian authorities sprayed glyphosate over an increasingly large area, but the overall level of coca cultivation has grown, rather than fallen. In 1992, the authorities sprayed 944 hectares, while total coca cultivation covered 41,206 hectares. By 1998, a staggering 49,527 hectares were fumigated,

The balloon effect: coca cultivation by department
(% share of national cultivation)

	1991	1995	1999
Guaviare	57	51	28
Caquetá	23	28	30
Putumayo	6	12	37
Other	14	10	6
Total	100	100	100

Source: Colombian environment ministry [13]

but the area planted with coca bushes rose to 101,800 hectares. Similarly, Colombia's production of marijuana rose throughout the decade and it is now the second largest producer after the United States. Poppy cultivation fell, but its rise and decline does not correlate with times and intensity of fumigation missions.

Spraying campaigns have simply forced coca growers to move to other areas: the so called 'balloon effect'. In 1991, according to the environment ministry, 51% of Colombia's coca was grown in Guaviare. The government's mid-1990s spraying campaign reduced Guaviare's share of coca-cultivation to 27.8% by 1999. Cultivation was simply displaced to the more southerly Amazonian department of Putumayo whose share of national cultivation rose from 5.9% to 36.8%. When Caquetá was targeted in 1999, more *cocaleros* fled to Putumayo, cutting down virgin rainforest as they went, and by 2000, 54% of all coca was grown there. The three departments' share of Colombia's total cultivation remained above 70% throughout the period.

Coca displacement in the Andes

Colombia has carried out the most sustained and extensive fumigation programme of the three main coca producing countries in the Andes (Colombia, Peru, Bolivia). Yet in Colombia cultivation has soared, while in Bolivia and Peru it has fallen – in Bolivia from 50,300 hectares in 1990 to 14,600 hectares in 2000; in Peru from 121,300 hectares to 34,000 hectares. Interestingly, Peru has barely used herbicides at all.[44]

The pattern of coca cultivation in the Andes has more to do with the changes in the structure of the drug trafficking industry, than the intensity of fumigation campaigns. During the reign of the Medellín and Calí cartels, coca was grown in Bolivia and Peru, then transported to Colombia for refining. When these powerful cartels were broken up (1993 and 1996-97), their production chains were abandoned and the new traffickers began to buy coca from domestic producers. Simultaneously, drug barons invested their earnings in landholdings in Colombia, so it made sense to start producing there. The 'air bridge' strategy pursued by the Clinton administration – which aimed to intercept coca paste being transported to Colombia from Bolivia and Peru, also encouraged the displacement of coca growing to Colombia.

The decline of coca in Peru was also aided by a naturally occurring fungus which wiped out much of the crop in the early 1990s, plus a change in the political situation. The Peruvian military defeated Sendero Luminoso guerrillas and regained control of the national territory, just as Colombia's civil war – which leaves vast tracts of land unsupervised by the government – was intensifying. The current distribution is not, of course, static, indeed one of most commonly voiced criticisms of Plan Colombia is that it is likely to displace coca cultivation to neighbouring countries.

Coca cultivation in the Andes 1985-2000
(in hectares)

	1985	1988	1990	1995	1999	2000
Colombia	13,500	34,000	40,100	50,900	122,500	136,200
Peru	90,370	110,400	121300	94,400	38,700	34,100
Bolivia	na*	48,925	50,300	48,600	21,800	14,600
Total	na*	159,325	171600	193900	183,000	184900

*insufficient data

Source: US State Department[15]

5 Plan Colombia

Plan Colombia was heralded as the most ambitious campaign against drug trafficking in history. The Plan involves six years of heavily militarised aerial fumigation of illegal crops. The United States' contribution to the Plan was to give Colombia its biggest ever military aid package, making the country the world's third largest recipient of US military aid, after Israel and Egypt. The level of military aid raised suspicions that Plan Colombia was a thinly disguised counterinsurgency offensive and led to fears that US could become embroiled in an intractable civil war.

Plan Colombia has already harmed the health of thousands of humans and animals and may cause irreparable damage to the Amazon rainforest, not only in Colombia, but also in neighbouring Ecuador, Peru and Brazil. Fumigation has prompted thousands of people to flee their homes and, in total, is expected to create one million refugees; it has intensified the war and undermined the peace process. Colombia's neighbours fear the war could spill over their borders and turn into a region-wide conflict.

The US transforms Plan Colombia

Critics have been careful to distinguish between Colombia's Plan Colombia and the United States' Plan Colombia. There are good reasons to do this. The original plan unveiled by President Andrés Pastrana in 1999 has little in common with the existing Plan Colombia, drawn up with Washington's help over the following year. The US input was so extensive that the first draft of Plan Colombia was written in English not Spanish.

Pastrana's original Plan Colombia published in May 1999 makes no mention of drug trafficking, military aid, military action or fumigation.

Its focus is on achieving peace and ending violence. The first line reads: 'The violence and insecurity which affect Colombian society are the main problems facing national life.' The document goes on to argue that a sustainable peace will only be achieved if poverty and underdevelopment in the countryside are addressed and if democracy is strengthened. After a short description of the human, economic and environmental costs of the violence, paragraph 5 states:

> 'Under these circumstances, it is clear that the solution of the armed conflict through negotiation is indispensable to tackle the root causes of violence...for these reasons, the government has decided to launch an integrated peace policy which will involve the development of future talks accompanied by political reforms aimed at strengthening democracy and the channels of participation and, side by side with this, the setting up and implementation of Plan Colombia, as an integral part of a development plan. Plan Colombia will involve actions prioritising and focusing on regions where violence has assumed a critical character and where it is associated with factors such as forced displacement and the presence of illicit cultivation.'

It goes on to say that violence 'has deep roots in the economic and political exclusion and...inequality and poverty.' It makes no mention of fumigation but talks about developing 'environmentally sustainable economic activities that give the population the ability to improve its income levels and quality of life in the medium and long term.'

The five key plans of action were:

- development of productive processes
- the promotion of human capital
- the construction of a peace infrastructure
- the strengthening of social capital
- promoting environmental sustainability

The only mention of security in the entire document was:

> 'Plan Colombia will also include programmes and policies for coexistence and civic security, based on a new orientation, which goes beyond the traditional model of security based on repression – police-justice-prison – and focuses on interventions with a greater preventative and pedagogic

content as part of an overall strategy to reduce violence, although it will not abandon measures of control.'

The document is full of jargon and could be dismissed as empty government rhetoric which would never have been put in to practice. Nevertheless, it was fundamentally a peace plan and it placed the problem of illicit crop cultivation in the context of rural poverty.

The final version of Plan Colombia

The final version of Plan Colombia, written by US officials, could not have been more different. It is entitled *Plan for Peace, Prosperity and the Strengthening of the State*. Drug trafficking and strengthening the military are its main preoccupations. The emphasis on peace has been transformed into an insistence on bolstering the state and the armed forces. The first line of the document reads:

'As Colombia stands both proud and threatened on the threshold of the 21st century, we are faced with the historic challenge of establishing and securing a society where the State can exercise its true authority and fulfil its essential obligations, as stated in our Constitution...The chief responsibility for us in government is to build a better, more secure country for this generation and future ones [paragraph two]... There is no question that Colombia suffers from the problems of a State yet to consolidate its power: a lack of confidence in the capacity of the armed forces, the police and the judicial system to guarantee order and security [paragraph 4]...'

The first mention of peace does not come until the second page and then the message has changed:

'Attaining peace is not a matter of will alone. Peace must be built; it can come only through stabilising the State, and enhancing its capacity to guarantee each and every citizen... their security and the freedom to exercise their rights and liberty [paragraph 8]... Negotiation with the insurgents, which my government initiated, is at the core of our strategy because it is one critical way to resolve a forty-year-old conflict [paragraph 9]...'

Drug trafficking was not mentioned in the original document, but in the

US version of the plan it has become the root cause of Colombia's problems and eight paragraphs are dedicated to it in the preamble:

> 'The decisive challenges for Colombia come from the spread of drug trafficking, and the economic, political and social impact of globalisation. [paragraph 3]...the enormous destabilising effects of drug trafficking, which, with vast economic resources, has constantly generated indiscriminate violence while undermining our values [paragraph 4]... The violence and corruption fuelled by drug trafficking generate distrust among foreign investors, putting a major roadblock in the path of modernising the way things work [paragraph 5)...In short, the hopes of the Colombian people and the work of the Colombian government have been frustrated by drug trafficking, which makes it extremely difficult for the government to fulfil its constitutional duty [paragraph six]

Another notable addition to the final version of Plan Colombia is 'a fiscal and financial strategy that includes tough austerity and adjustment measures in order to...recover the historically excellent prestige of Colombia in international markets.' Pastrana's original plan was not radical; it did not seek to overcome rural poverty by redistributing wealth (through land reform, for example), but through economic growth. Nevertheless it envisaged investing public, as well as private, money into rural development projects, an aim which seems incompatible with 'tough austerity measures'.

The ten elements of Plan Colombia

1. An *economic strategy* that generates employment supports the ability of the State to collect tax revenues and allows the country to have a viable counterbalancing economic force to narcotrafficking. The expansion of international commerce, accompanied by enhanced access to foreign markets and free trade agreements that attract foreign and domestic investment, are key to the modernisation of our economic base and to job creation. Such a strategy is crucial at a time when Colombia is confronting its worst economic crisis in seventy years, with unemployment reaching 20%, which in turn greatly limits the government's ability to confront drug trafficking and the violence it generates.

2. A *fiscal and financial strategy* that includes tough austerity and adjustment measures, in order to boost economic activity and recover the historically excellent prestige

of Colombia in the international financial markets.

3. A *military strategy* to restructure and modernise the Colombian Armed Forces and the National Police, to make them more capable to re-establish the rule of law and provide security throughout the country, and in combating organised crime and armed groups.

4. A *judicial and human rights strategy* to reaffirm the rule of law and assure equal and impartial justice to all Colombians, while pushing ahead with the reforms already initiated among the State security forces to ensure their proper role in defending and respecting the rights and dignity of each and every Colombian.

5. A *counternarcotics strategy*, in partnership with other producer and consumer nations, to combat the production and consumption of illegal drugs; and on a national level to allow us to obstruct the flow of millionaire resources from drugs to various insurgent and other armed organisations which is fuelling violence.

6. An *alternative development strategy* that will promote agricultural and other profitable economic activity for small rural farmers and their families. Alternative development will also consider economically feasible environmental protection activities that conserve the forest areas to stop the dangerous expansion of illegal cultivation throughout the Amazon delta and Colombia's vast natural parks, whose immense biodiversity and environmental importance to the entire globe is incalculable.

7. A *social participation strategy* aimed at collective consciousness-raising. This strategy aims at more accountable local governments, community involvement in anti-corruption efforts and in continuing to put pressure on insurgent and other armed groups to end kidnapping, violence and internal displacement of citizens and communities. Also, this strategy will include working with local business and labour groups, in order to adopt newer, more productive models in light of a more globalised economy, and to strengthen our agricultural communities in the face of rural violence.

8. A *human development strategy* to promote efforts to guarantee, within the next few years, adequate education and health, to provide opportunities to every young Colombian and to help vulnerable groups in our society, including not just those affected and displaced by violence but also those in conditions of extreme poverty.

9. A *peace strategy* that aims at a negotiated peace agreement with the insurgency on the basis of territorial integrity, democracy and human rights, and which should strengthen the rule of law and the fight against drugs throughout the country.

> 10. An *international strategy* to confirm Colombia's leadership in the consolidation of the principles of shared responsibility, integrated action and balanced treatment of the drug issue. The role of the international community is also vital to the success of the peace process provided it conforms to norms established in international law and is requested by the Colombian government.
>
> Source: Plan Colombia

Funding Plan Colombia

The United States' redesign of Plan Colombia turned it from a peace plan into a battle plan. Although there are ten elements of the Plan, a look at the funding shows that the military element is by far the most important.

Colombia had originally aimed to raise US$7.5 billion – of which US$4 billion was to come from the Colombian government and US$3.5 billion would come from foreign countries and multilateral agencies such as the World Bank and InterAmerican Development Bank.

These plans were derailed when in 1999 Colombia plunged into its worst recession in recent history, and signed a fiscal austerity plan with the IMF, making it extremely unlikely that it will be able to spend anything like the planned US$4 billion.[1]

Colombia also hoped to raise at least US$1 billion from Europe; but most European countries were sceptical about Plan Colombia and approved a contribution of just US$366 million (of which US$86 million were loans). European governments were piqued that they had not been consulted earlier and that the plan had been drawn up exclusively with the United States. Many member states were also worried about the militaristic nature of the plan (or at least irritated that all the lucrative military contracts had gone to the US). So unhappy was the European Union about associating itself with Plan Colombia, it made its contribution to a separate 'European peace initiative' and technically has contributed nothing to Plan Colombia.

Japan provided loans totalling US$170 million; the InterAmerican Development Bank (IDB), the Andean Development Corporation (CAF) and the World Bank provided a US$300 million loan and Canada made a contribution of US$40 million. The non-US contribution to Plan Colombia for the entire six year period 2000-2006 totalled US$876 million, (of which two thirds were loans) leaving the 'social side' of the plan severely under-funded.

Europe's peace initiative funding
US$m

Donor	Loan	Aid	Total
Germany		18.0	18.0
Austria		0.6	0.6
Belgium		10.1	10.7
Denmark		0.6	0.6
Spain	76.0	24.0	100.0
Finland		2.2	2.2
France		18.0	18.0
Low Countries		7.2	7.2
Ireland		0.9	0.9
Italy	10.0	5.0	15.0
Norway		20.0	20.0
Portugal		0.3	0.3
United Kingdom		7.02	7.02
Switzerland		8.5+12	20.5
Sweden		4+16	20.0
European Commission		126.0	126.0
Total	**86.0**	**230.37**	**366.97**

Source: Fondo de Inversiones para la Paz (FIP) & DNP[2]

*The European Union country funds were given in euros and totalled 330 million euros (the table above includes non-EU European countries). The European Commission's contribution was 140 million euros.

To put it another way: only US $270 million of non-repayable aid was given and the donors insisted that the funds were not to be used for Plan Colombia.

There was no shortage of cash for the 'military side'. The United States made a contribution of US$1.3 billion for the years 2000-2001 of which 78% was military aid. The package included 18 Blackhawk and 42 Huey helicopters, radar systems, reconnaissance aircraft and money to build US military bases across the region. The type of helicopters in the package prompted long debates in the Senate, as Republican Congressmen sought to win the multi-million dollar contracts for their states. Senators from Texas argued in favour of Hueys (manufactured by Textron, Texas), while Senators from Connecticut lobbied for Blackhawks, which are manufactured by Sikorsky Aircraft Corp, a subsidiary of United Technologies.

The Plan Colombia aid was passed as an 'emergency supplemental appropriation' and Colombia received US$330 million of military aid from the ordinary US budget, giving Colombia a grand total of US$1.1 billion of military assistance for years 2000-2001, the highest amount any Latin American nation has ever received.

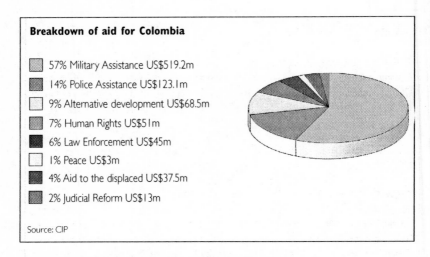

Breakdown of aid for Colombia

- 57% Military Assistance US$519.2m
- 14% Police Assistance US$123.1m
- 9% Alternative development US$68.5m
- 7% Human Rights US$51m
- 6% Law Enforcement US$45m
- 1% Peace US$3m
- 4% Aid to the displaced US$37.5m
- 2% Judicial Reform US$13m

Source: CIP

Andean regional counter drug initiative

In 2002, the Bush administration launched the Andean Regional Counter Drug Initiative, which is a continuation of Plan Colombia with an added emphasis on the bordering countries of Peru, Bolivia, Ecuador, Brazil, Venezuela and Panama. For 2002, Congress approved military and economic aid totalling US$782 million for the Andean Initiative. For 2003 the Bush administration requested US$731 million.

Andean Initiative funding For 2002*
US$m

	Military/Police	Social/Economic	Total
Colombia	243.5	137.0	380.5
Peru	75.0	119.9	194.9
Bolivia	48.0	74.5	122.5
Ecuador	15.0	31.9	46.9
Brazil	6.0	12.6	18.6
Panama	5.0	8.5	13.5
Venezuela	5.0	0.5	5.5
Total	**397.5**	**384.9**	**782.4**

Source: White House[3]

*The government originally requested US$731m of which 60% was to be spent on military aid, however congress changed the share of military aid in the final package to 51%

Britain and Plan Colombia

In Europe, Britain is viewed as one of the most enthusiastic supporters of Plan Colombia, along with Spain. Formally, the Foreign Office does not support or oppose Plan Colombia, describing it as 'a matter for Colombia and the United States'. The Foreign Office says it prefers to support the Colombian government's anti-narcotics and peace initiatives bilaterally.

Britain's contribution to the European Peace Initiative: US$20.5 million
US$7.02m (plus 17% to 19% of the European Commission's US$126m)

Other British government funding for Colombia
The Foreign and Commonwealth Office (FCO) has provided anti-narcotics funding since 1989 which has amounted to US$15m. A 'significant' proportion of this figure was spent on training Colombian anti-narcotics police, according to the Foreign Office. The SAS also trained the Colombian police, but no budgetary information is available.

Other FCO funding in 2001: in March, Donation for United Nations Human Rights Office of £250,00 and £50,000 for the UN Special Representative in Colombia. In September £150,000 to help child soldiers back to civilian life.

Department for International Development (DfID):
• DfID funds various projects (recent examples are shown below): £700,000 p.a
• DfID also contributes to the EC programme to Colombia. In 1999 the EC contribution was £10.9m of which the UK share was £2.1m.

1. Project to improve services and information for small farmers, in association with the Colombian agriculture ministry.
2. A Local Initiatives for Peace Project, in association with the World Bank
3. A project to improve the security and sustainability of groundwater supplies

Arms sales
• The UK is one of the main legal suppliers of small arms to Colombia along with the US, Germany and South Africa.

• UK weapon exports to Colombia totalled US$117,000 in 1999
US$3.5m in 1998
US$2.9m in 2000[1]
• Colombia's small arms imports from all countries between 1996 and 1999 totalled US$20m.

Military visits

Then Cabinet Office Minister Mo Mowlam arranged for visits by senior British military aimed at raising the Colombian military's 'awareness of human rights issues'. They included, in November 2000, General Sir Michael Rose, Former Commander of the SAS and in January 2001 General Sir Roger Wheeler, Former Head of the British Army, Former General Commanding Officer and Director of Military Operations in Northern Ireland and Chief of Staff during the Falklands Conflict.

Source: FCO, DFID, DTI, British Embassy in Bogotá[5]

Foreign mercenaries in Colombia

Plan Colombia raised fears in the United States that US troops could be drawn into someone else's war. The State Department therefore put a cap of 500 on the number of US military personnel to be sent to Colombia for the years 2000 to 2001.[6] The restriction only applies to Plan Colombia aid and not to other funds such as the Defence Department's budget or ordinary anti-drug programmes in Colombia. The cap may be exceeded for 90 days if US military personnel are involved in hostilities or if their imminent involvement in hostilities is 'clearly indicated by the circumstances.'[7]

The US government has contracted civilian personnel to carry out military duties in Colombia – in other words it is using a privatised army. One of the main benefits of using private contractors is that it obscures the true level of US intervention in Colombia. A cap of 300 was put on the number of US civilian contractors working on Plan Colombia in 2000-2001, but as with military personnel, this did not apply to contractors working on other US government programmes in Colombia. In 2002, the cap on troops and civilian personnel was changed from 500:300 to 400:400.

DynCorp Aerospace Technology has been contracted by the State Department to work in the Andes since 1991 and in 1998 it was awarded a new US$170 million five-year contract.[8] DynCorp pilots fly fumigation planes or the military helicopters that accompany such missions. These military helicopters have been involved in gunfights with Colombian guerrillas (60 times in the year 2000, according to the State Department).[9] DynCorp personnel also train and provide 'logistical support' to Colombian army anti-narcotics battalions, such as ferrying troops into battle and rescuing shot-down pilots. In short, mercenaries paid by the US government have been fighting counterinsurgency battles in Colombia.

Another benefit of using a privatised army is that the US public does not see American soldiers coming home in body bags. Two DynCorp employees were killed in 1997 when their aircraft crashed due to 'pilot error' and another died in 1998 in an air accident with 'unknown causes' but there was no blaze of publicity or flag waving ceremonies when their bodies were returned home.

DynCorp employees include many military veterans who have fought in Vietnam, the Middle East, El Salvador and Guatemala. They are paid US$110,500 a year, according to the US government (or up to US$10,000 a week according to *Semana* magazine).[10] They are the United States' frontline troops in the war against drugs.

There is some evidence that DynCorp staff have been involved in trafficking and consuming heroin, cocaine and amphetamines. On May 12, 2000, the Colombian authorities intercepted a package containing two bottles of liquid heroin which had been sent from DynCorp's Colombian office to its Florida airbase.[11] In 1994 a DynCorp pilot stationed on the Tres Esquinas military base in southern Colombia died of a cocaine overdose and, in 1999, the Colombian state prosecutor launched an investigation into amphetamine smuggling by ten DynCorp employees. Documents relating to these three cases have mysteriously disappeared.[12]

Five other private companies have been contracted by the US government to work in Colombia. These include AirScan, which conducts aerial surveillance, and Military Professional Resources Inc (MPRI) which was hired to train Colombian officers. The role of private contractors is obscured by a another layer of secrecy: the government is not required to release information about them and can use 'national security' as grounds to withhold data. Companies can also plead 'corporate confidentiality'.[13]

The SAS in Colombia

The British are even more secretive about their security services than the US. The government never discusses Special Air Services (SAS) operations and funding for its activities does not appear in the Ministry of Defence or Foreign Office budget. In Colombia, it is no secret that the

SAS trained anti-narcotics police and a special elite police corps in the 1980s and 1990s. The same elite corps which tracked down and killed drug baron, Pablo Escobar, but also had a far worse human rights record than the ordinary Colombian police force.[14]

'The Elite Corps, the frontline troops in the battle against drug trafficking... The Corps had been created in 1989 by President Virgilio Barco, when he was driven to despair by his inability to establish precise responsibilities in entities as large as the army and the police. Its formation had been entrusted to the National Police in order to distance the military as much as possible from the deadly contagions of drug trafficking and paramilitarism. It began with only 300 men, who had a special squadron of helicopters at their disposal and were trained by the Special Air Services (SAS) of the British government.'
Gabriel García Márquez,
News of a Kidnapping

'Members of the SAS are secretly helping Colombia fight the war against drugs. The SAS have given us great help in recent times, said General José Serrano, commander of the force. We are very grateful to the British government for this. Small teams of SAS specialists rotate routinely through Bogotá, and work with General Serrano's main unit, La Jungla. This battalion is responsible for locating and destroying drug laboratories in remote areas.'
David Smith,
SAS secretly helps Bogotá fight rebels

Mercenaries

There are also numerous former SAS men working in Colombia as mercenaries.[15]

- In 1990 the British QC Louis Blom-Cooper held an inquiry into allegations that the British, Israeli and US governments had turned a blind eye to the sale of arms to the Medellín cartel. In the course of the inquiry it emerged that British mercenaries had been training the cartels' death squads in Colombia.

'...a number of British mercenaries, several formerly with the SAS, had helped to train paramilitary forces of the Medellín cartel in 1988. They had worked with retired Colonel Yair Gal Klein, a former Israeli commando, who set up a security company, Spearhead. The Israeli government has just prosecuted Col. Klein for his part in the affair but the British government has turned a blind eye.'
'Arming of Colombian drug mafia attacked'
Financial Times December 6, 1990

- A group of former SAS members set up the security company Defence Systems Limited, which provides security for British Petroleum (BP) and other companies in Colombia. DSL was investigated by the Colombian authorities for training the Colombian police in 'lethal' counterinsurgency tactics.

Boost for the military

The militarisation of Plan Colombia and the extent of US involvement convinced Colombia's largest guerrilla group, the FARC, which had just agreed to peace talks, that the government was about to launch a counterinsurgency offensive. The US intervention meant the peace process was stillborn.

A FARC sign in the main square of San Vicente de Caguán read: 'Plan Colombia: the gringos supply the arms, Colombia supplies the dead bodies.' Colombia's military hardliners and paramilitaries interpreted it in the same way: carte blanche to wage war with the backing of the world's biggest military power. The message was reinforced on August 23, 2000 when Bill Clinton approved Plan Colombia using a presidential waiver on the grounds of 'national security'. This allowed him to over-rule the basic human rights conditions that Congress had attached to the aid and which the Colombian military had dismally failed to meet.

The first target area of Plan Colombia, Putumayo, experienced a horrifying paramilitary advance just before the fumigation started in late 2000. By terrorising the civilian population and prompting thousands to flee, the paramilitaries moved up through the department, pushing the guerrillas out of the strategic border area which was once their stronghold. The fumigations in Cauca were also preceded by an upsurge in paramilitary violence in the area.

The first year of Plan Colombia

The first official fumigation mission of Plan Colombia began in Putumayo, Colombia's southernmost department on the Ecuadorean border in December 2000. Putumayo is an isolated region deep in the Amazon rainforest. Thirteen percent of the population are indigenous and the remainder are settlers from other regions. It is one of the poorest parts of the country, a place where 19% of under fives suffer from chronic malnutrition and 86 babies in every 1,000 die before they reach the age of one (compared with 33 nationally).[16]

In December, January and February, planes sprayed farms with a glyphosate mixture twenty-six times the concentration recommended by the manufacturer.[17] The mixture contained a new additive, Cosmo Flux, which made the liquid stick to the skin of humans and animals, causing deep burns and welts. Soon after the spraying started, people began to complain of diarrhoea, vomiting, rashes, boils, respiratory problems and fainting. A second wave of spraying took place in mid 2001.

The Putumayo Public Health Department received 4,883 health complaints from three affected municipalities.[18] The local hospital reported 'a statistically significant increase in the incidence of fever, diarrhoea, abdominal pain, acute respiratory infections and skin infections.'[19] Other reported symptoms were paralysis, hair loss, nervous attacks, conjunctivitis, cramps and dizzy spells.[20] A separate study, which was also based on official figures, found that 178,377 animals had been reported dead, including cattle, horses, pigs, dogs, guinea pigs and fish and that only 12% of the 7,282 hectares sprayed contained coca plants, the remainder was pasture, food crops and uncultivated land.

Even families who had signed manual eradication pacts with the government and had switched to producing alternative crops had their farms sprayed, according to the national ombudsman. He wrote: 'It is hard to understand how the authorities can continue releasing resources from the national budget to carry out various alternative development and coca-substitution projects, only for them to be damaged by indiscriminate chemical fumigation.'[21] He concluded that the fumigation and intensification of the conflict had caused a 'humanitarian crisis' in Putumayo.[22]

Nariño

Nariño is on the Pacific Coast in the far south of Colombia (bordering Putumayo and Ecuador). It is another extremely poor area with 71% of the population living under the poverty line. Here fumigation had begun in 1999, and intensified with the onset of Plan Colombia. Among the targets of the spray planes was the indigenous reserve of Inga de Aponte, inhabited by 717 families. The community had already started replacing coca with alternative crops, but, once again, these were wiped out by the pesticides, as a delegation from Aponte testified to the Colombian senate.[23] In September 2002, the governor of Nariño, Parmenio Cuellar, called for a halt to the spraying saying 'It's the wrong approach'. He added: 'They do not carry out the aerial spraying with the chemicals they announced they would be using, but rather with other more toxic chemicals that harm children, vegetation, and animals.'[24] The fumigation in Nariño has also affected farms over the border in Ecuador. In the frontier provinces of Sucumbios and Carachi peasants have reported headaches, sore eyes and nausea, as well as wilting trees and plants.[25]

Throughout the year 2001, the fumigation missions moved up through the Colombia to Caquetá, Huila, Tolima, Cauca and Norte de Santander.

'We are risking our lives for a noble cause'

Major Vargas M. of the Colombian anti-narcotics police is in charge of all the fumigation campaigns in the country. He is young (late 30s, early 40s) and has a wary, irritable manner, suggesting he has spoken to many journalists about fumigation.

He showed a professional presentation on a laptop computer which stated that:
• illicit crop cultivation is damaging the environment
• glyphosate and Cosmo Flux have been declared safe by the World Health Organisation (WHO) and other international authorities (they have never been tested together)
• only large plantations, detected using satellite images, are sprayed

He said that coca is sprayed from an altitude of 15 metres or less and poppies are sprayed from 30m or less. (The recommended height to spray glyphosate is 10m).

'Planes cannot fly any lower because they are shot at by subversives.' he said.

'Peasants sow coca, marijuana and poppies, but they intersperse it with one or two maize plants. This is a tactic to avoid fumigation. When we spray the area, the peasants invite non-governmental organisations (NGOs) to come and look at the fumigated maize plants...'

'The [indigenous] people of Silvia complained to the ombudsman that their water supply [*aqueducto*] had been polluted. I went personally to the area and drank a glass of water from the *aqueducto* and I am fine.... Doctor Uribe, the best toxicologist in Colombia, looked at the skin complaints and found that none of them were caused by fumigation...It is the subversives that make peasants say such things.'

'Manual eradication is a good idea in theory, but it doesn't work. The peasants accept the tractors and aid, but the next year, they start planting coca again... We are fighting an unequal battle. We have to respect human rights, but the subversives don't.'

'We pilots have wives, mothers, girlfriends, worrying whether we will come home alive. We are risking our lives for a noble cause.'

Cauca

Cauca contains the majority of Colombia's indigenous communities including Guambianos, Paeces, Yaconas and Emberás. Floro Tunubulá, the country's first ever indigenous governor, was elected by a landslide in Cauca in the year 2000. Although strongly against illicit crop cultivation, he understood its roots: 'Poverty is forcing farmers to grow poppies and coca,' he says. Tunubalá travelled to indigenous reserves (*resguardos*) across the region to discuss the problem. With the support of the *resguardos*, all 41 mayors of Cauca, the chambers of commerce and a large number of community groups, he drew up an 'Alternative Plan'. This involved gradual voluntary manual eradication of illicit crops, and long term investment in the region's agriculture. The plan aimed firstly to encourage families to grow food for their own consumption and, secondly, to grow organic food for the national and international market. Despite the consensus in Cauca against fumigation and a voluntary agreement to start eradicating poppies manually, aerial spraying began in July 2001, ruining all chances of growing organic produce in the region.

Within eight days, the ombudsman of Cauca, Victor Meléndez, had received numerous reports of skin burns and rashes. The indigenous community of Silvia complained that their water had been poisoned. Meléndez, who was investigating the complaints, was particularly worried by the additives in the spray mixture: 'Cosmo Flux makes sure the chemicals are absorbed into the skin. We need long term laboratory tests before they are sprayed on people and animals.'[26]

My Alternative Plan aimed to tackle all the problems together: the environment, development, education, infrastructure and human rights. It was a regional plan and it had support across southeastern Colombia. In March 2001, I went to Europe to seek support for my Alternative Plan. There is a big demand for organic goods there, which we could supply. Most European governments were enthusiastic about my alternative plan, except for Britain and Spain, which said they supported the government's Plan Colombia.'

Floro Tunubalá, Governor of Cauca, interviewed by the author July 2001

Opposition to fumigation

Dressed in the traditional bowler hat and poncho of the Guambiano indians, Floro Tunubalá has led a crusade against fumigation. Four other governors, of Nariño, Huila, Tolima and Caquetá, joined him in his campaign to persuade the government to stop the fumigations. As the evidence grew of how the chemicals were harming human health, a minority of Colombian senators and congressional deputies began to voice fears and three bills were drafted calling for an end to aerial fumigation. In July 2001 a Colombian court suspended the fumigation, but this was later overturned. The Colombian ombudsman, all of the country's indigenous groups and the four main civic networks, the Permanent Assembly of Civil Society for Peace, Paz Colombia, Redepaz and Citizen Mandate for Peace have also called for a halt to fumigation.

Internationally opposition grew too. The Andean Parliament (August 2001) and the European Parliament (February 2001) both passed resolutions condemning the fumigation. The director of United Nations Drug Control Programme (UNDCP) in Colombia, Klaus Nyholm, expressed his concern about fumigating small peasant plots and called for international monitoring (July 2001). Major international charities have opposed fumigation including: World Wildlife Fund, Greenpeace, Oxfam, Cafod, Christian Aid, Save the Children, Caritas International, and Survival International. Nevertheless, spraying has continued and it is planned to last five more years.

Colombia's neighbours

Neighbouring countries (Brazil, Ecuador, Venezuela, Panama and Peru) are particularly worried about Plan Colombia. Their concerns include the fumigation affecting the Amazon rainforest, as well as the displacement of coca growing to their countries, an influx of refugees, the potential spillover of the conflict and growing US intervention in the region.

Ecuador

'There is enormous distress and deep concern in Ecuador over what have now become the first real, adverse effects of Plan Colombia on Ecuador.'
Heinz Moeller, speaking at OAS, February 2001

Ecuador has been the country most affected by Plan Colombia so far, since it lies next to Putumayo, the first target area of fumigation. The Ecuadorean government does not oppose Plan Colombia but wants international help to cope with the effects.

- **Fumigation.** Following numerous reports of ill-health and wilting plants in the border states of Sucumbios, Carachi and Orellana, the Ecuadorean government has demanded that the Colombian fumigating planes do not spray within 10km of the frontier. It has recommended that fumigation be suspended altogether. Peasants in Carachi and Sucumbios have also held protests.

- **Refugees.** Twelve thousand Colombians fled to Ecuador in the year 2000, and there were reports of more entering in 2001. A total of 30,000 Colombian refugees live in Ecuador, according to the UNHCR.

- **Paramilitary incursions.** The border between Colombia and Ecuador is deep in the rainforest. FARC guerrillas used to control most of this territory and frequently crossed to Ecuador to rest from the war and buy non-military supplies. Since the paramilitary offensive in Putumayo, violence on both sides of the border has escalated. Paramilitaries have reportedly set up camps in Ecuador and are waging a selective assassination campaign there.[27]

- **Troops.** Two thousand Ecuadorean troops have been moved to the border to try to stop armed groups and refugees entering.

Panama

'Although we are in no position to comment on whether or not the Plan should be implemented, I personally believe that it would not be a good idea.'
  Winston Spadafora, Panama's Interior Minister, August 2000.[28]

Security. The country disbanded its armed forces after the US invasion of 1989. The US army left Panama in 1999, and the government does not want incursions by guerrillas or paramilitaries used as a pretext for its return. Two thousand police officers have been sent to defend the frontier. At 266km it is the shortest border with Colombia and much of it is impassable terrain. The area on the Colombian side of the border is a paramilitary stronghold, particularly Urabá.

Refugees. 430 refugees entered Panama in the year 2000. 212 were repatriated. Approximately 7,000 Colombian refugees live in Panama.

Brazil

'The intensification of Plan Colombia is extremely dangerous. It could produce a Vietnam-isation of the region, that is to say, an extension of the conflict to neighbouring countries, especially Brazil.'
  President-elect Luiz Inácio Lula da Silva's party statement on Colombia, October 2002.[29]

Fumigation. Brazil has expressed concern about the impact of fumigation on the Amazon rainforest, pointing out it is a very 'fragile environment'. It was also strongly opposed to the proposed use of the poisonous fungus *fusariam oxysporum*. Plan Colombia fumigation has not yet taken place near the Brazilian border.

Troops. Brazil has sent 22,000 troops to defend its border with Colombia. It resents increasing US involvement in the region. On nationalist grounds, the Brazilian military has resisted attempts to get too involved with the US-sponsored war on drugs, although it has, on occasion, co-operated with the Colombian Armed Forces' counterinsurgency war.

Peru

'We support Plan Colombia, fundamentally in its social component.'
President Alejandro Toledo, February 2001.[30]

Peru has been the least critical of Plan Colombia, partly because the government is under strong US pressure to eliminate its own illicit coca cultivation and partly because it is a large recipient of US military aid. Nevertheless, the newly elected president Alejandro Toledo, (2001) emphasised that it is the 'social side' of Plan Colombia which he supports.

Venezuela

'Our concern is that the US's Plan Colombia (not Colombia's Plan Colombia) emphasises the military aspect, it has a strong military component, and Venezuela believes that if the objective is peace, it is counter-productive to try and resolve the problem using military methods.'
José Rangel, Venezuelan Foreign Minister, August 2000.[31]

Under populist President Hugo Chávez, Venezuela has been outspokenly critical of Plan Colombia. It has spoken out against US involvement and the military focus.

Spillover. Venezuela lies alongside Colombia's most conflict-ridden region. The situation along the 2,200km shared border is increasingly messy and violent. Both guerrillas and paramilitaries have made incursions into Venezuelan territory. Venezuelan landowners are now are now funding Colombian paramilitaries, according to Carlos Castaño.[32]

Refugees. There are between 50,000 and 75,000 Colombian refugees living in Venezuela, the highest number of all the neighbouring states, according to the UNHCR.

What are the alternatives?

Most coca is grown by poor farmers in the Amazonian south of Colombia. One solution would be to work with farmers to phase out coca gradually and replace it with other crops or animals. Local communities have experimented with a variety of products including tropical fruits (guava, palm chestnuts, *copoazu, minche, maraco,* and *borojo*), vegetables, herbs, fish and poultry. These projects try to choose goods that are suitable for extra local processing – like jam or herbal remedies – which allow the local farmers to add value to their products and secure a higher price. These projects would take time and will not be viable unless the government is prepared to invest money in improving local infrastructure and transport links.

Coca substitution schemes are likely to be most successful in the north and on the edge of the Amazon, which are closer to markets. In the most isolated regions, market-orientated farming may never be cost effective, or necessarily desirable. The Amazon is not suited for farming or ranching and its soil is quickly exhausted. The fragile ecosystem may not be able to sustain a continuing influx of migrants. The most effective measure would involve an agrarian reform in the more fertile central and northern regions of Colombia. More equitable wealth distribution and job-creating economic policies in the cities would also stop the urban poor from migrating south in search of work in the coca growing areas.

Even in regions like Cauca, where alternatives are viable, their success would depend on changing unfair international trading laws. At present rich countries espouse free trade which allows them to dump subsidised agricultural goods on third world markets while simultaneously raising an insurmountable wall of tariff barriers to stop poorer countries selling their produce in Europe or the United States. Europe's Common Agricultural Policy (CAP) throws a blanket of protection around all its farmers, while the United States abides by free trade only when it is sure that its agri-business corporations can produce a commodity cheaper than anyone else. As soon as foreign competitors threaten to sell a product at a lower price, the Americans cry 'unfair competition' and protective walls go up. Yet Europe and the US will not allow poor countries the same privilege and these double standards have had devastating consequences. Their destruction of the international coffee price agreement, for example, not only caused misery for peasants across Latin America but directly contributed to the rise of opium poppy cultivation in Colombia.

Reduce demand

Finally, the US and Europe need to consider their role in the drugs trade, given that they consume most of the world's cocaine. Without rich nations' insatiable appetite for drugs, there would be no market. This is not just a moral question, but a practical one. The present strategy does not work. A decade of fumigation has led not to a decrease, but an increase in illicit crop cultivation. Where there is a constant (or growing) level of demand, there will always be suppliers to meet the need: if production is targeted in one area it will simply be displaced to another.

The immense profits of drugs' trafficking make sure demand will be met. If one hectare's worth of coca paste can be bought for US$1,000 in Colombia and sold on the streets of New York for US$512,400 even if 99% of the smugglers' load were intercepted by the authorities they would still make a profit. If the authorities managed to intercept enough drugs to have an impact on the street price, this would simply make the business even more profitable and attract greater numbers of people to it.

The United States' anti-drug budget is enormous and ballooning fast. It grew from US$11.9 billion in 1992 to US$19 billion in 2002. For over a decade, the United States has spent 70% of this budget on attempting to reduce supply (including law enforcement at home) and just 30% on demand reduction.

Yet studies shows that treatment and preventive education are a far more effective way of reducing consumption. Rand, a think-tank established by the US military, analysed how much the government would have to spend on each method – treatment, domestic law enforcement, interdiction and 'source-control' (i.e. eradication of crops) – to decrease cocaine consumption in the US by 1%. It found that treatment was overwhelmingly the most cost-effective way of reducing cocaine consumption and its resulting social costs. It found that treatment was 7 times more cost-effective than domestic law enforcement, 10 times more effective than interdiction, and 23 times more effective than the 'source control' method.[33]

US anti-drugs operations abroad punish poor peasant farmers for their poverty. At home, the government's anti-narcotics strategy consists of criminalising mainly poor, black, inner-city crack and heroin consumers while turning a blind eye to middle class cocaine users. A massive US$8.4 billion, or 47% of the total drugs budget, was used on domestic law enforcement in the year 2000, despite the proven ineffectiveness of this policy.

It is now widely accepted that alcohol and tobacco cause more deaths than illegal drugs and that banning substances does not prevent people from acquiring them. Given the misery the war on drugs has caused at home and abroad, is it not time to consider legalising and regulating the trade in drugs?

6 The United States and Colombia

The war on drugs has been spectacularly unsuccessful. It has failed to reduce the production or consumption of drugs. It has caused misery, illness and environmental destruction. So why does the US continue to pursue this strategy and pour military aid into Colombia?

To evaluate US motives, we must take into account its history of almost two centuries of intervention in Latin America. The past record shows the US will intervene in any country in the hemisphere in order to protect its political and economic interests. Since James Monroe declared that Latin America was within the US sphere of influence in 1823, US forces have intervened militarily in Latin America more than 80 times. A more usual way of preserving US hegemony in the 20th century involved indirect intervention: the US installed, trained and funded despots from the 'Friendly Dictators' of the 1930s through to the military dictatorships of the 1970s. Its special forces trained counterinsurgency battalions and its intelligence services waged dirty tricks campaigns against the civilian left. US departments have tried to destabilise every left-leaning regime in Latin America. Salvador Allende in Chile is only one of many progressive Presidents toppled with US help: Ramón Grau San Martín, Jacobo Arbenz, João Goulart, Cheddi Jagin, Juan Bosch are others, to name a few. During the 1980s, the Reagan administration instigated an illegal war in Nicaragua, funded death squads in El Salvador and supported military governments in Guatemala in a war that claimed 200,000 victims.

The US State is not monolithic and there are frequently differences of opinion between the State Department, the Pentagon, the White House, the intelligence services and diplomatic staff. Similarly the influence that corporations wield depends on a variety of factors such as their strategic importance to the US and its geopolitical concerns. Sometimes policy is changed to suit companies simply because leading politicians, their families or friends, are shareholders.[1] It is not true to say, either, that the

United States has simply imposed its will on Latin America – at least not on the larger countries. In most cases there has been a convergence of interests between the ruling elites of Latin America and the United States. This has certainly been the case in Colombia. Although there have been moments of friction – the secession of Panama and, more recently, the drugs certification issue are the two most notable examples – historically the two countries have had one of the best bilateral relationships in the hemisphere. In the last two decades, the Colombian elite has itself begun to divide between hardliners and pragmatists favouring peace. The US, by favouring the most authoritarian elements within the Colombian elite, has helped to push the country inexorably towards all-out war.

There is some evidence to suggest that the 'war on drugs' is a strategy aimed at maintaining US dominance over Latin America. An overview of US policy towards Colombia in the 20th century shows that US forces were used to combat guerrillas (and the civic left) long before the drug trade existed. There is continuity of US policy towards Colombia through the Cold War to the Clinton years and George W. Bush. Despite the Clinton administration's claims that US aid was used only for counter-drugs initiatives and was given exclusively to Colombian military units vetted for human rights, the US continued to fund and train officers committing some of the worst atrocities of the dirty war. There are grounds for arguing that Plan Colombia is a counterinsurgency plan.

Since the accession of George W. Bush and particularly since the events of September 11th, 2001, some of the nuanced debates about where to draw the line between counternarcotics and counterinsurgency aid appear redundant. In early 2002, the Bush administration asked Congress to approve the first explicit counterinsurgency aid to Colombia since the Cold War – US$98 million to defend oil pipelines from guerrilla attacks. Under the auspices of the 'war on terror', Bush then asked Congress to allow all military aid to Colombia to be used against 'terrorist activities and other threats to national security.'

The US war on drugs

The war on drugs enables the US to maintain its hegemony over Latin America in two ways. The 'narco-guerrilla' theory allows it to justify its counterinsurgency activity in the post Cold-War world, while drug trafficking has been the pretext for a US military build up in the hemisphere. The recently constructed network of air bases and complex radar systems ensures that it will be well prepared to confront any 'unfriendly' forces in the future. The war on drugs also gave the bloated US military a new *raison d'etre* and an argument against spending cuts after the collapse of the Soviet Union. In Latin America, it strengthened the armed forces just as most countries were emerging from over a decade of dictatorship and were trying to assert civilian control over the military.

US rhetoric on drugs has always been entangled with other foreign policy considerations. The first 'war on drugs' was declared by President Richard Nixon in 1968 during the Vietnam war, after US soldiers began to come home suffering from heroin addiction. In 1971 drug trafficking was categorised as a 'threat to National Security' for the first time and two years later the Drug Enforcement Administration (DEA) was established.

The Reagan government seized upon the idea that drug trafficking could be defined as a national security threat and used as a rationale for military intervention. It invented the concept of the 'narco-guerrilla' to try to discredit the Sandinista regime in Nicaragua and the insurgencies in El Salvador and Guatemala. By falsely linking them with drugs, they hoped to convince waverers among the American public that the war in Central America was justified. As Special Forces commander Colonel John D. Waghelstein wrote:

'A melding in the American public's mind and in Congress of this connection would lead to the necessary support to counter the guerrilla/narcotics terrorists in this hemisphere...Congress would find it difficult to stand in the way of supporting our allies with the training, advice and security assistance necessary to do the job. Those church and academic groups that have slavishly supported insurgency in Latin America would find themselves on the wrong side of the moral issue.'[2]

The US congressional report into the Iran Contra affair not only showed that the Reagan administration had (illegally) sold arms to Iran to (illegally) arm the Contras, it also showed that the administration waged a smear campaign against the Sandinistas. One of the documents appended to the report, for example, is a strategy paper written by two fundraisers hired by National Security Council member Oliver North to raise money for the Contras. They decided to focus their publicity efforts on linking the Sandinistas to drugs because 'the chance to have a single issue with which no one can disagree with is irresistible.'[3] The administration went as far as sending a convicted drug trafficker to Managua airport to take pictures that supposedly showed Colombian drugs barons and Nicaraguan officials loading cocaine on to a plane. These photos were published on the front pages of the American press just before a Contra aid vote in Congress.[4]

The then newly created Office of Public Diplomacy in the State Department, headed by the Cuban-American Otto Reich, played a crucial role in the government's disinformation campaign. A report by the US Comptroller General later found that Reich had illegally disseminated propaganda to the American public. His activities were also condemned by the US Congress's General Accounting Office (GAO) and the Senate's Foreign Affairs Committee. He was George W. Bush's Assistant Secretary of State for the Western Hemisphere at the beginning of his term and was then made Special Envoy for Latin America.

The Communist/drugs/narco-guerrilla rhetoric was propagated repeatedly during the 1980s to drum home the message to the public. In 1985, Secretary of State George Shultz condemned the 'complicity of Communist governments in the drugs trade,' which he said was 'part of a larger pattern of international lawlessness by Communist nations.' Reagan declared: 'The link between the governments of such Soviet allies as Cuba and Nicaragua and international narcotics trafficking and terrorism is becoming increasingly clear. These twin evils – narcotics trafficking and terrorism – represent the most insidious and dangerous threats to the hemisphere today.'[5]

Ironically, as an US Senate inquiry later showed, it was Oliver North who conspired with drugs' traffickers to fund the Contras' counter-revolutionary war in Nicaragua.[6] The Reagan administration also worked with another notorious drug trafficking criminal, the Panamanian dictator General Manuel Noriega, a graduate of the School of the Americas and a longstanding CIA informant. As Irangate revealed, Noriega collaborated with Oliver North to aid the Contras and destabilise the Sandinista regime. By 1989, Noriega had outlived his usefulness and had become a political liability. President George Bush senior, who had worked with Noriega when he was head of the CIA, ordered US troops to overthrow him.

The Andean war on drugs

Throughout the 1980s, the United States had encouraged Colombia, Bolivia and Peru to eradicate coca crops and there were some raids on cocaine-processing plants, but it was not until the 1990s that anti-drugs campaigns in the Andes became highly militarised and the top priority of US foreign policy in Latin America. In 1989, the first Bush administration drew up an Andean Initiative that raised the level of military aid going to the region substantially.

The increase in US military activity in the Andes allowed President Bush to show his domestic audience that he was taking action on the drug problem. But there were also other factors: in both Colombia and Peru guerrilla groups were growing in strength and the US was also aware that it would soon lose its territory – and military base – in Panama, so needed good reasons to persuade other Latin American nations to host alternative bases. As the former Joint Chief of Staff Admiral William Crowe said:

'Certainly, I'll think we'll put more emphasis on the drug war. And if there are resources tied to it, why, you'll see the services compete for those and probably vigorously. We take some pride in being accomplished bureaucrats as well as military men. And I think it's legitimate for military men to try and perpetuate their institution.'"

Not all US military leaders agreed that fighting drugs was a job for the armed forces and some thought that the Middle East should be the US's top priority. However, the Southern Command (responsible for Central and South America) was keen: as its Commander-in-Chief General Maxwell Thurman said, 'It's the only war we've got.'[8]

In 1988-90 military think tanks formally defined anti-narcotics as a Low Intensity Conflict Mission and, as Coletta Youngers has shown, it was, from the beginning, doctrinally linked to counterinsurgency operations. Low Intensity Conflict is any conflict short of all-out war and is another definition of counterinsurgency. The theory incorporates the lessons of Vietnam and seeks to lessen US casualties, by advocating a greater use of national armies and paramilitaries, with a supporting role for US forces.

Counterinsurgency in action

The counterinsurgency agenda in Peru was explicit because it was the only way the United States could persuade the government to co-operate with the anti-narcotics effort. Defeating the extremist Maoist guerrilla group, Shining Path, was a top priority for Peruvian generals and they feared that coca eradication could hinder these efforts by turning coca-growing peasants against the army. Alberto Fujimori, who became President in 1990, held the same view: he wanted a free hand to wipe out the insurgents, but viewed coca growing as partly a social problem. He therefore turned down military aid in 1990 demanding more economic assistance. The only way the US could get the Peruvians on side was to explicitly support the counterinsurgency efforts. US Assistant Secretary of State for international narcotics, Matters Melvyn Levitsky told Congress: 'I want to be very frank in saying that where the insurgency and the drug traffickers are inextricably bound together, we have to deal with them together...We have an interest in helping them fight that insurgency.'[9]

In 1991 the US signed a military agreement with Peru which stated that 'counterinsurgency actions are a justifiable component of counternarcotics activities'. US military aid rose to its highest ever level to date in 1991. Fujimori then launched an all-out offensive against Shining Path, declaring a state of emergency in almost half of the country. In 1992 he seized dictatorial powers for himself and delivered a mortal blow to the guerrillas by capturing their leader Abimael Guzmán, whom he put in a cage to display to the world's press.[10]

Anti-narcotics aid has also been used for counterinsurgency purposes in Mexico. In 1997, the US Congress's investigative arm, the GAO, found that the Mexican government had used US-supplied anti-narcotic helicopters to transport troops used in quelling the uprising in Chiapas.[11] Bolivia has no guerrilla groups, although this has not stopped some military minds from advocating *preventative* counterinsurgency actions there.[12]

Throughout the 1990s the US encouraged the eradication of coca crops in the Andean countries and raised military spending there, but there were differences in the overall anti-narcotics strategy. The Bush administration spent most resources on interdiction, trying to intercept shipments of drugs coming through Mexico and the Caribbean by investing heavily in hi-tech military surveillance equipment. In 1994,

Clinton moved the focus to the source countries and followed the 'air-bridge' strategy – trying to intercept coca paste being transported from Bolivia and Peru into Colombia. This simply displaced coca growing to Colombia. The net effect of ten years of anti-narcotics efforts was 10,000 more hectares of cultivated coca in the Andean countries.

Colombia and the USA

In 1903 President Roosevelt declared: 'I do not think that Bogotá lot of Jackrabbits should be allowed to permanently bar one of the future highways of civilisation.'[13] The Colombian senate had just refused to ratify a treaty for the construction of a US canal in the Colombian region of Panama on the grounds that it would violate national sovereignty. Roosevelt then sent Marines to the province of Panama and 'encouraged' it to secede from Colombia. In November 1903, he signed a deal with the newly independent Panamanian government allowing the US to build a canal and giving it exclusive rights to the canal zone (10 miles wide and 40 miles long) 'in perpetuity'. In 1979, President Jimmy Carter agreed that the Americans would leave in 1999.

The 'theft' of Panama soured relations between Colombia and the United States in the early years of the twentieth century, but a payment of US$25 million in compensation in 1921 reduced tensions somewhat. Shortly after compensation was agreed, the Colombian government allowed US companies to search for oil in their territory.[14] US policy-makers were uneasy about the 'socialistic' reforms of Liberal governments in the 1930s, but were relieved that – unlike Mexico and Bolivia – Colombia's oil wells were not nationalised. US-Colombian relations grew much stronger during the Presidency of Eduardo Santos (1938-42) who gave his full backing to Allies in War War II. He allowed the US to build air and naval bases in Colombia and let the embassy set up a sophisticated counter-espionage system throughout the country. German airlines were nationalised and relations with the Axis powers were severed. Colombia was the only Latin American country to send troops to Korea in 1950-53, where they gained valuable counterinsurgency experience. President Laureano Gómez sent 1,000 soldiers to join the UN forces, even though Colombia was in the midst of the worse phase of *la Violencia*.

US interference in the Colombian labour movement during the Cold War

'The US embassy played a direct role in labor negotiations in the oil industry after the [Second World] war; the evidence suggests that the objectives went considerably beyond containing Communist influence to restricting organized labor power itself. In efforts to create a new labor code in 1948, for instance, representatives of the oil companies met with the Colombian minister of mines and petroleum, the minister of labour and embassy officials. The embassy sought to exclude any provision for compulsory arbitration from the new code of labor as well as to transfer the authority to declare the legality of a strike from local labor judges to superior labor tribunals in the departmental capitals. Embassy officials were pleased in 1948 when the Socony-Vaccum Company was able to negotiate a new contract with its workers without the intervention of...[the oil workers union] Fedepetrol...

State Department officials encouraged such prominent Liberals as Carlos Lleras Restrepo to use their influence to purge communists from the labor movement.US officials introduced him to AFL and CIO leaders and to Department of Labor officials in Washington....

[In 1957]...there was a major strike against a Bogotá steel fabrication plant, in which Sears Roebuck had a financial interest. The embassy claimed that the strike was guided by Communist labor organizers affiliated with the Cundinamarca Federation of Labor. Under US pressure the CTC was induced to withdraw its support for the strikers, and the lengthy strike collapsed....

From Stephen J. Randall, *Colombia and the United States: Hegemony and Interdependence*[15]

The Alliance for Progress and counterinsurgency

It was during the Alliance for Progress years that Colombia became a showpiece of Latin American foreign policy for the US. The National Front (1958-74) allowed only two parties to compete in elections, but the regularly alternating governments contrasted favourably with the military regimes ruling many other Latin American countries. The National Front presidents, particularly the Liberals, agreed with the philosophy of the Alliance for Progress – moderate reform to undercut radicalism, coupled with repression of Communists. And, just as the repressive element had taken precedence in Latin America as a whole, attempts at distributive reform soon petered out in Colombia too.

Colombia was one of the first countries to send officers to the School of the Americas in Panama and 7,917 Colombian officers were trained by the US (in Panama and elsewhere) between 1950 and 1979 (82,767 military staff from across Latin American were trained in the same period).[16] Just as World Bank technocrats had found Colombia a good testing ground for their economic theories, US warfare experts saw that Colombia was a good place to try out counterinsurgency techniques. Since the formal ending of *la Violencia* in 1953, Colombia had experienced ongoing rural violence. There was concern regarding the Communist-influenced peasant resistance communities in the south. In 1962, a team from the Special Warfare Center at Fort Bragg, North Carolina, the USA's top counterinsurgency training school, made a two-week trip to Colombia. General Yarborough, the commander of the Warfare Center, headed the trip and in his final report wrote:

'A concerted country team effort should be made now to select civilian and military personnel for clandestine training in resistance operations in case they are needed later. This should be done with a view toward development of a civil and military structure for exploitation in the event the Colombian internal security system deteriorates further. This structure should be used to pressure toward reforms known to be needed, perform counter-agent and counter-propaganda functions and as necessary execute paramilitary, sabotage and/or terrorist activities against known Communist proponents. It should be backed by the United States.'[17]

The report, found by Michael McClintock in the Kennedy Library, proposed an 'intensive civilian registration programme...so that [everyone] is eventually registered in government files together with fingerprints and photographs,' and also advised the Colombian military to regularly question rural villagers who 'are believed to be knowledgeable of guerrilla activities.' In a section discussing how best to question suspected rural bandits, it read: 'Exhaustive interrogation of the bandits to include sodium pentathol and polygraph, should be used to elicit every shred of information.' Pentathol is a drug used by doctors to induce relaxation, but in the early 1970s it was reportedly used by some Latin American security forces in conjunction with other drugs, particularly derivatives of curare (or its synthetic form suxamethonium, or 'Scoline'), to induce 'paralysis, agony and terror.'[18]

The mission advised that five 12-man Special Forces detachments, psychological warfare experts and an administrative detachment should be sent to work with the Colombian army.[19] The main recommendations of this report were used by the Colombian military to draw up its comprehensive counterinsurgency strategy, Plan Laso (Latin American Security Operation). In 1964, under the aegis of Plan Laso, thousands of troops with air force reinforcements attacked the peasant resistance community of Marquetalia – a seminal moment in FARC history.[20] Marquetalia was an area of some 500 square kilometres in Tolima, southern Colombia, where up to 4,000 peasants lived. US-supplied helicopters bombed and machine-gunned the area in a bid to defeat the Communist and radical Liberal guerrillas who had refused to disarm after *la Violencia*. Families were evacuated, while a handful of guerrillas stayed on to fight.[21] The rebels eventually fled but formed the FARC two years later.

Throughout this period the Colombian military continued to work closely with the Pentagon. The army's 1969 guidelines to fight guerrillas is based entirely on US training texts and overseas special warfare courses, which as McClintock has documented, were always well attended by the Colombians. In 1973, US Congressmen revealed that the CIA was running a 'technical investigations course' in Los Frenos, Texas, which included a 'four-week practical', teaching Latin American officers assassination techniques and how to make explosive devices. The US press dubbed it the 'Bomb School' and in a letter to a Senator, an AID official wrote: 'The thrust of the instruction introduces trainees to commercially available materials and home-laboratory techniques...in the manufacture of explosives and incendiaries...Different types of explosive devices and 'booby-traps' and their construction and use by terrorists are demonstrated.'[22] Of the 165 international students who had graduated from the bomb school in September 1973, the highest number came from Colombia. The Colombian and United States military have a long history of collaboration that started well before the business of drugs existed in Colombia.

US military aid and training

Since the Second World War, Colombia had received generous military aid from the United States, and between 1950-66 it was the fifth largest recipient in Latin America. In the late 1960s, it became the fourth-largest recipient and in the 1970s and 1980s it was in third place. During the 1990s, it received more military aid than all other Latin American countries put together. Since 1950, the United States has trained more officers from Colombia than any other Latin American country.

Estimated Military & Police Aid 1996-2002*
US$m

Year	Military Aid
1987	6.47
1988	4.17
1989	9.60
1990	74.75
1991	52.36
1992	51.61
1993	31.74
1994	9.50
1995	11.19
1996	54.20
1997	86.50
1998	110.20
1999	305.80
2000	798.30
2001	465.30
2002**	622.92

Source: CIP and Latin America Working Group [23]

*International Narcotics Control, IMET & Expanded IMET Emergency Drawdowns, Section 1004 CounterDrug Excess Defence Articles Foreign Military Financing
**Request

1980s: drugs, diplomacy and the dirty war

Drugs soured relations between the United States and Colombian governments in the 1980s. In common with other Latin American governments, Colombians felt the Reagan administration acted in a high-handed manner. In particular they resented the US's unilateral system of certification introduced in 1986, in which aid and loans were cut if a foreign government's anti-drugs efforts were deemed inadequate by the State Department. The extradition of Colombian nationals to the US also provoked strong opposition from politicians and the general public. However, despite these diplomatic disagreements, the relationship between the US and Colombian military grew stronger. In the 1980s the US trained 7,260 officers from Colombia, more than double the number from any other Latin American country.

It was in this decade that death squads linked to the military emerged. A human rights report published in 1992 by the World Organisation against Torture, the American Association of Jurists, and eight other international groups, named 247 Colombian officers who were implicated in human rights abuses. Half of the officers cited were graduates of the School of the Americas.[24]

One of the first and most feared death squads was *Muerte a Sequestradores* (MAS) which had links to the Medellín cartel. General Carlos Julio Gil Colorado was closely linked to MAS and in 1992 was one of the highest-ranking officers indicted for involvement with paramilitaries in Santander. He was a graduate of the School of the Americas (SOA). Lieutenant Virgilo Anzola Montero used MAS to carry out assassinations and disappearances. He also covered up the torture and murder of five peasants by soldiers under his command. He too was an SOA graduate. Major Alejandro de Jesús Alvarez was another leading MAS member who attended the SOA.

General Harold Bedoya Pizarro was a Guest Instructor at the School of the Americas. He founded and led the terrifying AAA (American Anti-Communist Alliance), which was modelled on the Southern Cone police/military death squads.

In 1988, 20 workers on a banana plantation in Urubá were massacred, in one of the most shocking atrocities of the decade. SOA graduate General Daniel Enrique García Echeverry, who established and ran paramilitary forces wherever he was stationed, was strongly implicated in this mass killing. Another officer, Lieutenant Luis Felipe Bercerra Bohórquez, was attending the School of the Americas while there was a warrant out for his arrest for the Urubá massacre.

Killing Pablo 1989-93

During the 1980s, defeating the Medellín cartel was not a top priority for the United States (the war in Central America was.) However, when in 1989 the Medellín cartel murdered presidential candidate Luis Galán and blew up an Avianca passenger jet with two Americans on board, the US security and intelligence forces realised that Pablo Escobar had become too powerful and went all out to capture or kill him. The fact that US officials, including the ambassador, knowingly collaborated with the Cali cartel and Medellín cartel dissidents in order to get Escobar, suggests that it was not his drug trafficking that worried them, but the fact that he had built up an extensive business and military network which was independent of the US.

'Los Pepes'

After Pablo Escobar escaped from prison in 1992, a mysterious new death squad emerged, called Los Pepes (People Persecuted by Pablo Escobar), which began to target Escobar's family, friends and associates. It has long been assumed that Los Pepes was formed by the Cali Cartel. And while it is true that the Cali drug traffickers worked closely with the police to defeat Escobar, investigative journalist Mark Bowden, who interviewed many US intelligence agents and had access to US embassy files, has demonstrated that Los Pepes were the creation of the Colombian police. The police received strong logistical support from US intelligence services, which at one point had 17 spy planes flying over Medellín. In addition, Bowden shows that the paramilitary leaders Fidel and Carlos Castaño worked closely with the police to form Los Pepes, as did dissidents from the Medellín cartel.

USA and Los Pepes death squad

Joe Toft was the head of the US Drug Enforcement Administration (DEA) in Colombia.

'Toft felt guilty himself...He knew that the death squad hits matched the intelligence reports gathered at the [US] embassy and passed along to the [Colombian Police's] Search Bloc. He knew that some of the DEA's own sources were founding members of the group. Still, Toft was torn. On the one hand, Los Pepes were effectively dismantling the Medellín cartel and stripping away the layers of protection around Pablo. But on the other hand, he couldn't in good conscience support the group's violent, illegal methods. So he had morally held his breath. He had done nothing and had kept the worst of his misgivings and evidence to himself. Inside the embassy, he had been the most gung-ho all along...Now with Pablo dead, Toft worried that they had created a monster. They had opened a bridge between the Colombian government, its top politicians and generals, and the Cali cartel that would be difficult, if not impossible to shut down.'

Mark Bowden, Killing Pablo [25]

1990s: Colombia 'the most threatened nation in the region'

Colombia rose to the top of list of priorities for US policy makers in the 1990s. The danger in Central America had subsided - the Sandinistas lost elections in 1990 and the Guatemalan and Salvadoran guerrillas were involved in peace processes. But the crisis in Colombia deepened, particularly in the later years of the decade: criminal violence soared, the country became the world's leading cocaine exporter and in 1998-99 the economy collapsed. Most importantly, the guerrilla war, previously confined to rural areas and poor city suburbs, was spreading to every part of the country.

In 1990 military aid to Colombia increased to a record high of US$73 million. It included US$65 million of emergency anti-narcotics military aid as part of Bush's Andean Initiative. The US Ambassador of the time, Thomas McNamara, who had not adjusted to the post-Cold War newspeak, made no attempt to pretend that the aid would not be used for counterinsurgency activities: 'I don't see the utilisation of the arms against the guerrillas as a deviation. The arms are given to the government in order that it may use them in the anti-narcotics struggle, but they may also be used for other objectives.' [26]

After Clinton's election, most officials preferred not to shout about the US military assistance being used to fight guerrillas. Instead, the concept of the 'narco-guerrilla' was revived. General Barry McCaffrey, former Gulf War 'hero' and head of the Southern Command, was the leading proponent of this theory. In 1995 he told a congressional committee:

> 'Drug production and trafficking continue to be the major regional problems which affect all the nations of the Americas. In Colombia, for example, the murder rate is nearly 10 times greater than that of the U.S. Most of these deaths are directly related to narco-guerrilla activity.' [27]

This statement was doubly misleading: not only did the term imply that guerrillas were the main drug traffickers, a position that even the DEA did not hold, it also suggested that the guerrillas were responsible for most murders, which the Colombian intelligence services own statistics showed was not the case. What McCaffrey and other military strategists were really trying to draw attention to was the growing strength of leftwing guerrillas, who despite the Colombian army's efforts, were expanding their territorial control each year. In 1996, Clinton appointed McCaffrey head of the White House's Office for National Drug Control Policy or 'Drugs Czar'. General Charles E. Wilhelm, SouthCom commander between 1997-2000, also had his eye on Colombia, declaring it to be the 'most threatened nation' in the region. [28]

Just as military leaders were alerting US policy-makers to the dangers, relations between the Colombian and US governments had reached their nadir. President Ernesto Samper's (1994-1997) link to the Cali cartel was too overt and made a mockery of the US's war on drugs. Samper played on the Colombian public's dislike for US interference, using nationalist rhetoric to strengthen his domestic position (although in practice Samper was not averse to overturning the ban on extradition, for example, in order to please the Americans). In 1996-97, Colombia was decertified, which meant ordinary grants and loans were suspended. In spite of this, special funds were channelled through the International Narcotics Control budget and emergency presidential 'drawdowns', giving Colombia a total of US$56 million military aid in 1996 and US$86 million in 1997, more than any other country in the hemisphere except Mexico.

Plan Colombia

The Clinton administration was nevertheless greatly relieved when the friendly Andrés Pastrana was elected. His willingness to work with the US enabled the Pentagon and State Department to transform Plan Colombia into a strategy which met US security needs, while presenting it as a Colombian initiative.

Pastrana was elected in 1998 and in that year, as President elect, he launched a peace process with the FARC. Although US military leaders had been calling for a robust offensive against Colombian guerrillas since the mid-1990s, some pragmatists in the State Department were willing to explore other options. In December 1998, members of the Clinton administration secretly met with the FARC in Costa Rica to discuss the eradication of illicit crops and the terms of the proposed demilitarised zone. It is possible that some US officials believed that, given that the guerrillas had remained undefeated for 40 years, securing a peace deal was the best way of defending US interests. Alternatively, they may have simply been sounding out the enemy, while preparing for war. In any case, the peaceful option was closed in March 1999 when the FARC murdered three US citizens – indigenous campaigners working with Colombian U'wa indians. The US administration immediately broke off all contact with the FARC, and although it continued to give formal support to the peace process, took an increasingly sceptical view of it.

Genesis of Plan Colombia

- May 1999 the 'soft' Spanish version of Plan Colombia is published. No mention of military aid.

- 15 July 1999 Minister of Defence Luis Ramírez and Armed Forces Chief of Staff Gen. Fernando Tapias visit Washington. Request US$500m of military aid.

- 16 July 1999, U.S. 'Drug Czar' Barry McCaffrey proposes US$1bn in 'emergency drug supplemental assistance' for fighting the drug war in South America. He also states that differentiating counter-drugs and counterinsurgency operations is counterproductive.

- 26 July Barry McCaffrey visits Colombia.

- 8-9 August 1999 US Under Secretary of State Thomas Pickering visits Colombia. Expresses support for Pastrana's peace process. Reportedly advises the government not to make more concessions to the FARC.

- 20-22 September 1999, Pastrana visits Washington to seek US$3.5bn foreign aid for 'Plan Colombia'.

- In October 1999 the militarised English final version of Plan Colombia is published. The State Department admits it played a 'extensive' role in designing the plan:

  'The Colombian Government did consult extensively with the United States Government as it refined its strategy, just as the U.S. has worked closely with all other countries committed to combating the illicit drug trade.'[29]

- 11 January 2000 Clinton administration submits proposal for US$1.3bn Colombia aid package to Congress

- June 2000 Congress approves (slightly modified) aid package. House of Representatives and Senate reach compromise on differing versions.

- 13 July 2000 President Clinton approves the US$1.32bn aid package

- 23 August 2000 President Clinton waives human rights conditions, allowing military aid to be released

Source: Center for International Policy (CIP)

Military build up

Plan Colombia not only greatly increased aid and training for the Colombian military, it also provided a pretext for a build up of US forces in the hemisphere.

The United States had agreed to leave Panama in 1999, after having had exclusive rights to the Canal Zone since 1903. Panama had not only been the perfect place for a transatlantic canal, but also an extremely good base for military operations, located between Central and South America and near to the Caribbean. The Howard Air Force Base in Panama was the main location from which the Department of Defense, the US Coast Guard and the US Custom Service conducted their operations.

On May 1, 1999, the United States stopped using Howard airbase. In the late 1990s it signed four ten-year agreements for the use of airfields in Manta (Ecuador), Aruba (Dutch Antilles), Curação (Dutch Antilles) and San Salvador (El Salvador). It has been using Manta, Aruba and Curação for counter-drug operations since spring 1999 and San Salvador since August 2000.[30] The Plan Colombia aid package included US$116 million for upgrading these air bases known as 'Forward Operating Locations'.

The United States has also built up an impressive radar and intelligence system around the Andean ridge with radar sites at Iquitos and Pucallpa in Peru, Tres Equinas, Leticia, San José del Guaviare, Marandua, and Riohacha in Colombia, and San Andrés (a Colombian Caribbean island). Of the Plan Colombia aid, US$162.3 million was for radar and intelligence-gathering equipment. The States also has the use of military training bases in Iquitos (Peru) and Tolemaida (Colombia) and three right in the heart of FARC-dominated territory in Tres Esquinas (Putumayo), Larandia (Caquetá) and San José del Guaviare (Guaviare).

'Push to the South'

The primary strategy of Plan Colombia was a 'push to the south' – the heart of guerrilla territory. The strategy was outlined to Congress by McCaffrey, Brian Sheridan and other officials.[31] Most of Colombia's military aid in Plan Colombia, US$416.9 million, was to fund this 'push'. Three new Colombian army battalions were created and trained by the US to operate in Putumayo and Caquetá. The first was assembled in April 1999 and has been based in Tres Esquinas since December 1999. US Special Forces trained the second battalion in July-September 2000 at Larandia base, in Caquetá and a third was trained in January-April 2001. These three battalions were given 14 Blackhawk and 45 Huey helicopters as part of Plan Colombia. They also have use of 33 older Huey helicopters, which were approved in a 1999 US aid package.

When testifying to Congress, US officials during the Clinton era used a variety of arguments to explain why the principal strategy of Plan Colombia was to advance into areas in the south controlled by guerrillas and all agreed there was a thin line between counterinsurgency and counternarcotics. Some argued that the FARC had become drug traffickers.[32] Others said that guerrillas would only be attacked if they hindered anti-narcotics efforts. This line was interpreted in different ways, implying varying degrees of engagement. Brian Sheridan, Assistant Secretary of Defence for Special Operations and Low Intensity Conflict, stated that: 'Only those armed elements that forcibly inhibit or confront counter-drug operations will be engaged.'[33] General Peter Pace, commander of the Southern Command, interpreted this as helping the Colombian military to 'provide security' in the target area of Plan Colombia and beyond:

'The combined capabilities of the Colombian military and Colombian police is not sufficient to provide security for the entire country...As a result of that, the military support that we are providing, in the form of assisting them to train their counternarcotics brigade and assisting them, though our State Department, to obtain helicopters and to marry up the helicopters with the counternarcotics brigade is, in fact helping them very much.'[34]

Indeed General Pace was frank enough to admit that Plan Colombia had very little to do with drugs at all:

Senator Sessions: Colombia is the oldest democracy in this hemisphere, I believe, except the United States. It has 38 million people; they've been allies and friends of ours, they are a significant trading partner of the Untied States and their nation is in jeopardy...They have real emigration because of the terrorism and the attacks and the Marxist guerrillas taking over substantial portions of their country. And we suggest the only way we can help them is to help them fight drugs. And I think we need to be much more realistic about that. And it will be a tragedy if we stand here and allow them to fall or to be undermined or have their economy destroyed as a result of this guerrilla effort.

General Pace: Sir I agree with you that this is a fight for democracy in Colombia, to support that democracy. It is not an expectation of being able to wipe out coca. If you did wipe out every coca plant in the world, some other drug would be fed to the demand side...I agree with you sir, this is supporting our friends and neighbours, supporting a fellow democracy while we also assist ourselves.[35]

'Push to the South'

Regaining Putumayo from the FARC has been a long-term aim of the Colombian state; it is after all a national border and it also contains oil. As Plan Colombia was being drawn up and it became clear that the guerrilla-controlled regions of the south would be its main focus, the paramilitaries began to announce plans to 're-take' the region. The paramilitaries have been an advance guard of Plan Colombia, trying to ensure that the type of mass peasant protests that accompanied fumigation in Guaviare did not occur. Most importantly, they aim to destroy the FARC and its support in the region. The strategy appears to have been successful, as the FARC have been pushed out of southern Putumayo and an armed strike in October 2000 can be seen as a last-gasp attempt to stop the paramilitary-military advance.

The pattern of events during this advance was terribly predictable:

- In January 9, 1999 paramilitaries arrived in the village of El Tigre: 26 people were dragged from their homes and killed. Fourteen other people were 'disappeared'.
  Source: 'The Sixth Division'. Human Rights Watch Report. 2001

- Their bodies were thrown in the river with stomachs split so that they would not float. A number of houses were burned down with the inhabitants locked inside. During the massacre, the XXIV brigade set up a roadblock to prevent people leaving the village.

Source: Question and Answer with a Human Rights Worker, during a Witness for Peace delegation in July 2001. Notes taken by Justin Podur

- In November 1999, fifty paramilitaries arrived at the village of El Placer. Twelve civilians were pulled from their houses and shot dead in nearby fields. The XXIV brigade was in town several days before the incursion but left. Army soliders returned several hours after the massacre. Two hundred people were extrajudicially executed in 1999, according to Amnesty International.

  Source: Amnesty International USA, Colombia Report 1999/Testimony of Andrew Miller, Amnesty International USA, Acting Advocacy Director for Latin America and the Caribbean, before the US House of Representatives Committee on Government Reform and Oversight Subcommittee on Criminal Justice, Drug Policy and Human Resources

- The killings continued the following year. The United Nations High Commission for Human Rights stated that Putumayo was one of the departments worst affected by 'collective executions by paramilitary groups' in the year 2000. The UN report also described the obvious collusion between the armed forces and the paramitliaries:

  'It is common knowledge that a paramilitary roadblock stands at the entrance to the settlement of El Placer, only 15 minutes away from La Hormiga (Putumayo) where a XXIV Brigade army battalion is stationed. Eight months after the Office reported to the authorities that it had seen it, the roadblock was still there. The military authorities denied its existence in writing. This [UN] Office also observed that paramilitaries were still operating at the Villa Sandra estate between Puerto Asís and Santa Ana in the same department, a few minutes away from the Brigade XXIV base....the existence and maintenance of this position are public knowledge – so much so that it has been visited repeatedly by international journalists who have published interviews with the paramilitary commander. Reports received by the [UN] Office even speak of meetings between paramilitaries and members of the security forces at the Villa Sandra estate. In late July, the Office warned the authorities of an imminent paramilitary raid on the inner city area of La Dorada, municipality of San Miguel (Putumayo), which indeed took place on 21 September. The paramilitaries remained in the area for several weeks despite the fact that it is only a few minutes away from the army's La Hormiga base.

  Source: Report of the United Nations High Commissioner for Human Rights on the human rights situation in Colombia, published in English, February 8, 2001

- It is not known how many people died in Putumayo in the year 2000. A journalist who travelled with a Witness for Peace delegation spoke to the priest of St Francis of Asís church in Puerto Asís, the second-largest town in Putumayo. Of the 207 funerals performed in his church in that year, 97 of them were assassinations, he told her. These figures only related to people who lived in or near Puerto Asís and who had Catholic burials.

Source 'The Time of Coca: On the Colombian front of the drug war' by Rose Marie Berger, Witness for Peace Delegation, January 2001

- The priest later fled Putumayo, as did the local legal registrar (*personero*) who had bravely kept a record of the paramilitary-military atrocities in the year 2000.
  Source: 'The Sixth Division', Human Rights Watch Report, 2001

- On the day fumigation started in Putumayo in December 2000, three truckloads of paramilitaries entered the village of Puerto Caicedo, announcing their intention to take the departmental capital Mocoa by the end of 2001. Within one month of their arrival 15 people had been killed, the local priest told Human Rights Watch.

Another Puerto Caicedo resident said:

'The paramilitaries asked around to see who had applauded when guerrillas held a meeting and criticised Plan Colombia. They promised to make these same people applaud to the sound of bullets.'

Source: 'The Sixth Division', Human Rights Watch Report, 2001

- The number of people fleeing Putumayo rose sharply: 1997: 27, 1998: 278, 1999: 368, 2000: 7,248, 2001: 17,143.
  Source: National Ombudsman's Office[36]

- A report about Putumayo by the National Ombudsman concluded that:

'The intensification of the armed conflict and the fumigations have provoked a severe humanitarian crisis in the communities of small farmers, Afro-Colombians and indigenous people in the region.'[37]

Clinton and human rights: half-truths and lies?

As the American public, press and politicians began to worry that the country was being dragged into another Vietnam, the Clinton administration went to great lengths to stress that Colombia was not a counter insurgency operation. Firstly, officials argued that US military aid would only be used in anti-narcotics operations. There were few grounds to have confidence in this claim: in 1997 a congressional end-use monitoring report (EUM) looking at an aid package for two Colombian brigades containing 700 rifles, machine guns, pistols, shotguns, grenade launchers and 60mm mortars found that they were used for narcotics operations only '50% of the time...with the remainder of the time performing security and public order missions.'[38] On December 13, 1998 Colombia's Combat Air Command One used US anti-narcotics-aid planes to bomb and fire rockets at the village of Santo Domingo, killing seven children and 11 adults.[39] In October 2000, another congressional investigation found that the US embassy in Bogotá did not have the means to monitor how aid was being used.[40]

The Clinton government was also aware that it was bolstering the Colombian military at a time when human rights abuses had reached an unprecedented high. Even the State Department's human rights report showed that the paramilitaries were responsible for most massacres and that the military were collaborating with them. American human rights activists assiduously documented each new atrocity and campaigned hard to stop their government from funding the perpetrators. In 1997 Congress approved an Amendment to the Foreign Operations Appropriations Act which banned the US from giving anti-narcotics aid to any foreign military unit whose members had violated human rights. This is called the 'Leahy Provision' (named after Senator Patrick Leahy who proposed it). However, there are very few Colombian military units that have not been implicated in human rights abuses, so the policy has been implemented in a patchy way and ignored completely for the most part.

In other cases the letter of the law was obeyed, but not the substance: for example the XXIV Brigade based in Putumayo was going to play a central role in Plan Colombia's 'push to the south'. However, in 1998, in a well publicised case, the Brigade disappeared three civilians, whose bodies, when found and exhumed, bore signs of torture. US aid for the brigade was suspended in October 1999. In January 2001, when a Human Rights Watch mission went to southern Colombia, it found that the new 'clean' anti-narcotics battalions were housed on the XXIV Brigade's base in Larandía, Caquetá and sharing their facilities. The Chief of Staff of the Counter Narcotics Brigade (which contained both new battalions) told the mission: 'During the December fumigation, both counter narcotics battalions were based at the XXIV Brigade facilities in

Santa Ana, outside Puerto Asís. They also assisted us with intelligence, civic military outreach and psychological operations during the fumigation.'[41]

Another example is Brigadier General Mario Montoya Uribe, a former School of the Americas guest instructor, with links to the AAA death squad in the 1980s. Until his promotion in October 2001, he was the commander of the Colombian army's southern forces, which included the XXIV brigade. In the Colombian press he was presented as the leader of Plan Colombia and he was certainly its spokesman for visiting foreign journalists. His forces were technically separate from the three new anti-narcotics battalions, but were operating in their target area of Plan Colombia and indispensable to it. According to US sources quoted in the Wall Street Journal, they also used US military aid:

> 'Brig. Gen. Mario Montoya Uribe, who heads all military operations in the south, is so attuned to U.S. worries, that when asked the rules for using the new helicopters he declares that only members of the U.S.-vetted battalions can fly in U.S.-purchased equipment. An American military officer standing nearby doesn't correct the general, but he later says that as far as Washington is concerned, any of Gen. Montoya's 10,000 men can use the transport, if they're on a clear drug mission.'[42]

Clinton's disregard for human rights was shown in August 2000 when he used his presidential waiver to override the human rights conditions that Congress had attached to the Plan Colombia aid. The President does not have the right to override the Leahy Provision, which is part of US law. If the US government funds military units guilty of human rights abuses, it is acting illegally.

- More Colombian School of the Americas (SOA) graduates have been implicated in human rights abuses than SOA graduates from any other country.[43]

- Colonel Gabriel Ramón Díaz Ortiz, the commander of the XXIV Brigade in Putumayo whose record was so bad that US aid was cut, is a graduate of the School of the Americas.

- All the commanders of the brigades highlighted in the 2001 Human Rights Watch report are graduates of the School of the Americas, including those of the XXIV Brigade in Putumayo, the V Brigade which oversaw the paramilitary take over of Barrancabermeja, and the III brigade in Valle del Cauca, where the Alto Naya chainsaw massacre of 2001 took place.

• The Human Rights Watch report also cited the case of three officers arrested for alleged links with paramilitaries who mysteriously escaped from military prison in 1999-2001: Major Diego Fino, Major David Hernández, and Lt Carlos Alberto Acosta. All three were SOA graduates.

• The General cited by the UN High Commissioner in February 2001 as a glaring example of an officer who had repeatedly colluded with paramilitaries yet not been prosecuted by the Pastrana government, General Rito Alejo del Río, is also a SOA graduate.

• US-trained officers were involved in almost all the worst atrocities of the 1990s including the Trujillo massacres, the Mapiripán massacre (1997) and Alto Naya (2001).[44]

US links to the Mapiripán massacre[45]

• Army Colonel Lino Sánchez was charged by the attorney general of being the 'intellectual author' of the massacre, along with Carlos Castaño. He was commander of an army brigade which received US Special Forces training just 80km from Mapiripán a month before the massacre took place, according to respected Colombian newspaper *El Espectador.*[46]

• Days before the massacre, over 100 paramilitaries arrived at San José de Guaviare airport, which doubles as an anti-narcotics airbase and is home to many US contract pilots. No police or army officers attempted to apprehend the illegal gunmen or seek reinforcements to stop the massacre. The US embassy's narcotics assistance section representative was at the base the day the paramilitaries touched ground, according to the former chief of police José Serrano.[47]

Furthermore, the Colombian paramilitaries are using the very counter insurgency methods that the US schools and manuals have been teaching officers since the 1960s. The key to counterinsurgency theory is to target civilians because without their support guerrillas cannot survive. Nowadays, counterinsurgency is called 'asymmetrical' or 'nonlinear' warfare. An example of US military thinking is given in this article published in 2001 in *Military Review*, 'the professional journal of the US army':

> 'Guerrilla fighters are civilians. If they are not carrying weapons, they are almost impossible to identify as adversaries. Civilians who are not guerrillas might be passing information to the enemy or to US forces.'[48]

These are exactly the grounds used by paramilitary leader Carlos Castaño to justify civilian massacres. The article goes on to state:

> 'Apart from civilian populations, there are a number of non-governmental organisations (NGO), government organisations from neutral countries, national and international businesses and religious organisations whose interest might be for, against or neutral to US interests...While such organisations [NGOs] are for humanitarian reasons, how many could harbour a sniper or saboteur? How many might relay information about US forces if they felt it would further their interests? Also, simply conferring with representatives of extreme political organisations can sometimes lend them a legitimacy that could be detrimental to US interests.'[49]

There is a strain of thought within the US military which believes that paramilitary violence is unpleasant, but justified, if it rids the region of insurgents.

Vital interests

US officials themselves are happy to admit, in a matter-of-fact way, that Plan Colombia is broadly aimed at defending US interests in the hemisphere.[50] 'Colombia's problems spill over into neighboring countries, they threaten the regional stability that is essential to the growth and sustainment (sic) of strong democracies and free market economies throughout the region,' said General Charles E. Wilhelm in February

2000.[51] A good example of this thinking was given during Senators' questioning of George W. Bush's nominees for key defence posts:

> **Senator Roberts:** And look at the vital national interests involved here: drugs, immigration, energy and trade. All four – as a matter of fact, I think it probably rates a higher priority than the Balkans. I'm not going to ask you to get into that. But, and if anybody doesn't think that it doesn't affect the pump price in Boston or Topeka in terms of energy, take a look at Hector [sic] Chávez, who could be the next Fidel Castro in regards to Venezuela....But at any rate, could you comment on that in terms of our strategic national interest? And Doug, you can start off, if you'd like. I don't want to risk anybody down there in terms of a civil war. But I think in terms of Colombia and stability of the region it's very important. Am I right?
>
> **Douglas Feith, Under Secretary of Defense for Policy (speaking when nominee)**
> Senator, I agree with you that the stability of the whole Andean region, the whole northern part of South America is an important US national security interest...making sure that our neighbors remain peaceful and reasonably stable is a very important interest of ours....
>
> **Peter W. Rodman, Assistant Secretary of Defense for International Security Affairs (speaking when nominee)**
> Well, I share the sentiment. We have decided as a country to emphasize the counternarcotics effort. I mean, that's – that's what two administrations and the Congress have decided. But I think, inescapably, we also have a stake in Colombia as a long-standing democracy and a friend. And I wouldn't call it nation-building, because I think that phrase brings to mind, you know, more ambitious things that we may not, in other parts of the world, want to attempt. But I think we do have a stake and we shouldn't shy away from saying it – a stake in helping Colombia, which is a friend, to survive...I think the Western Hemisphere is – if we don't have a vital interest in the Western Hemisphere, then, you know, we don't have a vital interest anywhere. This is a friendly country, a pivotal country, that we have a stake in.[52]
> *Excerpts from Senate Armed Services Committee Hearing (confirmation of nominees). June 5, 2001*

Occidental Petroleum's testimony to the Senate

Two years after Oxy's Larry Meriage gave the following testimony, the Bush administration asked Congress to approve the first counterinsurgency aid for Colombia since the Cold War: US$98m to protect oil installations in Arauca, the region where Oxy's operations are located.

'Thank you, Mr. Chairman. I am honored to have the opportunity to testify before this distinguished subcommittee regarding the U.S. response to the crisis in Colombia. This is a subject of paramount importance to my company, Occidental Petroleum Corporation (Oxy), and one that I believe should be at the forefront of America's foreign policy agenda.

In my testimony today, I will present a private sector perspective on Colombia based on nearly three decades of business experience in the country. I will offer our observations highlighting the vital U.S. economic interests in Colombia and how those interests are being undermined by the dramatic rise in narcotics' cultivation that is tied directly to the sharp increase in violence perpetrated by subversive groups operating throughout the country. I also want to call attention to the critical importance of foreign investment in Colombia's energy sector and, finally, to present our thoughts on the aid package submitted by the Administration....

....Despite efforts by units of Colombia's armed forces to maintain security in the area surrounding Caño Limon production facilities, units of both the FARC and ELN have attacked the government operated 483-mile pipeline that transports oil from Caño Limon to the Caribbean port of Covenas over 700 times since operations began – 79 times in 1999 alone. These attacks have caused nearly $100 million in losses (including lost production) and more than 1.7 million barrels have been lost....

...our new exploration project in North Santander has received nearly universal support in Colombia – including the strong backing of President Pastrana. Only two groups are intent on blocking the project – leftist guerrillas who seek to undermine the country's democratically elected government and several fringe non-governmental organizations (NGOs) in the U.S. Both groups are united in their opposition to oil exploration and development.

The opposition of Marxist rebels is driven by their goal of toppling the Colombian government. They attack foreign oil interests, while couched in ideological terms related to excessive foreign involvement in Colombia's oil industry, in practical terms is bent on depriving the government of vital oil revenues. The guerrillas know that oil projects in remote areas will lead to a stronger central government presence in parts of Colombia they have long dominated.

The opposition of these NGOs to this project is part of their global drive against the development and use of fossil fuel. These groups have deliberately and irresponsibly misrepresented the facts in their campaign to halt this project, thereby serving as de facto allies of the subversive forces that are attacking oil installations, electric power stations and other legitimate businesses enterprises that are vital to Colombian civil society.

...It is clear that urgent action must be taken. The 'Plan Colombia' put forward by the Pastrana Administration presents a comprehensive strategy designed to address the range of challenges faced by Colombia. U.S. support of President Pastrana will be critical to the Plan's success, which is why we strongly support the provision of a substantial supplemental aid package....

...I would urge you to consider support of counternarcotics operations in the northern regions as well as the south. This will help augment security for oil development operations, which, as noted earlier, are fundamental to the success of 'Plan Colombia'.

Testimony of Lawrence P. Meriage
Vice President, Executive Services and Public Affairs
Occidental Oil and Gas Corporation
Before the House Government Reform Subcommittee on Criminal Justice, Drug Policy and Human Resources Hearing on Colombia
February 15, 2000[53]

Colombia has the potential to be as important an oil supplier as Venezuela to the US. Many of the country's potentially oil-bearing sedimentary basins cannot be explored because they lie beneath territory controlled by guerrillas. Furthermore guerrillas are cutting oil companies' profits by repeatedly bombing pipelines and other infrastructure.

It is not simply Colombia's mineral wealth that is of interest to the US. It is a geopolitical issue too. Historically, the United States has intervened most often in Central America and the region has no important mineral deposits and captures only a miniscule proportion of total US foreign investment. What concerns US strategists is that if one country rejects its model – is allowed to curtail the free market, nationalise foreign companies or reject capitalism entirely – it would set an example, jeopardising its dominance of the entire hemisphere. Colombia is in a crucial strategic position, bordering five other countries and providing a bridge between Central and South America. The US is particularly concerned about Venezuela, its third-largest oil supplier, whose populist President, Hugo Chávez, is highly critical of US policy. Chávez's nationalist stance has worried US military analysts and provides extra reason for wanting to shore up support in Colombia. A FARC-run Colombia next to a Chávez led Venezuela would be nightmare scenario for the US.

The US is worried that the guerrilla war could spill over Colombia's borders to Brazil, Peru, Panama, Venezuela and Ecuador. Politically, the guerrillas cannot be allowed to win because this would send the dangerous message that it is possible to defeat the US. In blunt terms, there are up to 20,000 guerrillas in Colombia whose avowed aim is to defeat 'US imperialism'. It is inconceivable, given the US's history of intervention in Latin America, that it would ignore such a threat.

George W. Bush and September 11th

Since the accession of George W. Bush and particularly since September 11th, 2001, the US government has been willing to state openly that it will help the Colombian government defeat the guerrillas. The US position on the FARC had been gradually hardening throughout 1999-2001. State Department officials were frequently reported to be 'losing patience' with the guerrillas and the arrest of three suspected members of the Irish Republican Army flying out of the demilitarised zone in August 2001 reinforced their position.

Plan Colombia undermined the peace process by strengthening the confidence and the technical capacity of the Colombian armed forces and convincing the FARC that the government was preparing for war. However, it was not until September 11th, 2001 that the trudge towards war turned into an unstoppable stampede, as the more overtly interventionist stance and the belligerent rhetoric of the US encouraged hawks in Colombia.

Almost immediately after September 11th, parallels were drawn with Colombia. Speaking to ABC TV on September 23, Secretary of State

Colin Powell said that Colombian insurgents were 'terrorists with a global reach' who posed a threat to US interests.[54] In October 2001, US Ambassador Anne Patterson made two high-profile speeches in which she compared Colombia's armed groups to Osama bin Laden's Al-Qaeda and said: 'My government is concerned by the use of the demilitarized zone as a base for terrorist acts.' She stated that 'the United States must do more to combat terrorism in Colombia,' and concluded that, 'Plan Colombia remains the most effective anti-terrorist strategy we could design.'[55]

Other politicians, such as Republican Congressman Cass Ballenger, went further: 'We don't know how many terrorist organisations are currently operating inside the *despeje* [Colombia's demilitarised zone], but if recent history is any guide, we can be sure the *despeje* is crawling with terrorists.'[56]

AUC are declared terrorists

On September 10, 2001, the Colombian paramilitary group *Autodefensas Unidas de Colombia* (AUC) were added to the State Department's list of Foreign Terrorist Organisations. Critics had long accused the US of hypocrisy for labelling the FARC and ELN terrorists, while ignoring the AUC, which was responsible for far more killings.

The AUC are now routinely included in all official US statements about terrorism in Colombia. However, the AUC's operational capability stems from its close relationship with the armed forces and while the US continues to provide generous military aid to that institution, the paramilitaries are likely to remain strong.

Countdown to war

On January 8, 2002, 14 Blackhawk helicopters were delivered to the Colombian government, the last batch from the Plan Colombia aid package. On January 9, President Andrés Pastrana suspended the peace talks and announced that the armed forces would re-enter the demilitarised zone in 48 hours. The announcement was met by expressions of concern from European and Latin American governments, and from the United Nations. The United States issued a more neutral statement saying it supported the decisions taken by the Pastrana government. With the help of UN negotiator James Lemoyne, the peace process was temporarily salvaged and the FARC agreed to work more rapidly towards a ceasefire.

In early February the Bush administration announced the first explicit counter insurgency aid for Colombia since the Cold War: US$98 million to fund a new Colombian army unit to defend the Caño Limón oil pipeline and other oil infrastructure in Arauca from guerrilla attacks. The pipeline and the Arauca oilfields are operated by the US company Occidental Petroleum.

On February 20, Pastrana abandoned the peace process, after accusing the FARC of hijacking a plane and kidnapping a congressman. For the first time he defined the FARC as 'terrorists'. Aircraft, including US-supplied Blackhawks, bombarded the former demilitarised zone, an area inhabited by 100,000 civilians. Ground troops began to advance from the bases which had benefited from newly-trained battalions under Plan Colombia and, having spent US$162 million of the Plan Colombia funds on sophisticated radar equipment across the Andean ridge, the US stepped up intelligence sharing with the Colombian military.[57] On February 24, US Special Forces were filmed in the capital of the demilitarised zone, after it had been 're-taken' by government troops.[58]

On March 21, the Bush administration formally asked Congress to allow all military aid, past and present, to be used for counterinsurgency purposes. It requested that Congress lift the restrictions limiting military aid to anti-narcotics operations and allow the Colombian armed forces to use it for a 'unified campaign against narcotics trafficking, terrorist activities, and other threats to its national security.' Colin Powell best expressed the new philosophy:

'It's terrorism that threatens stability in Colombia. And if it threatens stability in Colombia, it threatens stability in our part of the world, in our neighborhood (sic), in our backyard. And I think that's something that should be of concern to us.'[59]

7 Facts & Figures

Appendix I

Guerrillas
Paramilitaries
Armed forces
Political parties
Peace and civil society groups
Private contractors

Guerrillas

FARC - Fuerzas Armadas Revolucionarias de Colombia

Colombia's largest guerrilla group.
Website: http://www.farc-ep.org
Year of formation: 1966
Number of combatants[1]
1966:350
1986:3,600
1995:7,000
2001:16,000-20,000

Number of municipalities with FARC presence[2]
1985:173
1991:437
1995:622

Zone of Influence: a presence in at least 622 (60%) of Colombia's 1,050 municipalities; controls over a third of national territory, although mainly in sparsely populated areas. Particularly strong in the southern departments of Huila, Caquetá, Meta and Putumayo, as well as the southeastern department of Guaviare.[3]

Leadership: Pedro Antonio Marín (alias Manuel Marulanda Vélez), also known as 'Tirofijo' (1930-) has led the group since its foundation Commander-in-Chief of the FARC. Born in 1930 to a peasant family in the coffee growing region of Quindio. Migrated to the resistance communities of Tolima in 1949 when his Liberal-supporting village was terrorized by the Conservative police during *la Violencia*. Became a leading Liberal guerrilla fighter and changed his name to Manuel Marulanda, after a murdered trade union leader. Has remained a guerrilla ever since. Joined the Communist Party in the 1950s. Part of a small group of guerrillas who fought in Marquetalia in 1964, a resistance community attacked by the military. In 1966, founded the FARC and became one of the six-strong military command. Has remained in charge ever since. Is described as sharp-witted, pragmatic, a good-listener, but inflexible once he has made up his mind.

Seven-member secretariat:
Manuel Marulanda Vélez alias Tirofijo, Alfonso Cano, Raúl Reyes, Timoleón Jiménez, Iván Márquez, Jorge Briceño alias Mono Jojoy, Efraín Guzmán.

Ideology: traditionally thought of as a pro-Soviet group because of its longstanding relationship with the Communist Party. But other elements have influenced its philosophy: it was created by Liberal, as well as Communist, guerrillas, so its leaders are not ideologically 'pure' Marxists. It is fundamentally a peasant army whose discourse is a mixture of revolutionary agrarianism and anti-imperialism.

Since the fall of the Soviet Union, it has emphasised its radical nationalist credentials and describes itself as Bolivarian (after independence leader Simón Bolívar). Its most recent manifesto has largely social democratic demands such as a mixed economy, a welfare state and civil rights. Structurally, it is centralist and imposes strict military discipline on its members.

Support Base: poor peasants and unemployed rural workers, particularly in lowland areas where waves of poor migrants have settled. They achieved broader support in the cities in the 1980s when it helped to create the Unión Patriótica (UP), which acted as a pole of attraction for left-wingers, trade unionists and community activists. The UP disintegrated after 3,000 of its supporters were killed by rightwing deathsquads.

In 2000 the FARC launched the Bolivarian Movement for a New Colombia, a clandestine broad front modelled on the UP. It has also tried to establish a network of contacts in poor urban neighbourhoods. Given its clandestine nature, it is hard to gauge their true level of support in the cities, but its popularity appears to be diminishing – certainly the organised labour and popular movement has become more critical of it in recent years.

Source of Funds: the most important source of income is taxing the drug trade (imposing a levy on coca paste sales and charging traffickers for the right to use jungle laboratories and airstrips in areas the guerrillas dominate). The second most important source of income is kidnapping.

Peace Process 1998-2002: In 1999 government troops were pulled out of an area the size of Switzerland (42,000 sq km) in the departments of Meta and Caquetá in southern Colombia. The aim was to create a neutral 'demilitarised zone' for peace talks. The FARC was already dominant in the region and rapidly gained total control of the zone. Peace talks with President Andrés Pastrana stalled repeatedly and achieved little. No ceasefire was agreed and the war intensified. In February 2002, the peace process collapsed and troops were sent to re-take the demilitarised zone.

History:[1] The FARC was formed in 1966, but its roots can be traced as far back as the 1930s when communism inspired peasants and rural workers developed a tactic they called 'armed self-defence'. Peasant families would occupy public lands or an absent landowner's estate and set up community militias to defend themselves. These peasant communities were concentrated in the Sumpaz and Viotá regions of Cudinamarca and Tolima.[5]

During *la Violencia*, peasants in these regions revived the old 'resistance communities' in order to withstand the onslaught from the ultra-rightwing Conservative government of 1950-53. Many Liberal peasants (among them Manuel Marulanda) migrated from Cauca, Huila and Quindio to these guerrilla-controlled areas after their villages were terrorised by the Conservative police and army.

After a coup in 1953, the dictator General Gustavo Rojas Pinilla offered an amnesty to all the guerrillas. The Communist-influenced guerrillas in Tolima and Cundinamarca did not trust the military government and refused to give up their arms. Instead they took to the hills, where they were joined by radical Liberal guerrillas who did not want to give up the struggle either.

In 1955, Rojas launched a major offensive against the guerrillas, known as the War of Villarica. This prompted the first wave of 'armed colonisation': hundreds of peasant families marched south in two long columns, protected by guerrillas, and established communities in El Pato

(Caquetá) and El Guayabero (Meta). Others settled in Riochiquito (Cauca) and Marquetalia (Tolima).

These armed self-sufficient peasant communities were dubbed 'Independent Republics' by the Conservative government in 1964, which launched an air and ground offensive against the Marquetalia community. Although the families were forced to flee and the rebels dispersed, it was a Pyrrhic victory. On July 20, 1964 rebels from Marquetalia, other regions of Tolima and Riochiquito (Cauca), held a meeting and issued 'The Guerrillas' Agrarian Programme'. During the following year they held meetings with guerrillas from the southern bloc (Huila, Caquetá, Cauca and Valle) and in April 1966 they formed the FARC. They agreed to switch from a defensive strategy to an offensive one, in which the self-defence milita were turned into mobile fighting units and sent across the country. At this time it had 350 fighters.

Relationship with Communist Party

Moscow was not promoting armed revolution in the 1960s, but trying to reach accommodation with governments. But the Colombian Communist Party did not want the FARC, which was quickly gaining peasant support, to come under the influence of the Cubans or Chinese. There was much debate within the Colombian party, but it agreed on this line at its Tenth Congress in 1966: 'Although a revolutionary situation does not exist in the country, it would be negative and fatal for the Colombian revolutionary movement to passively allow the annihilation of the peasants' organisations using the argument that one should wait until a revolutionary situation has completely matured before launching an armed struggle.'

The FARC and the Communist Party were not synonymous, but many of its most important leaders were Communists. Marulanda joined the party in the 1950s. Two 'political commissars' of the Communist Party were also sent to work with the guerrillas in 1964 and over the next two years helped constitute the FARC. These were Jacobo Arenas, a member of the party's central committee and the student leader Hernándo González (who died in action a year later).

Defectors: In 1972 Jaime Báteman Cayón, Alvaro Fayad, Iván Marino Ospina and Carlos Pizarro were expelled from the FARC and Communist Party. They went on to form the populist guerrilla movement M19. They argued that the peasant-based FARC were struggling for land and not for a seizure of state power.

In 1984, a section of the FARC which did support peace talks with the government formed the Ricardo Franco Front. This faction waged war on the traditional FARC and is also alleged to have carried out a purge of 134 of its own members. Throughout its history, the FARC has not tolerated dissenters and frequently shot dead 'traitors' and 'grasses'.

FARC influence in the countryside

The FARC found it easiest to expand in areas of recent settlement, such as Caquetá, Guaviare and Meta, where the state was barely present. In many areas, especially in the early years, they encouraged peasant communities to pool resources and set up rudimentary education and health posts. They were the forces of law and order, settling neighbour disputes and meting out punishments such as mending a hole in the road. Where villages existed, they tried to find out who were the most respected figures and encouraged them to organise communal activities such as sharing tools, working on each other's farms and clubbing together to buy seeds at a better price.

These communistic experiments were less common following the 1980s coca boom and the influx of thousands of new migrants. However, coca growers did tend to view the FARC as the natural authority in the region and supported them against the government, whose presence in the region was limited to militarised fumigation campaigns. The FARC were popular because they stopped the advance of property speculators and cattle ranchers, who waited until the poor *colonos* went bankrupt and bought up their land.

Many large landowners also supported the FARC in the early years because they provided protection from rural banditry in areas where the state was weak. Later, when the guerrillas grew stronger, the landowners turned against them and formed their own militia.

Expansion in the 1980s and 1990s

The FARC survived the 1960s and 1970s, but began to expand rapidly in the 1980s for three main reasons: 1) land concentration and the coca boom accelerated peasant migration to the lowlands, 2) a wave of popular struggle in the late 1970s was met by state repression, convincing activists to support the armed struggle and, 3) the Sandinista revolution of 1979 and guerrilla offensives in El Salvador and Guatemala raised hopes of victory.

In May 1982, at its Seventh Congress, the FARC altered its gradualist strategy and prepared to seize power. It added the words *Ejército Popular*

(Popular Army) to its name, becoming FARC-EP and changed its military structure.

In November 1982, President Belisario Betancur declared an amnesty for all guerrillas and invited them to participate in peace negotiations. The FARC decided to take advantage of this new political opening and agreed to a truce in March 1984. A demilitarised zone called 'La Casa Verde' (The Green House) was created in the Sumapaz region of Meta, 50 miles south of Bogotá. The truce broke down in 1985 after the M19 guerrillas stormed the Palace of Justice.

In 1985 the FARC formed the Unión Patriótica (UP), with candidates for the elections in 1986 and 1990. The FARC has been criticised for exposing UP members to violence, by not calling a ceasefire and instead pursuing a dual strategy of electoral participation and armed struggle. For most though, the massacre of 3,000 UP supporters, most of whom were not guerrillas, was evidence of the Colombian elite's intolerance and the impossibility of achieving change through parliament.

In 1987, the FARC formed a coordinating body with two other guerrilla groups, the ELN and EPL, called the Coordinadora Guerrillera Simón Bolívar (CGSB) and fighting continued for the rest of the decade. In 1989 the M19 and most of the EPL made peace with the government and in 1991 a constituent assembly was elected. The CGSB offered to lay down its arms if the Armed Forces would also agree to a ceasefire. In 1990, the military invaded *La Casa Verde*, re-igniting the war. The CGSB were offered six out of the 70 seats in the constituent assembly, which it rejected because the number did not reflect its real strength in the country.

In the 1990s, the rural crisis and the government's fumigation campaigns (which led to mass peasant protests in 1995-96) boosted support for the FARC. The guerrillas have pursued a military rather than a political strategy; even its attempt to build up a support base in the cities is aimed at creating a network of helpers who will provide logistical support for armed action, rather than an organisation of political agitators.

Taxing the drug trade has enabled the FARC to improve its military capability. From 1996 it could launch multi-front attacks with columns of up to 1,000 fighters using mortars and homemade cylinder bombs. In 1999, for example, it attacked military and police posts in three towns just 60km from Bogotá, cutting off the capital from southern departments.

In 1998, both presidential candidates courted the FARC. The guerrillas decided to talk to the Conservative Andrés Pastrana, rather than the discredited Ernesto Samper who was embroiled in a drugs' funded scandal. For that reason, the FARC was said to have 'chosen' Colombia's president in 1998.

Despite the 1998-2002 peace process, the war intensified. The demilitarised zone enabled the FARC to reinforce its dominance in that area, but paramilitaries have pushed it out of southern Putumayo and some areas of the northeast. The paramilitary advance in the northeast has been so devastating that it has forced the FARC and ELN – historic enemies – to fight together in this region.

Ejército de Liberación Nacional (ELN)

Colombia's second-largest guerrilla group.
Website: http://www.eln-voces.com/
Founded: 1964
Number of combatants:[6]
1966: 18 combatants
1973: 250
1986: 800
1995: 5,000
2000: 3,500 - 4,500

Zone of Influence: strongest in northeastern departments round the oil industry (Arauca, Casanare, Santander), but pushed back by rightwing paramilitaries in late 1990s. Also active in southwest, around Cali.

Leader: Nicolás Rodríguez Bautista 'Gabino'. Founding member of ELN in 1964. Joined when he was a student in Bucaramanga, northern Colombia. Became leader following the death of Manuel Pérez in 1998.

Manuel Pérez (d. 1998)
Joined 1969. Was a priest working with the popular movement in Cartagena and was inspired by the example Camilo Torres, a priest who died in combat a few months after joining the ELN (1966). When Pérez joined, the ELN had 60 or 70 members. He became leader in the early 1980s and developed the strategy of targeting the oil industry. He died of natural causes in 1998.

Five-member central command: Nicolás Rodríguez Bautista, Antonio García, Pablo Beltrán, Ramiro Vargas, Oscar Santos.

Ideology: Pro-Cuba. Originally believed in Che Guevara's *foquista* theory, briefly summarised: a group of dedicated men could create the conditions for revolution, the countryside should be the focus of activity and the vanguard should try to establish an enclave or *foco* in the countryside from which to lead the revolution. Two of its best known members were priests, influenced by liberation theology.

Support base: the ELN was founded by students and intellectuals from the city. Universities remained its best recruiting ground in the early years, but in the 1990s most of its members came from the urban poor and the peasantry.

Main activities: their main focus is attacking the country's oil infrastructure; it bombed the Caño Limón pipeline (which runs out of Colombia's second-largest oil field) 127 times in 2001.

Funding: Kidnapping and extortion. The ELN specialises in mass kidnappings. For example in the year 2000 it kidnapped the entire congregation of a church in Cali. It is thought to be the only armed group that does not have links to the drugs' trade.

Peace Process 1998-2002
Signed the 'Heaven's Gate' agreement with Colombian civic groups in Germany in 1998. This called for a national convention to be held in Colombia in which 'civil society' would be invited to discuss peace and social reform. The ELN demanded that the government create a second demilitarized zone in which to hold the convention. In mid-2000 the government agreed to create a demilitarized zone in northeastern Colombia. It was to be 4,000 square km, a tenth of the size of the FARC's zone, and was to be internationally monitored. The chosen site was in an economically strategic area and a stronghold of paramilitarism. The proposals sparked mass protests and roadblocks, and the zone was never created. In June 2002, the Pastrana government broke off talks with the ELN, saying its preliminary demands, which included financial support for demobilised fighters and compensation for releasing hostages, were unreasonable.

History‾

The ELN was founded in 1964 by middle class students and intellectuals from Santander. One of the founding members, Fabio Vásquez Castaño, had been part of a group of scholarship students in revolutionary Cuba in 1962, who had asked for and received military training in Havana. Vásquez was originally a member of the radical Liberal youth movement Juventud del Movimiento Revolucionario Liberal (JMRL).

The ELN was formally founded by 18 men on July 4, 1964 on a ranch in Santander. Among them was Vásquez, Víctor Medina Morón (the former regional general secretary of the Santander Communist Party) and the current leader of the ELN, student Nicolás Rodríguez Bautista. On January 7, 1965, the group rode into the town of Simacota, Santander and distributed the Manifesto of Simacota.

Initially the ELN made rapid headway in northeastern Colombia, winning support from displaced peasants, students and oil workers. Their most famous recruit was the Catholic priest Camilo Torres, who was known locally for his work with the poor. He was killed in action within months of joining. The ELN's work in the cities was helped by its link with Torres, who had been the leader of the Frente Unido del Pueblo (FU). By the end of the 1960s the army had managed to track down and kill most of the ELN's urban supporters.

The ELN guerrillas never implanted themselves in rural communities in the same way as the FARC, and this made it easier for the military to defeat them. In 1973 most of the group was wiped out in a massive counterinsurgency drive, Operation Anorí. For the next decade, the group suffered an internal crisis and was bedevilled by splits.

The ELN re-emerged as a force in the 1980s, after an upsurge in popular protest was met by state repression. Its new leader was another priest, Manuel Pérez (who joined in 1969), who encouraged the ELN to look outwards and try to make links with community groups and trade unions.

Unlike the other main guerrilla groups, the ELN refused to enter peace talks 1984, so winning over those who did not want a compromise. In 1986 it launched a campaign against foreign domination of the oil industry, extorting money from foreign companies and bombing pipelines. The bombing of pipelines generated heated debate on the left, many of whom disapproved of the tactic. The ELN demanded the nationalisation of major oilfields, a ban on foreign exploration and a national debate on energy policy.

In 1987 it joined the Coordinadora Guerrillera Simón Bolíviar (CGSB) with the FARC and remained in the alliance until 1994, despite tensions between the two. Since then the tactics of the two guerrilla groups have differed: the FARC has focused on building up its military capability, while the ELN has tried to open a dialogue with 'civil society'. It has sought peace since 1996, but rather than bi-lateral talks with the government, it wanted to create a national forum to discuss social reform. While the FARC refused to talk to the discredited Samper government (1994-98), the ELN signed a draft agreement in 1998 to launch the national convention process. It was not ratified because of the unexpected death of leader Manuel Pérez. In July 1998 the ELN organized a meeting in Germany with the Church, NGOs and unions, where it was agreed to hold a national convention in Colombia. President-elect Pastrana (1998-2002) did not attend the Heaven's Gate meeting in Germany but endorsed its outcome.

The ELN's peace strategy has coincided with a paramilitary offensive in the ELN's heartland, the northeast, which has weakened the group and eroded its support base. The ELN's membership is estimated to have fallen from a high of 5,000 in 1998 to 3,500 by 2001.[8]

Ejército Popular de Liberación (EPL)

Membership:[9]
1968: 80
1990: 800
1991: 200
1995: 400

The Ejército Popular de Liberación (EPL) was formed in December 1967 as the armed wing of the Maoist Communist breakaway party, the Partido Comunista de Colombia – Marxista Leninista (PCC-ML). It was dominated by urban middle class intellectuals who advocated Mao's theory of 'prolonged popular war' in the countryside. It operated in the northwestern departments of Antioquia and Córdoba and gained influence in the banana growing region of Urabá. It won some support among militants of the mass peasant movement, ANUC. It suffered serious military defeats and its strength was also sapped by a series of internal splits which resulted in new factions such as the Marxist-Leninist League, the Marxist Leninist Tendency and the Pedro León Arboleda (PLA) group. By the mid 1970s, the EPL faced extinction, but it re-emerged as a force in 1980s.

In 1980 the PCC-ML and EPL formally broke with Maoism.[10] In September 1984, it signed a one year truce with the Betancur government, but this collapsed in 1985. In 1985, it joined the Coordinardora Guerrillera Simón Bolívar (CGSB) with the FARC and ELN.

In March 1991, most of the EPL demobilised along with M19, but a dissident faction remained active. The dissident EPL suffered a severe blow when the Colombian army captured their commander Francisco Caraballo and 14 other leaders in 1994.

In 1995, the EPL had about 400 members, 13 fronts and was strongest in Urabá, (northern Antioquia, Chocó and Córdoba). Rightwing paramilitaries made rapid advances in this region in 1995-96 and the FARC also began to move in at the same time. Most of the EPL was eliminated in the three-way fighting. Paramilitary leader Carlos Castaño has admitted ordering killings that were made to look like tit-for-tat EPL-FARC murders, thereby exacerbating the antagonism between the two guerrilla groups.[11] Castaño also state that some EPL fronts joined the paramilitaries to defend themselves from the FARC and that the paramilitaries gave demobilised EPL guerrillas land in Córdoba.[12]

In 1998 the remnants of the EPL published proposals for peace talks with the Pastrana government, but formal talks never began.

Ejército Revolucionario Guevarista (ERG)

Small breakaway from the ELN. Operates in northwestern departments of Chocó, Risralda and Antioquia.

Ejército Revolucionario del Pueblo (ERP)

Small breakaway from the ELN. Founded 1996. Operates in northern department of Sucre.

Grupo Jaime Báteman Cayón

A guerrilla group formed from M19 dissidents who opposed the 1990 peace process. Operates in Valle del Cauca and Cauca. It is named after an M19 leader who was killed in an air-crash in 1983.

Former guerrilla groups

▓ Movimiento Diecinueve de Abril (M19)

A guerrilla group founded by members of the populist movement Anapo, and defectors from the FARC. Formed in late 1973, demobilised 1990. It was named after the date of the 1970 presidential election which many Anapo supporters believed they had lost due to government fraud.

Ideology: Radical nationalist. Populist. Non-aligned. Similar cross-class populist platform as the Sandinistas in Nicaragua. Its first act was to steal Bolívar's sword – a symbol of Colombian nationhood.

Members: Formed by middle class intellectuals. At its height never had more than 1,000 fighters, but became extremely popular amongst the urban poor, particularly in Cali and Bogotá. Failed to establish a rural base. Most active in Cauca and Valle.

Founders: Former FARC members including Jaime Báteman Cayón (d.1983), Alvaro Fayad (d.1986), Iván Marino Ospina (d.1985), Carlos Pizarro (d.1990), (expelled from the FARC and Communist Party in 1972 for arguing that the peasant-based FARC were struggling for land and not for a seizure of state power). Former Anapo members including Carlos Toledo Plata, Andrés Almarales (d.1985), Israel Santamaría.

History

M19 specialised in spectacular actions such as stealing 5,000 weapons from a military arsenal (1979) and occupying the Embassy of the Dominican Republic (1980). It also cultivated a Robin Hood image by, for example, hijacking dairy trucks and distributing the milk in shantytowns. It created a national sensation and rapidly won support among the urban poor. After military setbacks in the cities in the early 1980s, it tried to establish a base of rural of operations in Cauca, but failed to win support from the peasantry. In August 1984 it signed a ceasefire with the Betancur government, but called it off ten months later, complaining that the president and military had violated the terms of the agreement.

On November 6, 1985, thirty-five M19 guerrillas seized the Palace of Justice in Bogotá and took all of the Supreme Court judges hostage. The rebels intended to hold a symbolic trial of President Betancur for failing to implement agreed reforms. The military responded by storming the building and in the ensuing battle all twelve judges, scores of civilian employees and all but one of the guerrillas were killed. The Palace of Justice tragedy irrevocably weakened M19 as it lost much public support and some of its most able leaders, including Andrés Almarales. In 1989, it started peace talks with the Barco administration and in March 1990 it surrendered its weapons to the government.

On April 26, 1990, M19's leader and presidential candidate, Carlos Pizarro, was assassinated aboard an Avianca airliner. Thousands of mourners protested in the streets of Bogotá and Cali. Antonio Navarro Wolff became M19's presidential candidate and in the 1990 elections won 754,740 votes, 12.5% of the vote, the highest percentage the left had ever won. Navarro Wolff was appointed health minister by President Gaviria, a post he held for a year before resigning to take part in the Constituent Assembly.

A part of the peace deal was a constituent assembly to write a new constitution. M19's party, Alianza Democrática M19, received 992,613 votes, 26.7% of the total, and elected 19 members to the assembly, making it the second-largest party behind the Liberals who captured 25 seats. The abstention rate in the elections was extraordinarily high, however, at 74%. The new constitution included many new civil and socioeconomic rights.

Alianza Democrática-M19[15]

Within a few years of winning almost a third of the national vote in 1991, AD-M19 had declined into obscurity. It failed to make the transition from a vanguardist guerrilla force into a broad-based political party. It focused exclusively on national issues, ignoring the need to build the party at a local level. It proved unable to translate its widespread support into a network of activists. Almost all of M19's founding members were killed between 1980-90. Its remaining leaders were incorporated into the political system or found themselves isolated with no political base.

In the October 1991 congressional elections, AD-M19's vote dropped to 10% in the lower house (17 seats) and 9.4% in the senate (9 seats), although Vera Grabe, who headed the party's senatorial list, won more votes any other candidate. The total number of votes it received was 420,000, compared with almost one million in December 1990.

AD M19 remained in the Gaviria cabinet until November 1992. Health minister Navarro Wolff was replaced by Camilo González Posso (1990) and then Gustavo de Roux (mid-1992). AD-M19 was critical of Gaviria's neoliberal programme, but failed to secure concessions, such as increases in public health spending. AD-M19, to some extent, became identified with the austerity measures of the government and lost the opportunity to become a coherent opposition force.

AD-M19 concentrated on building national alliances and its fragility at local level was illustrated by the 1992 municipal elections. It secured just 260 councillors nationwide (compared with 4,200 for the Liberals) and its total vote for mayoral candidates was just 86,430. By 1994, AD-M19's presidential candidate, Navarro Wolff, won just 219,214 votes, 3.79% of the total.

Quintín Lame

Indigenous guerrilla group founded by Paeces and Guambianos in Cauca in 1985. Demobilised 1991. It was named after indigenous leader Martin Quintín Lame (1880-1967). It was formed to protect indigenous communities from both the army and the FARC. Local landowners paid a protection fee to the FARC, which then went on to repress indigenous communities who organised land occupations and other civic actions to defend their territories. It had a cordial relationship with M19, which gave it military training. Quintín Lame did not engage in major military actions and when it demobilised in 1991, it had 157 fighters. It was given one seat (with a voice but no vote) in the 1991 constituent assembly. In addition, civic indigenous organisations won 2.7% of the vote and won two seats.

Partido Revolucionario de los Trabajadores (PRT)

Small guerrilla group founded in 1982. Origins unclear, some claim formed by dissidents of the Maoist Partido Comunista de Colombia – Marxista Lenista (PCC-ML).[14] Other sources claim it is a breakaway from ELN. Demobilised 1990. Granted one seat (without a vote) in the 1991 constituent assembly.

Movimiento Obrero Estudiantil Campesino (MOEC)

Guerrilla group formed in 1959 by students inspired by the Cuban revolution. Mixture of radical Liberals, dissident Communists and nationalists who wanted to link up the rural 'guerrilla-bandits' of *la Violencia* with workers and students in the cities. Split between two factions, one which prioritised guerrilla struggle and another which advocated political work with urban dwellers. The guerrilla wing tried to unite with Liberal 'bandits' in Cauca and Vichada, but early armed actions were unsuccessful and most fighters were killed. In late 1964 the MOEC split into various fractions, the largest of which were the Maoist Movimiento Obrero Independiente Revolucionario (MOIR) and the Fuerzas Armadas de Liberación (FAL), which eventually petered out after its members were killed or joined other groups.

Ejército Revolucionario de Colombia (ERC)

Foquista guerrilla group formed 1961 in Antioquia. Annihilated by the army.

Autodefensa Obrera (ADO)

Also known as Movimiento de AutoDefensa Obrera. (MAO). Trotskyist guerrilla group. Founded in Bogotá circa 1974. Most notorious act was the 'trial' and execution of former interior minister Rafael Pardo in 1978. Signed a ceasefire in 1984.

MIR- *Patria Libre*

Small guerrilla group formed by dissidents of the Maoist Partido Comunista de Colombia-Marxista Leninisista (PCC-ML). Merged with ELN in 1987.

Paramilitaries

Paramilitaries is a term used to describe various types of illegal rightwing armed groups which work alongside the armed forces. They include private militia funded by landowners and businesses; drug traffickers' hit squads and 'social cleansing' death squads. The largest paramilitary network is the Autodefensas Unidas de Colombia (AUC).

Paramilitaries became legal in 1968 with the enactment of Law 48 which authorised the military to arm and 'mobilise' civilians to defend public order. Paramilitarism was outlawed in 1989, but was re-instated in 1993 when the government legalised 'private security and vigilance co-operatives (Convivir). These groups of rural armed civilians were supposed to provide intelligence and other support to the armed forces, but many of them soon turned into fully-fledged paramilitaries. They were outlawed in 1999.

Autodefensas Unidas de Colombia (AUC)

Colombia's most organised paramilitary network, formed in 1997.

Members:
1990: 1,800
2001: 8,000 – 11,000[15]
Its operational capacity is increased by the logistical support or free passage frequently awarded to it by the Colombian military.

Ideology: 'Anti-subversive', 'patriotic', authoritarian. Believes that 'private property is fundamental'.[16]

Areas of influence: strongest in northern Colombia, but can operate anywhere in Colombia with impunity (except FARC strongholds in Caquetá, Meta, Huila, Tolima and Putumayo). The AUC has recently made inroads into southern Putumayo.

Tactics: the AUC targets civilians and rarely engages in armed combat with guerrillas. In rural areas, its defining tactic is the civilian massacre, which is aimed at undercutting support for the insurgency. In cities and towns, it selectively assassinates civic activists, trade unionists, leftwingers, human rights workers, liberal lawyers and journalists, as well as 'undesirables' such as prostitutes and gays. The AUC constitution prohibits its members from attacking state forces.

Leaders: Carlos Castaño, founder and leader. Military commander, Salvatore Mancuso.

Members: Almost all the commanders are retired military officers.[17] Other members are: ex-police officers, reservists, peasants and the urban unemployed. A paramilitary earns more than an army private (and more than a guerrilla who does not earn money, but is fed and clothed.) Some killings are carried out by hired gunmen, who earn up to US$395 per assassination[18] (1999 prices).

Source of funding: donations/extortion from ranchers, landowners and businesses. Some wealthy Colombians see paramilitaries as the best defence against guerrillas and voluntarily donate large sums of money. Trafficking, refining and manufacturing drugs. Taxing coca cultivation and the drugs' trade.[19]

Relationship with army: There is abundant evidence documented in United Nations reports (among others) of close collaboration between the military and the AUC. This consists of logistical support, such as providing army vehicles, communication equipment, uniforms and weapons to the AUC and sharing intelligence. The army also turns a blind eye to AUC roadblocks and camps. A common tactic is for the army to 'make itself scarce' when paramilitaries commit atrocities or to fail to respond to warnings of AUC incursions. Many AUC members are retired or even off-duty officers.

History

The AUC is an umbrella group uniting many regional paramilitary forces. The first of these forces was the Autodefensas Campesinas de Córdoba y Urabá (ACCU) founded by the brothers Fidel and Carlos Castaño in the late 1980s.

In the mid-1990s, the ACCU managed to secure control of Urubá (a region near the Panamanian border) by waging a campaign of massacres and assassinations, primarily against the civilian left. During this offensive it also managed to eliminate most of the remaining EPL guerrillas, who once had a strong presence in this region. The ACCU then moved further south, working with other paramilitary groups to eliminate 'subversives' in the rest of Antioquia and Chocó, as well as the Bolívar, Sucre and Santander.

In 1994 Fidel Castaño was reportedly killed and Carlos became commander of the ACCU. He began to organise the disparate regional paramilitary organisations into a national force and in 1997 the AutoDefensas Unidas de Colombia (AUC) was proclaimed.

The group's next target was the FARC stronghold of Guaviare, in southeastern Colombia and the Mapiripán massacre (1997) was the first stage of this campaign. Since then, the AUC have continued to expand into guerrilla strongholds such as southern Putumayo. It is also fighting an ongoing battle to secure control of the north and in particular strategic and resource-rich Magdalena Medio. The takeover of the oil refining town of Barrancabermeja was part of the Magdalena Medio offensive. The attempt to destroy all civic organisations and close down all democratic space in Barrancabermeja provides a glimpse of the paramilitaries' authoritarian project for Colombia.

During the 1998-2002 peace process, the paramilitaries demanded a seat at the negotiating table. The Pastrana government refused to recognise them as a legitimate belligerent force. The guerrillas would not have been willing to participate in talks which involved the AUC.

In 2001, Carlos Castaño resigned as the AUC's military commander in order to become head of its new 'political directorate'. The change appeared to result from internal feuding within the AUC (in his biography Castaño criticised some members for digressing from the AUC's 'anti-subversive' mission and using AUC forces to settle personal scores and to accumulate personal wealth). The impact of the changed AUC structure is not yet clear – Castaño himself says the new military high command is just a 'figurehead', suggesting that he remains in charge of overall strategy.[20] The AUC has not launched its own political party, but at a local level it supports particular candidates. After the March 2002 congressional elections, Salvatore Mancuso, the AUC's military commander, claimed that 30% of those elected were paramilitary supporters.

During 2002, opponents of Alvaro Uribe described him as the 'paramilitary candidate'. The Liberal Party candidate, Horacio Serpa, for example, complained that paramilitaries were ordering voters to back Uribe. Castaño's view is that Uribe is 'the man closest to our philosophy' and that the 'the social base of the Autodefensas consider him their political candidate.'[21] Castaño was wary that an Uribe victory could undermine the influence of the paramilitaries by strengthening the official armed forces. 'We would receive little recognition for our anti-subversive struggle,' he said.[22]

Following Uribe's election, Castaño sought accommodation with the new hardline government and the United States, by temporarily resigning and then announcing a purge of drugs' traffickers from the organisation. 'The best way to recover what is salvageable from the self-defence forces is to start afresh with a rigid review and restructuring under a clear commitment and centralised and hierarchical command.' This tactic failed to prevent the US requesting his extradition on drugs' trafficking charges in September 2002. Without Castaño, the AUC could fragment into separate regional forces.

www.colombia-libre.org/colombialibre/pp.asp

▨ Fidel Castaño (d.1994?)

Co-founder of the ACCU. Born on a farm in Antioquia. Left home aged 16 and became involved in drug trafficking and smuggling. Invested his fortune in large tracts of land in Urabá. In 1981 FARC guerrillas kidnapped and murdered his father. In the early 1980s he made links with *Muerte a Secuestradores* (MAS). While Carlos, his younger brother, became involved in the military side of MAS, Fidel continued his business dealings and took care of the money. In the mid-1980s he and Carlos set up their own armed group, Los Tangueros, named after Fidel's ranch Las Tangas and began an offensive against 'subversives' in Urabá. Los Tangueros eventually became known as the ACCU. In 1994 Fidel disappeared aged 36. According to Carlos Castaño, he was shot dead on January 6, 1994 by an EPL guerrilla, who later joined the AUC. Others believe he may have left the country.

▨ Carlos Castaño

Founder and leader of AUC. Born in Amalfi, northeast Antioquia. Raised on a modest farm, but his father moved onto a bigger estate after Fidel Castaño made his fortune. In 1981, when Carlos was aged 14, FARC guerrillas kidnapped and killed his father. After the death, he left school and began to work as informant for the local army unit, the Bombshell battallion, which had links to the MAS death squad. Carlos then began to carry out killings for the MAS and was supplied with weapons by army officers.[23]

In 1983, aged 18, Carlos went to Israel for one year to receive military training in a privately run course. In the mid-1980s he returned and founded Los Tangueros death squad with his brother Fidel. In 1994 Carlos took over as commander of Los Tangueros. In 1994, it was officially renamed the AutoDefensas Campesinas de Córdoba y Urabá (ACCU) and its statutes were drafted. The ACCU expanded southwards, uniting disparate regional paramilitary forces, and in 1997, the AutoDefensas Unidas de Colombia (AUC) were formed.

In June 2001 he resigned as the AUC's military commander and became its political director. In June 2002, he resigned as national leader, but three months later announced he was reforming the organisation, purging it of drug traffickers.

Carlos has longstanding links with drug traffickers. In an interview in the year 2000 he said drug trafficking provided 70% of the AUC's funds.[24] Two years later he offered to act as a mediator between 50 major Colombian drugs' traffickers and the United States.[25] He also admits working with the Cali Cartel to defeat Pablo Esobar.[26] In September 2002, the United States requested the extradition of Castaño on drugs' related charges. In 2002 twenty-two arrest warrants were outstanding against Carlos Castaño.

▨ Salvatore Mancuso

Son of an Italian immigrant. Born on a ranch in Córdoba. Studied agricultural engineering in Bogotá and attended Pittsburgh University for one year to study English. Then returned to ranching/meat exporting in Córdoba. Kidnapped for three days by EPL guerrillas in 1984. Formed his own (legal) defence force and was an informant for the army. In the late 1980s joined Fidel Castaño's paramilitary group, which later became the Autodefensas de Córdoba y Urabá (ACCU). Carlos Castaño describes him as a 'blue-blooded Dandy'. 'When he joined the Autodefensas we gained social status...we already had the backing of the middle class in Córdoba, but after recruiting a high society boy like Mancuso, we acquired the support of people we lacked.'[27]

In 2001 Mancuso became military commander of AUC, aged 36. He is one of Castaño's closest associates (he resigned temporarily from the AUC with Castaño in 2002). In 2002 he was convicted *in absentia* for involvement in the murder of a mayor and was sentenced to 11 years imprisonment. Two warrants for his arrest are outstanding. In September 2002, the United States requested the extradition of Mancuso on drug trafficking charges.

Former paramilitary groups

Convivir

(Cooperativas para la Vigilancia y Seguridda Privada). Armed civilian squads established by the government in 1993. Their objective was to help the armed forces with intelligence gathering and other civilian functions, but many soon evolved into death squads. Outlawed in 1999.

Muerte A Secuestradores (MAS)

There are two different organisations using MAS as their name. One was the death squad formed by the Medellín Cartel in 1981 after M19 guerrillas kidnapped the sister of the Ochoa brothers. The other was a paramilitary network formed by army officers and ranchers in 1982 in the Magdalena Medio which developed links with drug traffickers. MAS assassinated hundreds of civic leaders, trade unionists, and peasant activists in northern Colombia in the 1980s. A report by the Attorney General in 1983 named 59 serving officers as members, including numerous School of the Americas graduates.[28]

Alianza Anti-Comunista Americana (AAA)

Extremist death squad active in the late 1970s.

Armed forces

www.fuerzasmilitares.mil.co

Army: 146,000 www.ejercito.mil.co
Police: 120,000 www.policia.gov.co
Airforce: 10,000 www.fac.mil.co
Navy: 5,000 www.armada.mil.co

Defence Ministry
Colombia has had a civilian defence minister since 1991.
www.mindefensa.gov.co

Colombia has compulsory military service. High school graduates (*bachilleres*) are exempt from serving in combat units. The Uribe government has pledged to recruit 10,000 professional soldiers by 2004 and abolish compulsory national service.

Unlike many Latin American countries which have suffered recurrent military coups, the Colombian military took power only once in the 20th century (1953-1959) in the midst of civil war. The Colombian armed forces do, however, act with a high degree of autonomy and impunity. Their direct responsibility for human rights abuses has fallen since the early 1990s, since collaboration with illegal paramilitaries has risen sharply.

Political parties

Liberals and Conservatives

The Liberal and Conservative parties were founded in the mid-nineteenth century and every elected Colombian president since has belonged to one of the two parties.[29] Both originally represented landowners and merchants, but soon developed mass followings. Party loyalties were cemented during numerous bi-partisan wars in the nineteenth century. During this period the Conservatives were identified with the Catholic Church and centralism, and the Liberals with anti-clericalism and federalism. In the 20th century, the moderate centre of both parties have had similar philosophies (economic orthodoxy, free trade and a small state in the first half of the century, with a tendency towards greater state intervention and protectionism in the post-war period). In the early 20th century the Liberals, at times, articulated the demands of the popular movement and the party has had numerous radical fractions. Many of today's guerrillas (notably the FARC) descend from the Radical Liberal tradition.

In 1958, after a violent civil war and period of social upheaval, *la Violencia* the two parties agreed to formally alternate power. The National Front lasted until 1974. Today the Conservative Party and Liberal Party do not have clearly differentiated philosophies: both broadly favour neoliberal policies (trade liberalisation, privatisation, fiscal and monetary orthodoxy). They do not have different positions on the internal conflict (a party's stance is determined by tactical questions such as the public mood, the military outlook, the leader's attitude, etc.). Party affiliation largely depends on family ties, regional location and career opportunities.

▒ Conservative Party

Founded 1848. Originally named Partido Conservador Colombiano, renamed Partido Conservador Social in 1987. In the early 20th century, the party split into two factions, the Moderate (Unionist) Conservatives who favoured free trade and a small state, and a smaller ultra-right faction, the Historic (Independent) Conservatives, who sympathised with the Falange in Spain and looked back to the golden days of the Spanish Empire. Since the dismantling of the National Front in 1974, only two Colombian presidents have been Conservatives: Belisario Betancur (1982-86) and Andrés Pastrana (1998-2002). The party's popularity slumped during the Pastrana years, as the economy plunged into recession and the war intensified. Due to the low ratings in the opinion polls, the Conservative candidate in the 2002 presidential elections, Juan Camilo Restrepo, pulled out of the race.

www.partidoconservador.com.co

▒ Movimiento de Salvación Nacional (MSN)

A faction of the Conservative Party which became formally independent of it in 1990. Led by rightwinger Alvaro Gómez Hurtado, leader of the 'historic' Conservatives and son of past President Laureano Gómez (1950-53). The MSN did surprisingly well in the elections for the 1991 constituent assembly where it gained 11 seats and Gómez Hurtado became one of its presiding officers.

▒ Liberal Party

Founded 1849. In the early 20th century, it divided into two factions, the Moderate Liberals (who favoured economic orthodoxy) and the Radical Liberals, who represented the rising middle class and advocated protectionism, state intervention and social welfare. Under the banner of Radical Liberalism, Jorge Eliécer Gaitán mobilised huge crowds of poor

Colombians. His murder in 1948 sparked off *la Violencia*. In the post-Violencia period, some radicalised Liberals continued to fight as guerrillas, but the official party lost its anti-establishment edge. The party (both Radicals and Moderates) participated in the National Front 1958-74. Since 1974, five of Colombia's seven presidents have been Liberals. The current President, Alvaro Uribe, is a dissident Liberal.

www.partidoliberal.org.co

Frente Social y Político/ Polo Democrático

A leftwing alliance formed in 2000 to contest the 2002 presidential elections. Its candidate Eduardo Garzón was the former leader of Colombia's main trade union federation, the Confederación Unitaria de Trabajadores (CUT). As well as union backing, it had the support of many grassroots civic groups. In 2002, it became a broader alliance, (principally by winning the support of Vía Alterna). It changed its electoral name to Polo Demócratico and chose the former M19 guerrilla Vera Grabe as its vice-presidential candidate. It came third, with 6% of the votes cast.

The Frente Social y Político opposes the neoliberal model and advocates a mixed economy with state ownership of strategic sectors. It supports a negotiated settlement ('without the involvement of the US'). It condemns both the human rights violations committed by the Colombian state and violations of international humanitarian law by armed groups (i.e. guerrillas or paramilitaries). It sees itself less as a political party, more as a network of social movements, which retain their autonomy within it. It believes that peaceful extra-parliamentary activity is more important than elections.

www.luchogarzon.com

Vía Alterna

Electoral alliance formed in 1998 by former M19 guerrillas, the Alianza Social Indígena and independents. Advocates an 'independent, non-clientelist programme, committed to serving the interests of the most vulnerable section of the population.' Its most famous member is former M19 guerrilla leader, Antonio Navarro Wolff, who was elected a lower house congressman (1998-1990) and senator (2002-2006).

www.viaalterna.com.co

Partido Comunista de Colombia (PCC)

Founded 1930. The Colombian Communist Party's relationship with the FARC has dominated its history. It has given the party a higher profile than it otherwise might have had, but it has also forced it to take political positions that were contrary to the original Soviet-directed line. Although the party supports armed struggle, it does not advocate the immediate overthrow of capitalism, but fairer land and wealth distribution within a mixed economy, civil rights and an end to US dominance.

The Communist Party maintains a public, formal separation from the FARC. Although the guerrillas grew in strength in the 1990s, the Communist Party struggled to keep its political organisation intact. The party was unable to hold a national congress between 1991-1998 because so many of its central committee members had been killed, forced into exile or into hiding. The internal crisis was compounded by the collapse of the Soviet Union. The Colombian Communist Party had been rigidly pro-Soviet and it fell into ideological disarray when the eastern block began to disintegrate.

The party has to some extent recomposed itself but cannot operate freely. It focuses on achieving 'peace and democracy' and advocates a negotiated settlement. It also campaigns against the neoliberal model and the IMF. It aims to mobilise the 'popular and democratic' movement in order to weaken the far right and establish a just peace.

http://www.partidocomunistacolombiano.org/

Movimiento Bolivariano por una Nueva Colombia

Clandestine political movement of the FARC, founded March 2000.
www.movimientobolivariano.org

Partido Comunista de Colombia – Marxista Leninista (PCC-ML)

Founded 1965. Maoist breakaway from the Communist Party. Closely linked to the EPL. Opposed EPL demobilisation in 1991 and continues to support the dissident wing of the EPL which continued fighting. Formally abandoned Maoism in 1980, arguing that it had over-emphasised the role of the peasantry and underestimated the role of the proletariat and the importance of legal and political work.

www.pcdec-ml.com

Movimiento Obrero Independiente Revolucionario (MOIR)

Maoist group formed in 1969, as a breakaway from the Movimiento Obrero Estudiantil Campesino (MOEC). Pro-China, pro-Albania. Has stood in congressional elections since 1974.

www.moir.org.co

Esperanza, Paz y Libertad

Party formed by EPL guerrillas who demobilised in 1991.

Former parties and movements

Alianza Democrática-M19 (AD-M19)

Party formed by M19 guerrillas after demobilising in 1990. See M19.

New Liberalism

Breakaway group from the official Liberal Party formed in 1982. Published a 12-point programme calling for: congressional reform, state intervention in urban development, controls on foreign investment, restoration of moral values, human rights, trade union rights, indigenous rights, reform of the national television network and end to oligarchic rule. Luis Carlos Galán was the group's presidential candidate in 1982, winning 10% of the vote. Galán rejoined the official Liberals and was assassinated in 1989 while campaigning for the party's presidential nomination. Julio César Gaviria was going to be New Liberalism's presidential candidate in 1990, but became the official Liberal candidate after Galán's murder.

Unión Patriótica (UP)

Political party formed in 1985 by the FARC and the Communist Party, following the 1984 truce. Also contained many non-aligned leftwingers and trade unionists. The party was decimated – three thousand members were assassinated by death squads between 1985-1990, including two of its presidential candidates, Jaime Pardo Leal (d.1987) and Bernado Jaramillo (d.1989).

The UP advocated constitutional reform, decentralisation, grants of land to peasants, increased health and education spending, a civilian defence minister. It defined itself as a popular front for peace and democracy and became increasingly independent of the FARC/CP as it grew larger. It became the main leftwing opposition force in the 1980s, but this was not reflected in its electoral support. In the 1986 congressional elections, it won 6 lower house seats and 3 senate seats. It also elected 18 deputies in departmental assemblies and 335 municipal councillors. Its 1986 presidential candidate, Jamie Pardo Leal, received 328,752 votes, 4.5% of the total.

A Luchar

A leftwing coalition loosely identified with the ELN in the 1980s. Focused on social protest, rather than elections.

Frente Popular (FP)

Electoral front launched by the post-Maoist Partido Comunista de Colombia – Marxist Leninista in the 1980s.

Alianza Nacional Popular (Anapo)

Populist movement founded by the former dictator General Rojas Pinilla in 1960. Became the main opposition party in the 1960s, attracting all those who were excluded by the traditional parties' power-sharing agreement. Specially popular with the lower middle class and the very poor. Rojas stood as Anapo's presidential candidate in 1970, but lost in what many believe was a fraudulent election. Leftwing Anapo members went on to form the M19 guerrilla movement.

Asociación Nacional de Usuarios Campesinos (ANUC)

A grassroots peasant movement created in 1967 by the Radical Liberal President Carlos Lleras Restrepo (1966-70), who aimed to overcome landower opposition to agrarian reform by organising pressure from below. ANUC gradually became independent from the government and increasingly radical, but it became bogged down by internal divisions after attracting all sorts of leftwing groups, particularly Maoists.

Peace and civil society groups

There are hundreds of local and sectoral organisations which promote peace, human rights and social justice. These include groups of the displaced, peace communities, trade unions, church groups, women's groups, student networks and indigenous communities. The main national networks and organisations are listed below.

Assamblea de la Sociedad Civil por la Paz

Founded in 1998 by over 800 grassroots campaign groups, human rights organisations and trade unions. It grew out of a peace assembly organised by the oil workers' trade union (USO) in 1996. It seeks to strengthen social movements and mobilise civilians for 'peace with social justice'. It calls for a ceasefire, humanitarian agreements, and civilian participation in peace accords. It opposes Plan Colombia for being 'pro-war, not pro-peace'.

It also seeks to 'defend the right for a dignified life for all'; to 'develop a culture and pedagogy for peace' and to 'strengthen the social movement for peace and create spaces for dialogue and a political solution to the armed conflict'. It describes itself as 'democratic, autonomous, participatory, broad and pluralist'. Its main activities are information sharing, workshops, conferences, vigils and mobilisations.

www.porlapaz.org.co

Comisión de Conciliación

A commission founded in 1995 by the Colombian Bishops' Conference which promotes dialogue, a negotiated settlement to the conflict, humanitarian accords and respect for human rights.

Comunidades de paz

Groups of villages in the conflict-ridden region of Urabá (northwestern Colombia), which have attempted to create autonomous peace communities, rejecting threats or overtures from all armed groups. Although they have won national and international recognition, armed groups continue to attack the communities, making it very hard for them to survive. Some of the communities have fled en masse to less isolated regions.

www.comunidadesdepaz.org.

Mandato por la Paz

Mandato por la Paz began as a campaign for 'a citizens' mandate for peace', which persuaded 10 million Colombians to vote for 'peace, life and liberty' in the national elections of October 1997. It called for a ceasefire, a negotiated settlement and for the norms of international humanitarian law to be respected by all armed groups. It also called for an end to the recruitment of child soldiers, kidnapping, forced displacement, aggression against the civilian population, assassinations and massacres. The campaign was supported by Unicef and Unesco, and over 100 non-governmental organisations including Redepaz and País Libre.

www.colnodo.apc.org/colombiapaz

Planeta Paz

NGO founded in 2000 that encourages popular participation in peace initiatives and encourages discussion about post-conflict scenarios.

www.planetapaz.org

Redepaz

The Network of Initiatives for Peace and Against War (Redepaz) is the most longstanding network of peace organisations. It was created in 1993 and draws together NGOs and local peace initiatives. Its mission is to 'broaden and consolidate the social movement for peace, through initiatives of citizens' power'. It holds regular discussions and encourages the creation of peace groups, such as students for peace, women for peace, ecologists for peace. It is currently leading a campaign to establish 100 municipalities for peace.

www.redepaz.8m.net

Codhes

Consultaría para los Derechos Humanos y el Desplazamiento (Codhes) was founded in 1992 to highlight the problem of forced displacement. It provides emergency humanitarian aid, as well as long term economic and psychological support to displaced communities. It supports displaced organisations which campaign for basic necessities or for recognition of their civil rights. Codhes also monitors the levels of displacement and

seeks to raise awareness of its causes.
www.codhes.org.co

Cinep

Centro de Investigación y Educación Popular (Cinep) was founded by Jesuits in 1962. It aims to combine academic research with direct action in poor communities. It is 'committed to the social economic and political transformation of Colombia in favour of the excluded'. It is most well known for cataloguing human rights abuses and political violence. In association with the Catholic Church's Justicia y Paz organisation, it maintains a database of political violence. It also researches socio-economic and cultural issues.
www.cinep.org.co

CUT

The Confederación Unitaria de Trabajadores (CUT) is Colombia's largest trade union confederation. It was formed in 1986 after a wave of mass mobilisation and strikes. It brought together independents, Liberals, Conservatives and Communists, who previously had competing union federations. The CUT now accounts for 80% of unionised workers and is particularly strong in the public sector (including the oil industry). Although CUT leaders come from across the political spectrum, they have suffered perhaps more than any other group from paramilitary assassinations. The CUT campaigns for labour rights, wages and conditions and human rights.
www.cut.org.co

País Libre

País Libre is a charitable foundation that supports victims of kidnapping. It was founded in 1991 in response to a call from Francisco Santos Calderón, who was then the news editor of Colombia's best selling newspaper *El Tiempo* (and is now the vice president of Colombia). He published a 'Letter to a Kidnapped Person', a plea to remember the victims, after he was kidnapped for eight months by drug traffickers.
www.paislibre.org.co

Region	Number of Resguardos	Population
Amazon (Putumayo, Caquetá, Amazonas)	88	29,073
Centre (Arauca, Boyacá, Casanare, Huila, Norte Santander, Tolima)	104	26,973
North (Cesar, Córdoba, Guajira, Magdalena)	31	144,1992
Orinoquía (Guainía, Guaviare, Meta, Vaupés, Vichada)	106	447,740
Pacific (Antioquia, Caldas, Cuaca, Chocó, Nariño, Quindio, Risaralda, Valle del Cauca)	238	152,293

Source: Interior Ministry[30]

Indigenous Colombians

There are 701,860 indigenous people in Colombia (1.7% of the population), according to the National Census of 1993-97. There are 80 different ethnic groups, 64 languages and 300 dialects. Under the Colombian constitution, indigenous communities have the right to live in self-governing reserves (*resguardos*). There are 567 *resguardos* in Colombia, covering 36.5 million hectares and inhabited by 800,271 people, according to Interior Ministry's Indigenous Affairs division. (Slight discrepancies exist in the figures provided by different government departments).

Private contractors and mercenaries

DynCorp Aerospace Technology

DynCorp Aerospace Technologies was founded in 1946 and is based in Reston, Virginia.[31] It is a 'technology and services company' with over

US$1.8 billion in annual revenues and more than 23,000 employees worldwide. It is one of the largest U.S. defense contractors and its contracts with US government agencies account for 98% of its business.

DynCorp has been contracted by the State Department to work in the Andes (Colombia, Bolivia and Peru) since 1991 and in 1998 was awarded a new US$170 million five-year Colombia contract.[32] Dyncorp pilots fly fumigation planes or the military helicopters that accompany such missions. These military helicopters were involved in 60 gunfights with Colombian guerrillas in the year 2000, according to the State Department.[33] Dyncorp personnel also train and provide 'logistical support' to Colombian army anti-narcotics battalions, such as ferrying troops into battle and rescuing shot-down pilots. Dyncorp pilots in Colombia have been involved in various drugs scandals.

In September 2001, the International Labor Rights Fund, a U.S. non-profit group, brought a lawsuit against DynCorp on behalf of families reportedly harmed by aerial fumigation.

www.dyncorp.com

Northrop Grumman Corporation

Northrop is an aerospace and defence services company. It has 80,000 employees and projected revenues of US$18 billion for 2003. In 1998 the US Air Force Combat Command awarded Northrop Grumman Technical Services a contract to operate and maintain its 'Counter Narcotics Surveillance and Control System'. The five-year contract includes performing maintenance, system operations, and logistic support of seven radar sites and 10 associated ground satellite stations in Colombia, Peru, Venezuela, and Panama.

www.northgrum.com

Eagle Aviation Services and Technology (EAST) Inc.

A company subcontracted by DynCorp to carry out aerial crop fumgiation in Colombia. EAST has worked in Colombia for 10 years and three of its pilots have been killed in two crashes. In 1999-2000, EAST had contracts worth US$30 million with the US Defense Department for engineering, supplies and other services at Laughlin Air Force Base in Texas. EAST was also the company used by Oliver North to fly arms to the Contras during the 1980s Iran-Contra scandal.[34]

Military Professional Resources (MPRI)

MPRI is a defence contracting company founded in 1988 and which employs mainly retired US military officers. In 2000, it signed a US$4.3 million one-year contract with the US Defense Department to carry out a review of the Colombian armed forces. This involved 'advice and assistance in developing specific plans and programs to assist the Ministry of Defense and the armed forces of Colombia in institution building, long-range planning and inter-agency co-operation to enhance their counter-drug capabilities'.[35] The contract was not renewed in 2001.
www.mpri.com/channels/home.html

Defence Systems Ltd (Defence Systems Colombia)

Defence Systems Limited is a private security company founded in 1981 by ex-SAS officers Alistair Morrison (OBE) and David Abbot. It specialises in protecting mining and petroleum companies, but has also been hired to protect US and British embassies and airports. It is run from premises opposite Buckingham Palace, has 14 regional offices in five continents and 4,000 employees. In 1997 it was taken over by the Florida-based company Armor Holdings Inc.

Its unit in Colombia, Defence Systems Colombia, is hired by BP to advise on security around its oil drilling sites and pipelines. The Colombian prosecutor investigated whether DSC trained Colombian police in 'lethal' counter insurgency tactics. In 1998, the prosecutor said that it could not confirm or discard the allegations and decided to continue the investigation to try to establish whether the training was confined to defensive tactics to protect BP's utilities, or whether it included full counter insurgency techniques. The prosecutor has since put the case in abeyance, pending further evidence.
www.amorgroup.com

Appendix 2

Drug facts at a glance

Production

In 1999 Colombia produced:

- 80% of the world's cocaine
- 2% of the world's heroin
- 1% of the world's marijuana (including international wild growth)

- All of the world's coca is grown in Colombia, Bolivia and Peru
- Three quarters of the world's heroin comes from Asia
- Marijuana is grown in at least 120 countries all over the world

Consumption

North America
Consumes an estimated 60% of world's cocaine and 3% of the world's heroin. Contains: 51% of world's cocaine users, 8% of world's heroin users, 15% of world's cannabis users.

Europe
Contains: 16% of the world's cocaine users, 20% of the world's heroin users, 15% of the world's cannabis users.

Marijuana
The US regards Mexico, Colombia and Jamaica as the most important cannabis producers. However, some independent experts say that the United States is the largest marijuana producer in the Americas.[36] It is noteworthy that although the US government has calculated the exact amount of marijuana produced in Latin American countries, it has no idea how much is grown in the US.[37]

Half of all the cannabis consumed in the US is produced domestically, according to the Transnational Institute.[38] Marijuana is the most important cash crop in Kentucky, California, Alabama, Connecticut, Hawaii, Tennessee, West Virginia, Virginia, Maine and Rhode Island.[39] Nationally, cannabis is the fourth most important cash crop and is ranked higher than tobacco, wheat or cotton.

The US began to spray domestic cannabis plants with Paraquat in the late 1970s, but stopped after the government accepted that smoking Paraquat-tainted cannabis could cause permanent lung scarring. The US then was accused of hypocrisy when it encouraged fumigation abroad, so in the 1990s it re-started domestic fumigation. Only Hawaii, however, has been sprayed on a large scale. Here too, people complained of headaches, nausea and diarrhoea following the fumigations.

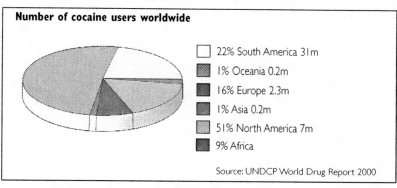

Number of cocaine users worldwide

- 22% South America 31m
- 1% Oceania 0.2m
- 16% Europe 2.3m
- 1% Asia 0.2m
- 51% North America 7m
- 9% Africa

Source: UNDCP World Drug Report 2000

Prevalence of drug use, selected countries 1998 (as % of population*)

	Cannabis	Opiates	Cocaine**	Amphetamines	Ecstasy
United Kingdom	9	0.5	1	1.3	1
Germany	4.1	0.2	0.6	0.4	0.8
France	4.7	0.3	0.2	0.6	0.3
United States	12.3	0.5	3.2	0.7	
Canada	7.4	0.2	0.7	0.7	
Mexico	1.1	0.1	0.3	0.3	
Colombia	5.6	0.3	1.6	0.5	
Peru	2.1	-	1.5	-	
Argentina	2.3	0.03	1.2	-	

*UK, Canada, Mexico, Argentina   % of population above 5 years old
  US, Colombia   % of population above 12 years old
  Germany, France   % of population above 18
**Includes *basuco*, unrefined coca paste, which is smoked mainly in Andean countries

Source: UNDCP World Drug Report 2000 [0]

Glossary

colono	peasant settler
Defensoría	Ombudsman's Office
ejército	army
Fiscalía	State Prosecutor's Office. Has the power to investigate and prosecute
Iran Contra Affair	In 1984-6, US officials in the Reagan administration sold arms to Iran in order to raise funds for the Contras, an irregular army trying to overthrow the leftwing Sandinista government (1979-90) in Nicaragua. This was illegal in two ways: firstly because Congress had banned the US from supplying arms to Iran and Iraq, and secondly because it prohibited the US government from giving aid to the Contras.
latifundio	large estate
latifundista	landowner of large estate
llanos	eastern plains of Colombia
Magdalena Medio	Central Magdalena river valley covering parts of Cundinamarca, Antioquia, Santander, Bolívar, Boyacá. The Magdalena Medio is the country's most strategic and resource-rich region, containing the country's best lands, its oil refineries, its most important river network, as well as gold, emeralds and coal to the north. It is one of the most contested and violent areas of the country.
pájaro	lit bird. Hired gunman

Proceso 800	State prosecutors' investigation into funding of political parties by drug traffickers. Launched after President Ernesto Samper was accused of accepting drugs money in the 1994 presidential election.
Procuradoría	Attorney General's Office. With investigatory powers.
sapo	lit. frog, slang for 'snitch' or 'grass'
sicario	hired gunman
Urabá	Banana-producing region on Atlantic Coast of Colombia on Panamanian border (covering northern Antioquia and northeastern Chocó). Ones of the most contested and violent areas of the country.
vacuna	lit. vaccine. Extortion or 'taxes' charged by guerrillas.

Sources of further information

Center for International Policy (CIP), Colombia Project
www.ciponline.org/colombia

Washington Office on Latin America (Wola)
www.wola.org

Latin America Working Group
www.lawg.org/colombia.htm

Human rights

United Nations High Commission for Human Rights Office in
Colombia
www.hchr.org.co

Human Rights Watch
www.hrw.org

Amnesty International
www.amnesty-usa.org/countries/colombia
www.amnesty.org.uk

Consultaría para los Derechos Humanos y el Desplazamiento (Codhes)
www.codhes.org

Colombian Ombudsman's Office/Defensoría del Pueblo
www.defensoria.org.co

Peace Brigades International
www.peacebrigades.org/colombia.html

Colombian Vice President's human rights office
www.derechoshumanos.gov.co

Equipo Nizkor (Spanish human rights centre)
www.derechos.org/nizkor/colombia/eng.html

Drugs, fumigation and environment

Transnational Institute: Drugs & Democracy Project
www.tni.org

Acción Andina
www.cedib.org/accionandina/index.php

Mama Coca
www.mamacoca.org

Fumigation
www.fumigation.org

Narco News
www.narconews.com

Corporación Unidades Democráticas para el Desarrollo
www.ceudes.org

Amazon Watch
www.amazonwatch.org

European NGO Council on Drugs and Development
www.encod.org

Indigenous rights

Organización Nacional Indigena de Colombia (Onic)
www.onic.org.co

Etnias de Colombia
www.etniasdecolombia.org

Women

Red Nacional de Mujeres de Colombia
www.colnodo.apc.org/%7Ewwwrednl/index.html

Arms and military

Stockholm International Peace Research Institute
www.sipri.org

School of the Americas Watch
www.soaw.org

Colombian peace networks

Asamblea Por La Paz
www.porlapaz.org.co

Planeta Paz
www.planetapaz.org

Barranca Vive
barranca.porlapaz.org.co

Paz Colombia
www.galeon.com/pazcolombia

Others sites of interest

Centro de Investigación y Educación Popular (Cinep)
www.cinep.org.co

Fundación País Libre
www.paislibre.org.co

Pastoral Social
www.pastoralsocialcolombia.org

Colombia indymedia
colombia.indymedia.org

Solidarity groups

Colombia Solidarity Campaign UK
www.colombiasolidarity.org.uk

Colombia Peace Association UK
www.colombiapeace.org

Colombia Human Rights Network US
www.igc.org/colhrnet

Colombia Support Network US
www.colombiasupport.net

ABC Group (UK development agencies working together on Colombia)
No website but have two email services for information about Colombia
cpw@abcgroup.globalnet.co.uk
colombiaforum@abc.globalnet.co.uk

Notes

FOREWORD

1   J. Pearce, (1990) *Colombia: Inside the Labyrinth* London: Latin America Bureau, p. 287
2   C. Berquist, R. Peñaranda, G. Sánchez, (2001), *Violence in Colombia 1990-2000 Waging War and Negotiating Peace*, Wilmington: Scholarly Resources, p.13
3   Amnesty Internacional (December 2002) *Colombia: Seguridad. a qué precio?La falta de voluntad del gobierno para hacer frente a la crisis de derechos humanos* London: Amnesty International
4   C. Echandía 'Evolución Reciente Del Conflicto Armado en Colombia: La Guerrilla', in Jaime Arocha *et al* (1998) *Las Violencias: Inclusión creciente* Bogotá: CES pp.35-65
5   US State Department, *Country Report on Human Rights in Colombia* 2000 mimeo p.1
6   Nazih Richani (2002) *Systems of Violence: The Political Economy of War and Peace in Colombia* New York: State University of New York Press
7   Ibid., p.87
8   Strategic Forecasting LLC, 28/01/03
9   Ibid., p.123
10 Strategic Forecasting LLC, op. cit.
11 J. Habermas, 'The European Nation-State Its Achievements and its Limits. On the Past and Future of Sovereignty and Citizenship,' in Gopal Balakrishnan (ed) (1996) *Mapping the Nation* London:Verso pp. 268-281. Let me first explain what the modern state gained by its unique fusion with the homogenizing idea of the nation. This first modern form of collective identity had a catalytic function for the transformation of the early modern state into a democratic republic. The national self-consciousness of the people provided a cultural context that facilitated the political activation of citizens. It was the national community that generated a new kind of connection between persons who had been strangers to each other, so far. By this, the national state could solve two problems at once: it established a democratic mode of legitimation on the basis of a new and more abstract form of social integration. p.284
12 J. Pearce, (1990) *Colombia: Inside the Labyrinth* London: Latin America Bureau p.198
13 D. Pecaut, (1997) 'De la Violencia Banalizada al Terror: El Caso Colombiano' in *Controversia* No. 171, Diciembre pp.9-32
14 'Land purchases by drugs, traffickers,' writes Alejandro Reyes 'has changed the terms of the Colombian agrarian problem. In the first place, it has contributed to increasing the levels of property concentration in a few hands, with the accompanying displacement of peasants to the colonisation frontiers and towns. In the second place, it has overvalued land, reducing the incentives of agrarian entrepreneurs and ranchers to market their goods. In the third place, it contributed to the funding of private counterinsurgency strategies which sought to recuperate security by force, contest

guerrilla territorial control and in many occasions terrorised the rural population, increasing the levels of violence. In the fourth place, it reinforced a traditional pattern of inefficient concentration of the best land in ranching, prejudicing agriculture and forests. In many regions, drugs traffickers have substituted the old landlords and have further impoverished the social leadership in the affected regions.' A. Reyes, 'Compra de Tierras por Narcotraficantes' in F. Thoumi *et al* (1997), *Drogas Ilícitas en Colombia* Bogota: Planeta Colombia Editorial, p.343

15 El Colombiano, 6/5/2002

16 The final toll of UP activists, leaders and electoral candidates who have been murdered is not confirmed, but in December 1993, the Renacer Foundation and the Colombian Commission of Jurists, presented and official petition before the Interamerican Human Rights Commission asking that the Colombian Government should respond to charges concerning 1,554 UP members victims of homicide, forced disappearance, attacks and threats, actions described as 'genocide'. *Observatorio de los Derechos Humanos en Colombia Newsletter* no 21, March 2002

17 See for instance, Human Rights Watch (1996) *Colombia's Killer Networks: The Military-Paramilitary Partnership and the United States* New York: Human Rights Watch

18 The armed forces were deemed responsible for over 60% of the political killings in Colombia until 1994, when overnight almost and under intense international scrutiny at the time from human rights organisations, the record changed and abuses attributed to them fell to 4% or so, while those attributed to the paramilitary rose to over 40%.

19 D. Pecaut (2001), p.193

20 Richani, op. cit., p.45

21 Ibid., p.44

22 Human Rights Watch World Report 2002

23 Castaño withdrew altogether in 2002 after the US had named the AUC a 'terrorist' organisation and warrants were issues for Castaño's arrest for drug trafficking.

24 A military operation against the occupation by the M19 guerrillas of the Palace of Justice resulted in the deaths of some 120 people, including 12 Supreme Court judges. It marked the end of Belisario Betancur's peace process. The guerrillas also undoubtedly broke the truce. But arguably, given the nature of the peace process and Colombia's history of State abuse of amnesties granted to demobilised guerrillas in the wake of the Violencia civil war, the State had particular responsibility to build trust.

25 *Cien Días*, March 1989, p.7

26 This was the theme taken up by my Colombian MA student Carolina Maria Rudas Gomez, in her final dissertation: 'Living with Violence: The dynamics of socialization spaces in contemporary Colombia' (Bradford, September 2000, mimeo) Carolina explored how living with violence influence the construction and evolution of each different socialization space. She identitifed three responses. First that of passivity induced by fear and silence; the second is the re-creation of violent socialized spaces; finally a non-violent response that creates new social bonds and serves as a motor of social activity and social change.

27 Although recent studies of post-cold war civil wars have included Colombia. They have tended to define 'civil war' along the following lines taken from M. Ross, *Oil, Drugs and Diamonts: How do Natural Resources Vary in their Impact on Civil War?* June 2002, mlross@polisci.ucla.edu. Ross argues that civil wars:
   · Occur within the recognised boundaries of a single state
   · Involve combat between the state and at least one organised rebel force
   · Result in at least one thousand deaths during a single calendar year

28 D. Pecaut, (2001) *Guerra contra la sociedad* Bogotá: Editorial Planeta

28 M. Kaldor (1999) *New and Old Wars: Organized Violence in a Global Era* Cambridge: Polity Press

29 Collier P. and Hoeffler A. (1998) *On economic causes of civil war.* Oxford Economic Papers 50, pp. 563-573

30 WHO (2002), *Violence: A Global Public Health Issue* WHO: Geneva

31 Ibid., statistical appendix Table 7, p.300

32 D. Pecaut, (2001) op. cit., p.187. Saul Franco uses the figure of 338,378 for the twenty years 1975-1995. S. Franco, (1999) *El Quinto: No Matar* Bogotá: TM Editores

33 Institute for Forensic Medicine reported 62,123 cases of domestic violence in 1999, of which 41,528 were conjugal violence, 9,896 were child abuse and 10,699 were cases of abuse by other family members. The Institute also estimated that 95% of all abuse cases are never reported to the authorities and reported 13,703 cases of probable rape during the year. US State Department, 2000, op. cit., p.68

34 E.g. D. Meertens (2001) 'Victims and Survivors of War in Colombia, Three Views of Gender Relations,' in C. Berquist *et al. Violence in Colombia 1990-2000* Wilmington, Delaware: Scholarly Resources, pp.151-170. Maria Clemencia Castro and Carmen Lucia Diaz, (1997) *Guerilla. Reinsercion y Lazo Social* Bogotá: Almudena Editores

35 D. Meertens (2001) op. cit., p.156

36 Ibid., p.157

37 Ibid., p.159

38 Ibid., p.162

39 Interview with women from Mate de Monte, an environmental NGO in Yopal, May 2002

40 Quoted in *Colombia Forum* Issue 30, May-August 2002

41 Maria Clemencia Castro and Carmen Lucia Diaz, op. cit., pp. 206-207

42 Some other examples are: Jaime Arocha, Fernando Cubiles and Myriam Jimeno, (1998) (eds) *Las violencias:Inclusión Creciente* Bogotá: LCES; Saul Franco, (1999) *El Quinto: No Matar* Bogotá: TM Editores. The Univerity of Antioquia have set up an interdisciplinary research team to work on violence, see Pablo Emilio Angarito (ed), (2001) *Balance de los Estudios Sobre Violencia en Antioquia* Medellín: Universidad de Antioquia; Outside Colombia, Caroline Moser and colleagues have begun to open up this line of research, see for example C. Moser and C. McIlwaine, (2000) *Urban Poor Perception of Violence and Exclusion in Colombia,* Washington: Wold Bank; C. Moser and F. C. Clark, (2001) (eds) *Victims, Perpetrators or Actors? Gender Armed Conflict and Political Violence* London: Zed Books.

43 J. Pearce (2000) Complex Violences in Latin America: The case of Colombia Paper delivered to Institute of Latin American Studies Seminar, mimeo

CHAPTER 1: HUMAN RIGHTS

1 Political assassinations, disappearances and combat deaths. Figures of Cinep and Justicia y Paz database on human rights, cited in Mauricio García Durán, 'War, negotiations and mobilization for peace (1980-2002) in Leal, C and Bonilla D (eds) *Colombia: Land in Turmoil,* Duke University Press, forthcoming, p.3.

2 Figures include political killings, social cleansing, combat and crossfire deaths. October 1995 to June 2001. Colombian Commission of Jurists. Violaciones de derechos humanosy violencia sociopolitica en Colombia. Derecho a la vida. Homocidios

sociopoliticos, ejecuciones extrajudiciales, desapariciones forzadas, muertes en combate y en fuego cruzado. Total de víctimas y muertes en combate, porcentaje total de autoría por períodos, según presuntos autores Octubre de 1995 a Junio 2001. Data emailed to author by Colombian Commission of Jurists, 29 July 2002.

3   Colombian police figures, cited by País Libre, see www.paislibre.org.co

4   Colombian Commission of Jurists, op. cit.

5   Ibid.

6   DAS figures cited in C. Echandía Castilla, *El Conflicto Armado y las Manifestaciones de Violencia en las Regiones de Colombia*, Presidencia de la República de Colombia, Oficina del Alto Comisionado para la Paz Observatorio de Violencia, Santa Fe de Bogotá, 1999, p.65. The author of the book caution that the figures are low because murder is 'enormously' under reported.

7   The figure used for political assassinations (2,431), is that of CINEP/Justicia y Paz. *Noche y Niebla 18. Banco de Datos de Derchos Humanos y Violencia Política*, Oct-Dec 2000, Tabla No. 22 Víctimas de Violencia Político Social Por Persecución Política, según Distribución Geográfica, p43. If a wider definition of political killings is used, such as the 'socio-political' killings (which include political murders, 'social-cleansing' and combat deaths) catalogued by the Colombian Commission of Jurists, the proportion rises to about 22%. Combat deaths [Cinep/Justicia Paz 1,677]. *Noche y Niebla* 18, Oct- Dec 2000, Tabla 30 Combatientes Víctimas en Acciones Bélicas, p.49 [Ministry of Defence: 1,780] *Resultados Operacionales Fuerza Pública* 1999 y 2000, Ministerio de Defensa Nacional, Marzo de 2001, p.7.

8   *Colombia: Inseguridad, Violencia, y Desempeño Económico en las Areas Rurales*, Consejería para la Paz de la Presidencia de la República, Colombia, 1999, Director de Investigación: Jesus Antonio Bejarano Avila

9   Figures cited in G. Sánchez 'Prospects for Peace', C. Bergquist, R. Peñaranda, G. Sánchez (eds), *Violence in Colombia: The Contemporary Crisis in Historical Perspective*, Scholarly Resources, USA, 1992, p.12. British figures from UK Home Office.

10   1990-1998 figures cited in C. Echandía Castilla, *El Conflicto Armado y las Manifestaciones de Violencia en las Regiones de Colombia*, Presidencia de la República, Oficina del Alto Comisionado para la Paz, Observatorio de Violencia, Santa Fe de Bogotá, 1999. The 1982 figure is from G. Sánchez, 'Prospects for Peace' in C Bergquist, R Peñaranda, G Sánchez G (eds), *Violence in Colombia: The Contemporary Crisis in Historical Perspective*, Scholarly Resources, USA, 1992, p.13. The 1999 figure is from the police website, www.policia.gov.co. The 2000 figure is from Homicidio y Control de Armas en Colombia, Ministerio de Defensa, Serie 2001, No. 2, Bogotá, julio de 2001

11   Human Rights Watch Report *War Without Quarter: Colombia and International Humanitarian Law*, Oct 1998, Section IV 'Paramilitary Violations of International Humanitarian Law'.

12   Attorney General's Report, 'Formato Nacional de Acta de Levantamiento de Cadaver, July 20, 1997, quoted in Human Rights Watch, *War Without Quarter: Colombia and International Humanitarian Law*, Oct 1998, Section IV 'Paramilitary Violations of International Humanitarian Law'

13   The figure of 'at least 22' is given by Colombian government's news service, Ancol, 13.02.2001.

14   'The lack of a precise body count is due to several factors. Because it is in a coca growing area, Mapiripán has a large, transient workforce made up mostly of young men, who work the coca fields, and young women, who work as prostitutes; permanent residents often do not know their names or recognise people only by their nicknames. Also, many

of the bodies were thrown into the Guaviare River, and little attempt was made to search its banks for remains. Before dumping the bodies, witnesses say, paramilitaries eviscerated them to make sure they would not float. Finally, people abandoned the area so quickly after the massacre it was difficult for authorities to confirm if those who were missing were dead or forcibly displaced.' *Human Rights Watch Report, War Without Quarter: Colombia and International Humanitarian Law*, Oct 1998, Section IV 'Paramilitary Violations of International Humanitarian Law'

15 On 12.2.2001 General Jaime Humberto Uscategui was sentenced for 40 months in prison by a military tribunal for 'omission' for failing to prevent the massacre. He was cleared of collaboration with the paramilitaries.

16 The ombudsman's office defines a massacre as the killing of more than three people.

17 *Masacres Ocurridas en Colombia 1998-1999*, Defensoría del Pueblo/ Naciones Unidas Alto Comisionado para los Refugiados, Santa Fe de Bogotá, 2000

18 Report of the United Nations High Commissioner for Human Rights on the human rights situation in Colombia, published in English, 8 February 2001, Clause 121

19 Interview with Carlos Castaño by journalist Germán Castro Cacycedo in *En Secreto* (Santafe de Bogota: planeta, 1996), pp.153-154, quoted in Human Rights Watch Report: *War Without Quarter: Colombia and International Humanitarian Law*, Oct 1998, Section IV 'Paramilitary Violations of International Humanitarian Law'

20 Report of the United Nations High Commissioner for Human Rights, op. cit., Clause 31

21 Ombudsman Eduardo Cifuentes cited in 'The Chainsaw Massacre is not a movie in Colombia', Agence France Presse, April 19, 2001, by Jacques Thomet, Bogotá

22 Comments cited in BBC Mundo.com, América Latina, 'Masacre de civiles en Colombia, 15.03.2001

23 Jacques Thomet, op. cit.

24 *Resolución Defensorial No 009 sobre la situación de orden publico en la region del Rio Naya'* quoted in Human Rights Watch Report: *The Sixth Division Military-Paramilitary Ties and US Policy in Colombia*, October 2001, p.52

25 Report of the United Nations High Commissioner for Human Rights, op. cit., Clause 34.

26 Cited in DESC *Derechos Económicos Sociales y Culturales*, Mayo del 2000, Bogotá, p.31

27 Amnesty International's Concerns at the 89th International Labour Conference', 5-21 June 2001, Geneva, p.4

28 *Panorama de los Grupos de Autodefensa*, Publicación de Vicepresidencia de la República de Colombia, December 2000

29 This section is based on Amnesty International Report, *Enough is Enough: Repression of Human Rights Defenders*, 1999 Amnesty International Report: *COLOMBIA Protection of human rights defenders: One step forward, three steps back*. 2000, and author's interview with two Credhos members in October 2001.

30 Ibid., p.1

31 Author's interview

32 Report of the United Nations High Commissioner for Human Rights, op. cit., Clause 136

33 Ibid., Clause 17. The full text of the paragraph quoted is: 'The Office has also experienced some difficulties in dealings with the Government. Bodies through which, since starting up operations in Colombia, it has been providing the State with support and advice for the promotion of activities and programmes aimed at overcoming obstacles and implementing international recommendations have been dismantled, sidelined by key Government policies, assigned piecemeal to collateral effects of the major problems faced, or have not had an impact commensurate with the magnitude of the crisis. For

example, the overwhelming majority of Governmental responses to Office communications about specific cases and situations (such as early warnings) have been unsatisfactory, inoperative and purely bureaucratic. Even though President Pastrana himself has taken serious note of these situations, the poor Governmental response to dialogue with the Office has not been substantially corrected and the potential of the Office has been greatly underutilized by the Government.' The report also stated: 'Since the Minister of Defence was designated to lead the Centre coordinating the campaign against the self-defence and other illegal groups... the Office has supplied information on the location of paramilitary bases and the movements of the different blocs. It has generally received unsatisfactory, pro forma responses giving no information on what the authorities have done.'

34 Human Rights Watch report: *The Sixth Division Military-Paramilitary Ties and US Policy in Colombia*, October 2001'The Sixth Division'

35 1993 figure cited in G. Sánchez 'Prospects for Peace' in C. Bergquist, R. Peñaranda, G. Sánchez (eds), *Violence in Colombia*, Scholarly Resources, USA, 2001, p.22. The 4% figure comes from Colombian Commission of Jurists. Violaciones de derechos humanos y violencia sociopolítica en Colombia. Derecho a la vida. Data emailed to author by Colombian Commission of Jurists, 29 July 2002

36 Human Rights Watch, op. cit.

37 Report of the United Nations High Commissioner for Human Rights, op. cit., Clause 133

38 Ibid., Clause 135

39 *Defensoría's* press office, interview with author 2002

40 'ONU teme impunidadad en la Fiscalía', *El Tiempo*, 1 November 2001

41 Annex to joint report by Human Rights Watch, Amnesty International and Washington Office on Latin America, *COLOMBIA Human Rights and USA Military Aid to Colombia II*, January 2001

42 Human Rights Watch report: *The Sixth Division Military-Paramilitary Ties and US Policy in Colombia*, October 2001

43 'Barrancabermeja besieged by Paramilitaries', Colombia Support Network report.

44 Ibid.

45 Human Rights Watch report: *The Sixth Division Military-Paramilitary Ties and US Policy in Colombia*, October 2001, citing Credhos.

46 These are figures of the police and public prosecutor's office (*fiscalía*) compiled by Credhos. People killed in combat have been excluded (a total of 11 between Jan-Aug 2001). The figures also exclude killings by FARC and ELN guerrillas. These numbered: January (13); February (10); March (1); April (1); May (1), June (1) *Informe sobre situación de Derechos Humanos en Barrancabermeja y en el Magdalena Medio*, Credhos/Christian Aid, 2001, pp.28-42. Other sources cite different figures: Medicina Legal states 200 people were murdered in January 2001 and 296 were killed from January to July

47 País Libre, www.paislibre.org.co

48 *Masacres Ocurridas en Colombia 1998-1999*, Defensoría del Pueblo/ Naciones Unidas Alto Comisionado para los Refugiados, Santa Fe de Bogotá, 2000, p.13

49 Report of the United Nations High Commissioner for Human Rights, op. cit., Clause 104

50 The calculations for 1997 (29% of 257,000) and 1998 (35% of 308,000) are based on the figures and percentages cited in *This Is Not Our War: Children and Forced Displacement in Colombia*, Consultoria para el Desplazamiento Forzado y los Derechos Humanos (Codhes) and UNICEF, Santafé de Bogotá, March 2000, p.13 and p.22. The

calculation for 1999 (28% of 288,000) are based on the figures and percentages cited in Codhes Informa 30, August 2000 *Boletín de la Consultoría para los Derechos Humanos y el Desplazamiento*

51 See Noche y Niebla 18, Oct-Dec 2000, Cinep y Justicia Paz, Maps on pp. 32, 37 and 43

52 Human Rights Watch letter to Commander Manual Marulanda, July 10 2001, p.5

53 The FARC admitted responsibility for the tragedy which occurred in the small village of Boyajá on date 2.5.2002. The bomb was apparently aimed at paramilitaries, who had entered Boyajá. The death toll was at least as high as 110 but, at the time of writing, it was not clear whether all of these victims were killed in the church. According to a BBC report, many were killed outside the church during fighting between guerrillas and paramilitaries. 'Pastrana pide misión de la ONU' by José Baig, BBC Mundo.Com, 6.5.2002. In total 45 children were killed. United Nations Representative Anders Kompass criticised the guerrillas, the paramilitaries and state authorities (for failing to act when warned of an imminent paramilitary incursion).

54 All information in this paragraph from Human Rights Watch 'Letter to Commander Manual Marulanda', 2001

55 InterAmerican Press Association except death figures for 2000, which are from the International Press Institute

56 Assassination figures: International Press Institute; kidnapping and threats figures (which refer to first half of 2001), InterAmerican Press Association

57 All three cases from International Press Institute

58 International Press Institute, 'death watch'

59 Ibid. and InterAmerican Press Association, press release, 6.7.2001

60 InterAmerican Press Association press release, 14.6.2000. Comments made to a conference at the University of Alcalá de Henares in Madrid, Spain, June 2000

61 *Codhes Informa* 30, August 2000 Boletín de la Consultoría para los Derechos Humanos y el Desplazamiento, For the period 1985-1994, Codhes has used the figures of the Conferencia Episcopal (Bishops Conference)

62 Ibid.

63 Figures 1995-1998 *This Is Not Our War: Children and Forced Displacement in Colombia*, Consultoria para el Desplazamiento Forzado y los Derechos Humanos (Codhes) and UNICEF, Santafé de Bogotá, March 2000, p.22. Figures for 1999 Codhes Informa 30, August 2000 Boletín de la Consultoría para los Derechos Humanos y el Desplazamiento 68 Urban displacement rose from 18% to 25% between 1998-1999. *This Is Not Our War: Children and Forced Displacement in Colombia*, (Codhes) and UNICEF, Santafé de Bogotá, March 2000 and *Codhes Informa 30.* op. cit.

64 Ibid., p.15

65 Ibid.

66 Ibid., p.50

67 Ibid., p.51

68 Ibid.

69 Full text available on UNHCHR website http://www.hchr.org.co/estadosexcepcion/ex0207-AC.html

70 The legislation needs to be approved by congress and will then be put to a referendum.

71 *Masacres Ocurridas en Colombia 1998-1999*, Defensoría del Pueblo/ Naciones Unidas 76

72 *Resultados Operacionales Fuerza Pública 1999 y 2000*, Ministerio de Defensa Nacional, Marzo de 2001, p.23. Citing: CDO GRAL FFMM-Inspeccion General – Oficina de Derechos Humanos Direccion Ponal 10 January 2001

CHAPTER 2: HISTORY

1   For pre-Columbian and colonial times, an excellent starting point is F. Safford and M. Palacios, *Colombia: Fragmented Land & Divided Society*, Oxford University Press, 2002, and M. Deas essays in L. Bethell (ed) *The Cambridge History of Latin America*, Vols III and V

2   H. Kline Colombia: Democracy Under Assault, Westview, Oxford, 1995 p.30

3   See M. Palacios in E. Posada Carbó *Colombia: The Politics of Reforming the State*, ILAS/Macmillan, UK, 1998, p.37

4   See H. Kline *Colombia: Democracy Under Assault*, Westview, Oxford, 1995 p.4

5   See Catherine LeGrand, 'Agrarian Antecedents of the Violence' in C. Bergquist, R. Peñaranda, G. Sánchez G (eds), V*iolence in Colombia: The Contemporary Crisis in Historical Perspective*, Scholarly Resources, USA, 1992

6   In the late nineteenth century the French had tried unsuccessfully to build a canal across Panama

7   G. Sánchez, 'The Violence: An Interpretative Synthesis' in C. Bergquist, R Peñaranda, G. Sánchez G (eds), *Violence in Colombia*, Scholarly Resources, USA, 1992, p.77

8   See G. Sánchez, 'The Violence: An Interpretative Synthesis' in C. Bergquist, R. Peñaranda, G. Sánchez (eds), *Violence in Colombia: The Contemporary Crisis in Historical Perspective*, Scholarly Resources, USA, 1992

9   J. Pearce, *Colombia: Inside the Labyrinth*, Latin America Bureau, London, 1990, p.49

10 For more on ANUC see L. Zamosc, 'Peasant Struggles of the 1970s in Colombia' in S. Eckstein, *Power and Popular Protest*, University of California Press, 1989

11 C. Bergquist, 'Waging War and Negotiating Peace, The Contemporary Crisis in Historical Perspective', in C. Bergquist, R. Peñaranda, G. Sánchez (eds), *Violence in Colombia*, Scholarly Resources, USA, 2001. See also 'The Labour Movement and the Origins of the Violence' in C. Bergquist, R. Peñaranda, G. Sánchez (eds), *Violence in Colombia*, op. cit. in which Bergquist shows how the Left overlooked small coffee growers and how the latter developed an affinity with the traditional parties

12 See A. Molano, *Selva Adentro. Una historia oral de la colonización del Guaviare*, El Áncora Editores, Bogotá, 1996 and A. Molano, 'Violence and Land Colonisation' in C. Bergquist, *et al*, op. cit.

13 See E. Pizarro, 'Revolutionary Guerrilla Groups in Colombia', in C. Bergquist *et al*, op. cit.

14 For more on Anapo see C. Abel and M. Palacios ,'Colombia since 1958' in The Cambridge History of Latin America, Vol VIII, p.643

15 For more on the popular movement in this period see J. Pearce, *Colombia: Inside the Labyrinth*, Latin America Bureau, London, 1990

16 Another example is Victor Carranza's paramilitary network in the emerald-producing region of Boyacá

17 Richani, op. cit.

18 See J. Pearce, *Colombia: Inside the Labyrinth*, Latin America Bureau, London, 1990, p.246. There was another short-lived death-squad called *Muerte A Secuestradores*, which was founded a year earlier, in 1981, after M19 guerrillas kidnapped Martha Nieves Ochoa, the sister of the Ochoa brothers, key players in the Medellín Cartel

19 For more information see Ana María Bejarano 'The Constitution of 1991: An Institutional Evaluation Seven years Later' in C. Bergquist, R. Peñaranda, G. Sánchez (eds), *Violence in Colombia*, Scholarly Resources, USA, 2001

20 The election of mayors had already been sanctioned by a law passed by congress in 1986.

21 The leftwing *Frente Social y Político* and the post-M19 parties support the constitution, but they are not strongly represented in congress.

22 For more on the decline of AD-M19 see Lawrence Boudon, 'Colombia's M19 Democratic Alliance' in *Latin American Perspectives*, Issue 116, Vol 28, No 1, Jan 2001

23 Kline, op. cit., p.74

24 Pastrana already had a good working relationship with US officials. It was US embassy staff in Bogotá who in 1994 gave him tapes of telephone calls which showed that his rival Ernesto Samper's campaign had links to the Cali Cartel. Pastrana showed the transcripts to the press within two days of Samper's election. The tapes were made by US intelligence agents, according M. Bowden, *Killing Pablo*, Atlantic Books, London, 2001.

CHAPTER 3: THE ECONOMY

1 Lachlin B. Currie *The Role of Economic Advisers in Developing Countries* (1981) quoted in J. Sheahan, *Patterns of Development in Latin America. Poverty, Repression and Economic Strategy*, Princeton University Press, US, 1987, p.280

2 For 1981-2000, Preliminary Overview of the Economies of Latin America and the Caribbean, 2000, United Nations Economic Commission for Latin America (ECLAC), p.86, for 1950-1980, E. Cardoso & A. Helwege *Latin America's Economy: Diversity. Trends and Conflicts*, Massachusetts Institute of Technology, US, 1992, p.10

3 Dornbush and Edwards define economic populism as 'an approach to economics that emphasizes growth and income redistribution and de-emphasizes the risk of inflation and deficit finance, external constraints, and the reaction of economic agents to aggressive non-market policies', p. 370 M. Urratia , 'On the Absence of Economic Populism' in R. Dornbusch and S. Edwards, *The Macroeconomics of populism in Latin America*, University of Chigaco Press, US, 1991

4 Keeping inflation low by controlling the money supply is the overriding aim of monetarist economic policy.

5 Urratia, op. cit., p.376 and p.381

6 Ibid. In 1923 24% of coffee was grown on farms of less than three hectares and only 23% was grown on farms of more than 35 hectares, p.16

7 R. Steiner 'Hooked on Drugs: Colombian-US Relations' in V. Bulmer-Thomas and J. Dunkerley (eds), *The United Sates and Latin America: The New Agenda*, ILAS, London, 1999, p.167. The first estimate refers to D. A. Andelman, 'The Drug Money Maze', in *Foreign Affairs*, July/August 1994, the second estimate is Steiner's. See also, M. Reina 'Drug Trafficking and the National Economy' in op. cit. C. Bergquist, R. Pearanda, G. Sánchez (eds)

8 Javier Fernández Riva, 'The Impact of Drugs on the Colombian Economy', unpublished conference paper, Institute of Latin American Studies, University of London, 29 April 1996 Figure 1 'Gross Revenues from Cocaine Exports', p.5 and comments p.6

9 Departamento Nacional de Planeamiento (DNP) '% de personas bajo LP y LI por zona. Nacional. 1978-1999', Fuente: Cálculos DNP-UDS-DIOGS con base en Dane. EH Nacionales. 1999 EH 103 (March) www.dnp.gov.co/archivosweb/Direccion_Desarrollo _Social/indicadore_sociodem... 2.8.01

10 DNP, % viviendas con energía, acueducto, alcantarillado y teléfono por zona. Nacional y departmental 1985-1993-1997. www.dnp.gov.co/ArchivosWeb/Direccion_ Desarrollo _Social/Indicadore_Sociodem...03/08/01

11 Infant mortality: DNP 1993 (% Tasa de Mortalidad infantil por zona. Nacional y Departmental 1993, www.dnp.gov.co/ArchivosWeb/Direccion_Desarrollo_Social/ Indicadore_Sociodem...03/08/01) Schooling rates: Dane 1997

12 DNP 1999, preliminary figures. Note Amazonian states not included. DNP '% de personas bajo LP y LI. Nacional y Departmental 1997-1999'. www.dnp.gov. co/ArchivosWeb/Direccion_Desarrollo_Social/Indicadore_Sociodem...02/08/01

13 Malnutrition: DNP 1995, Infant Mortality: DNP 1993

14 UNDP Human Development Report 2001, p.183

15 Ibid. The eight most unequal countries were Swaziland (60.9); Nicaragua (60.3); South Africa (59.3); Brazil (59.1); Honduras (59.0); Bolivia (58.9); Paraguay (57.7) and Chile (57.5).

16 Bloomberg News Database

17 'Spilling the Beans' by Joanna Blythman, *Guardian Weekend*, 4.8.01

18 Comments at 'Why Colombia' conference, Sheraton Park Lane Hotel, London, 17 May 2001

19 Human Rights Watch Report: *Colombia: Human Rights Concerns Raised by the Security Arrangements of Transnational Oil Companies*, April 1998

20 Figures taken from speech by Vice President Francisco Santos Calderón at the Johannesburg Sustainable Development Summit on 2 September 2002. Santos did not use the 1.9m figure in the speech, but said 'eight times the oil spilt Exxon Valdez disaster'. The author multiplied 240,000 bls by eight. Amazon Watch estimates that between 1986- 2002, 2.5m barrels were spilt.

21 'Machuca, el resurgir de un pueblo', Panorama, Nov-Dec 1999 published by Ecopetrol. The United Nations Economic and Social Council, Commission on Human Rights, 55th Session, 16 March 1999, point 25 states 'about 70 people' died.

22 *Informe de la Comisión Interinstitucional sobre la Situación de Derechos Humanos en los Departamentos de Casanare y Arauca*, Procuraduría General de la Nación; Fiscalía General de la Nación; Defensoría del Pueblo; Consejería Presidencial Para los Derechos Humanos; Asociación Nacional de Usuários Campesionos – UR; Fundación Comite de Solidaridad con los Presos Políticos, July 1995

23 Human Rights Watch Report: *Colombia: Human Rights Concerns Raised by the Security Arrangements of Transnational Oil Companies*, April 1998, citing 'Collaborative Agreement between BP Exploration (Colombia) and Colombian Ministry of Defence National Army, November 7, 1995. Since 1991, all oil companies were obliged to pay a 'war tax' levied by the government. BP had been cooperating with the army since at least June 1993, according to Human Rights Watch. The company agreed to show Human Rights Watch its 1995 contract with the defence ministry, but the details of agreements prior to 1995 remain confidential.

24 *Informe de la Comisión Interinstitucional sobre la Situación de Derechos Humanos en los Departamentos de Casanare y Arauca*, Procuraduría General de la Nación; Fiscalía General de la Nación; Defensoría del Pueblo; Consejería Presidencial Para los Derechos Humanos; Asociación Nacional de Usuários Campesionos – UR; Fundación Comite de Solidaridad con los Presos Políticos, July 1995, p.13

25 BP Press Release 21 October 1996 cited in J. Pearce, 'Development, Conflict and Corporate Responsibility. The Case of Casanare in Colombia. Confidential Report, November 1998, clause 4.34, p.54

26 Fiscalía General de la Nación, Unidad Nacional de Derechos Humanos, Fiscalía Regional Delegada, 20 January 1998, Bogotá, Colombia. RAD:166; RES: 133. p.30

27 J. Pearce, 'Development, Conflict and Corporate Responsibility. The Case of Casanare

in Colombia'. Confidential Report, November 1998

28   Interview with the author. His name cannot be published because he fears for his safety.

29   This account is based on interviews with the lawyers Marta Hinestroza and Carlos Sánchez; an unpublished report written by Sánchez and Hinestroza, *Filiales de la British Petroleum Destruyen Ecosistemas en Colombia*, 2002, and a briefing paper by Andy Higginbottom, 'BP's Colombia pipeline subsidaries have driven peasants off their land', 31 November 2002. There are claims against two pipeline companies, Ocensa, and ODC, in which BP has a 9.5% stake. Thirty-four properties are represented in the claim against ODC and 45 properties are represented in the claim against Ocensa. Each property housed an average of three families (approximately 30 people).

30   Interview with the author. 22.7.2002 London

31   Author's interview with BP's Ian Stewart 2001

32   Fiscalía General de la Nación, Unidad Nacional de Derechos Humanos, Fiscalía Regional Delegada, 20 January 1998, Bogotá, Colombia. RAD:166; RES: 133. p.28.

33   'Colombian legal inquiry clears BP', *FT*, 18 March 1998. DSL's managing director, Noel Philp, a former member of the SAS, told the *FT* in 2001 that it was the police themselves that provided the training and that DSL managers at BP installations simply 'liaise with the police trainers' (*FT* Investigation: The Private Military Business', 18 April 2001)

34   Telephone conversation and email correspondence with Fiscalía (prosecutor's office) 2002

35   'BP hands 'tarred in pipeline dirty war", by Michael Gillard, Ignacio Gómez and Melissa Jones, *The Guardian*, Saturday 17 1998. M. Gillard and M. Jones made the World in Action programme 'Secret Soliders', 30 June 1997, which led to the public prosecutor's initial investigation into DSC.

36   The news of the children's deaths was originally published in the Colombian newspaper *El Tiempo*. On 22 February 2000, Oxy's Colombian president, Guimer Domínguez, told *El Tiempo* newspaper that he regretted the accident and wanted an investigation. He added that while the company had asked the police to intervene, no company representatives had been present.

37   *Minerales Estratégicos para el Desarrollo de Colombia*, CD produced in 2001, by Unidad de Planeación Minero Energético (UPME); Empresa Nacional Minera Ltda (MINERCOL) and INGEOMINAS

38   J. Pearce, *Colombia: Inside the Labyrinth*, Latin America Bureau, London, 1990, p.106

39   'Minería para la miseria y el genocidio', Sintraminercol, 10.24.2000 http://alainet.org/docs/966.html

40   Stefano Farné, 'Employment and working conditions in the Colombian flower industry', Working Paper, International Labour Office, Geneva, November 1998, p.15. See also 'By the Sweat and Toil of Children', 1994, report by the US Department of Labour, Bureau of International Affairs.

41   FAO Press release 'FAO: Unsafe Application of Pesticides Causes Health and Environmental Damage - Training and Standards Required', 29 May 2000 http://www.fao.org/ag/AGS/agse/pre.htm

42   Flower companies 'try at whatever cost to avoid the establishment of a trade union in their firms', according to the ILO, although it notes that the rate of unionisation is nevertheless higher than the national average. Stefano Farné, 'Employment and working conditions in the Colombian flower industry', Working Paper, International Labour Office, Geneva, November 1998, p.14

43   United Nations Economic Commission for Latin America & the Caribbean (Eclac),

Foreign Investment in Latin America and the Caribbean, 2000

44 Cited in *Why Colombia?* Published by the Colombian Embassy, London, 17 May 2001

45 UK Foreign and Commonwealth Office (FCO) Colombia Briefing Paper 2001.

46 United Nations Economic Commission for Latin America & the Caribbean (Eclac), *Foreign Investment in Latin America and the Caribbean,* 2000

47 Cited in *Why Colombia?* Published by the Colombian Embassy, London, May 17, 2001

CHAPTER 4: DRUGS

1   * The names of all the coca growers in this chapter have been changed.
    Data from the Dirección Nacional de Estupefacientes cited in *Los Cultivos Ilícitos: Política Mundial y Realidad en Colombia,* Defensoría del Pueblo, Bogotá, August 2000, p.35

2   *This Is Not Our War: Children and Forced Displacement in Colombia,* Consultoria para el Desplazamiento Forzado y los Derechos Humanos (Codhes) and UNICEF, Santafé de Bogotá, March 2000

3   Annex to Melquisedec Sabogal, 'Crisis Social Agraria, Narcóticos y Guerra' in D. González Posso (ed) *Cultivos Ilícitos, Narcotáfico y Agenda de Paz,* Agenda Ciudadana, Bogotá, June 2000, p.49. The figures are taken from an internal document of the government's agrarian reform institute INCORA *Breves Comentarios sobre la propiedad de la tierra en Colombia,* de marzo de 1998, from the table entitled 'Evolución de la Distribución de la Propiedad Rural en Colombia 1960, 1989 y 1986' which cited the source: IGAC.

4   Food and Agriculture Organisation of the United Nations. FAO statistical database. www.fao.org Agriculture (PIN) Net Per-Cap PIN 89-91. Year 2000 = 93.3

5   IMF Country Report No 01/68 'Colombia: Selected Issues and Statistical Appendix'. Table 5 Colombia: Value of Agricultural Crops 1/ (Percentage changes; at constant 1975 prices). 1991-2000. Source: Colombian Ministry of Agriculture.

6   Departamento Nacional de Planeamiento (DNP) '% de personas bajo LP y LI por zona. Nacional. 1978-1999', Fuente: Cálculos DNP-UDS-DIOGS con base en Dane. EH Nacionales. 1999 EH 103 (marzo) www.dnp.gov.co/archivosweb/Direccion_Desarrollo _Social/indicadore_sociodem... 2.8.01

7   Exports figures: Dane (www.dane.gov.co). Coffee output figures: Food and Agriculture Organisation of the United Nations. FAO statistical database. www.fao.org, Coffee, Green Production (Mt). The value of Colombian coffee crops fell 23% 1991-2000, according to the IMF: IMF Country Report No 01/68 Colombia: Selected Issues and Statistical Appendix. Table 5 Colombia: Value of Agricultural Crops 1/ (Percentage changes; at constant 1975 prices). 1991-2000. Source: Colombian Ministry of Agriculture.

8   Coffee bushes grow at 1,400 to 1,800 metres above sea level. Poppies grow at 2,800 above sea level. According to Martin Jelsma, of Transnational Institute, many coffee farmers migrated to higher altitudes, in the same mountainous regions, to switch to poppies.

9   Direccion Nacional de Estupefacientes in *Los Cultivos Ilícitos: Política Mundial y Realidad en Colombia,* Defensoría del Pueblo, Bogotá, August 2000, p.35

10 Different sources quote different proportions ranging from 60% to 85%. The UNDCP Annual Coca Cultivation Survey 2001, March 2002, Country Office Colombia. See also environment ministry figures and Colombian anti narcotics police figures cited in *Los Cultivos Ilícitos: Política Mundial y Realidad en Colombia,* Defensoría del Pueblo, Bogotá,

August 2000, pp.40-41

11 *Encuesta Nacional de Calidad de Vida* 1997– Dane. In this survey, Amazonia is lumped together with Orinoquia (eastern Colombia) and figures for the region are only provided for urban administrative centres.

12 DANE 1973-1993 Estadísticas Municipales cited by by Darío González Posso, 'Situación y Perspectivas de la Seguridad Alimentaria en la Amazonia', Tratado de Cooperación Amazónica. Secretaría *Pro Tempore*, Publicacíon No. 64, November 1997, p.8

13 Cifisam was founded by the Vicariate of San Vicente del Caguán-Puerto Leguízamo

14 *Evaluación Económica de la Propuesta de Desarrollo: Granja Familiar Amazónica (Grafam)*, Centro de Investigación Formación e Información Para el Servicio Amazonico (Cifisam), PLANTE/UNOPS/UNDCP, Caquetá, Colombia, 2000 p.55

15 Studies cited in UNDCP *Annual Coca Cultivation Survey 2001*, March 2002, Country Office Colombia, p10. The studies were funded by the Colombian government development agency, Plante. S. Uribe, 'Encuesta para la caracterización socioeconómica de la población, producción agrícola y cocalera en las zonas de cultivos ilícitos,' 1999 and S. Uribe 'Costos de producción de pequeños y medianos cultivadores de coca en Putumayo, Caquetá y Guaviare' in *Los cultivos ilícitos en Colombia*.

16 This is based on the assumption that 6.4kg of cocaine were made from this hectare of coca - a reasonable assumption, as it is within the CIA and UNDCP's ranges. The street price of cocaine is taken from the UNDCP survey *Global Illicit Drugs Trends 2002*. The coca grower's net income was taken from S. Uribe's study cited in the UNDCP *Annual Coca Cultivation Survey 2001*, March 2002, Country Office Colombia, p.10. A coca grower's share of the final price ranges from 0.1% to 0.3% depending on which earning studies/conversion rates are used.

17 Ibid., p.9, citing US and Colombian governments.

18 Ibid., p.1. This conversation rate is based on an 'industrial setting'.

19 Ibid. CIA Coca Fact Paper: A Primer http://www.cia.gov/saynotodrugs /cocaine.html. (Page last updated 12.4.2002)

20 Ibid.

21 Ibid., Country Office Colombia, p.10. The studies were funded by the Colombian government development agency, Plante, S. Uribe, op. cit.

22 UNDCP survey Global Illicit Drugs Trends 2002

23 J. Orlando Melo, 'The Drug Trade, Politics and the Economy: The Colombian Experience' in E. Joyce & C. Malamud (ed) *Latin America and the multinational drug trade*. New York: St. Martin's Press, 1998, pp.79-81

24 A. Rabasa and P. Chalk, *Colombian Labyrinth: The Synergy of Drugs and Insurgency and Its Implications for Regional Stability*, MR-1339-AF, pp.14-16, Santa Monica, RAND 2001. Copyright RAND 2001

25 Nazih Richani 'The Paramilitary Connection' in *NACLA Report on the Americas*, Vol XXXIV, Sep/Oct 2000

26 *War Without Quarter: Colombia and International Humanitarian Law*, Oct 1998, Section IV 'Paramilitary Violations of International Humanitarian Law', p.1

27 'Carlos Castaño responderá ante justicia de E.U', 26 March 2002, *El Tiempo*

28 Nazih Richani, op. cit., pp.38-41

29 Email from Klaus Nyholm to author, November 22, 2002

30 J. Pearce *Colombia: Inside the Labyrinth*, LAB, London, 1990, p.193

31 *New York Times*, 11 November 1998

32 'Effects on Health and the Environment of Herbicides which Contain Glyphosate', Elsa

Nivia, November 2000, taken from www.usfumigation.org./NOvPressConfSpeakers /ElsaNivia/ElsaNivia.htm Elsa Nivia is the coordinator of the Pesticide Action Network, Colombia. Published with permission of the author.

33 In mid 2002 the State Department carried out the first study into the effects of mixing the EPA-registered formulation of glyphosate with Cosmo Flux 411F. In a report to congress in September 2002, it concluded that 'the chemicals used in the coca spraying, in the manner in which they are applied, do not pose unreasonable risk or adverse effects to humans or the environment'. The report did concede that there was 'the potential for acute eye toxicity, due to an inert ingredient in the particular glyphosate formulation used by the program', State Department Media Note, September 5 2002, State Department Report on the Aerial Spray Programme Colombia. This report was then criticised by independent experts, see: 'Official report fails to quell safety fears over Colombian anti-drug campaign', *New Scientist* vol 176 issue 2364 - 12 October 2002, p.9.

34 Acción Andina, *Counter-Fact Sheet: The Aerial Eradication of Illicit Crops: Answers to Frequently Asked Questions*, 02.09.2001

35 ICI suspended the sale of the additive, Atplus 300f saying it had not been tested for the purpose it was being used for. ICI had been selling the chemical to the Colombian company Cosmoagro, which manufactures Cosmo Flux. (Fumigation and Conflict in *Colombia: in the Heat of the Debate*, Transnational Institute, September 2001). The original expose was written by Hugh O'Shaughnessy, 'How global battle against drugs risks backfiring' in The Observer, 17 June 2001. A fortnight later, ICI pulled out. See: Antony Barnett and Solomon Hughes, 'ICI pulls out of cocaine war', *The Observer*, July 1, 2001.

36 *Fumigation and Conflict in Colombia: in the Heat of the Debate*, Transnational Institute, September 2001, p.5

37 Coletta Youngers, WOLA Briefing Series: Issues in International Drug Policy, June 2 1997

38 R. Vargas, *Fumigación y Conflicto: Políticas Antidrogas y Deslegitimación del Estado en Colombia*, TNI-Accion Andina, Tercer Mundo Editores, Colombia, 1999

39 *Evaluación Económica de la Propuesta de Desarrollo: Granja Familiar Amazónica (Cifisam)*, p.55

40 United Nations Pulls Out of Plans to Use Anti-Drug Biological Weapons in South America' Press release from Acción Andina (Bogotá), Sunshine Project (US/Germany), and the Transnational Institute (Amsterdam), 13 November 2000

41 Letter from Colombian Environment Minister Juan Mayr Maldonado to Senator Rafael Orduz, 4 January 2001, published on www.ceudes.org

42 Studies cited in *Los Cultivos Ilícitos: Política Mundial y Realidad en Colombia*, Defensoría del Pueblo, Bogotá, August 2000, p.32

43 Cited in *Los Cultivos Ilícitos: Política Mundial y Realidad en Colombia*, Defensoría del Pueblo, Bogotá, August 2000, p.40

44 Peru carried out a series of small scale spraying operations, mainly field tests with different herbicides, between 1987-90. The programme was suspended in 1990 and does not correlate with the years of rapid decline of coca hectares (1990-99).

45 International Narcotics Control Strategy Reports, 2000 and 1996, Bureau for International Narcotics and Law, US State Department

CHAPTER 5: PLAN COLOMBIA

1   Colombia's contribution was to be raised as follows:
US$800m from 'peace bonds' – debt-bonds which domestic companies were compelled
to buy (and which of course the government had to repay)
US$900m loans from international institutions (which again had to be re-paid)
US$2.25bn to come from the ordinary government budget

2   Cited in *El Plan Europeo: Por qué invertir en la paz de Colombia*. *El Espectador* and El
Banco Interamaricano de Desarrollo, Bogotá, August 200, p.11

3   White House Fact Sheet 'Andean Regional Initiative', March 23, 2002

4   Year 2000 figure (GB£2m) taken from 'We've tooled up the world' by Justine Smith
and Alex Williams, *Daily Mirror*, 28 May 2002, citing government's Annual Report on
Strategic Export Controls.

5   FCO and DIFD figures from emails to author. DTI export licence data taken from The
Norwegian Initiative on Small Arms Transfers (NISAT). Small Arms Transfer Database
http://first.sipri.org/index.php. Arms export values taken from export data on website
of British Embassy in Bogotá. Military visits information: telephone conversation with
FCO Colombia desk.

6   For the year 2002, Congress put a cap of 400 on US military personnel and a cap of 400
on US civilian personnel.

7   'US security assistance to the Andean region 2001-2001', p.6, Center for International
Policy (CIP). CIP analyses are based on US executive and legislative documents. This
quote is taken from Military Construction Appropriations Bill, 2000.

8   'Drug Control: The Department of State's Contract Award for Its counternarcotics
aviation Programme', US Congress, General Accounting Office report, 28 February
2001

9   State Department spokesman Richard Boucher said guerrillas had fired at private
contractors involved in fumigating missions 60 times in 2000. His comments to the
press, on 22.02.01, were made after admitting that 'private US citizens' had been
involved with a dogfight with FARC rebels on the weekend of 20.02.01. Latin
American Daily Report, 23.02.01.

10   'US Assistance to Colombia Will Take Years to Produce Results,' report by US Congress's
GAO, October 2000

11   The Canadian magazine *The Nation* broke the story, which was based on DEA
intelligence reports

12   *Semana* magazine, 16-23 July 2001

13   The DynCorp contract is a study in vagueness. The section dealing with search and
rescue says: 'This operation deals with downed aircraft or hostile action by narcotics
producers or traffickers'. It gives no further details. Julian Borger's Washington Diary,
Guardian Weekly, June 7, 2001

14   'No unit or section of the [Colombian] National Police is exempt from human rights
abuses and extortion. However, governmental and non-governmental representatives
agree that certain units – namely the police intelligence units of the DIJIN and the
Elite Corps – are particularly notorious for their abuse of citizens... The Elite Corps,
which performs a dual role as a counterinsurgency and counternarcotics force has a
reputation as being a more effective, but also more abusive unit than regular local police
units', pp.24-25, *The Colombian National Police. Human Rights and US Drug Policy*, May
1993, Washington Office on Latin America

15   See also: 'The Tough & the Toff: Two Men from Different Cultures United by the Lure

of War', *Daily Telegraph* November 21, 1993, in which Peter MacAleese a former SAS man talked to journalist Christy Campbell about his work as a mercenary in Colombia

16 Department of National Planning (DNP). Putumayo is so isolated that government statistics are incomplete: it does not, for example, have the poverty or indigence rate for this region.

17 Elsa Nivia. She estimates that if the impact of the additives are taken into account, the effect could be spraying the mixture at 100 times the recommended concentration. 'Las fumigaciones aéreas sobre cultivos ilícitos si son peligrosas: algunas aproximaciones' Conference paper, at University of California, Davis, May, 17-19 2001

18 Cited in national ombudsman's report: *Resolución Defensorial Nacional AL No.026. Derechos Humanos y Derecho International Humanitario en el Marco del Conflicto Armado y de las Fumigaciones de los Cultivos de coca en el departmento del Putumayo.* October 9, 2002, p.32

19 Illnesses reported to the *Personeros* (Official Legal Representative) of San Miguel and Valle del Guamués republished in 'Efectos de las fumigaciones aéreas en los municipios del Valle del Guamués y San Miguel, Putumayo, Diciembre 2000 – Febrero 2001' by Bernardo Pérez Salazar, published on www.mamacoca.org

20 Resolución Defensorial Nacional AL No.026. *Derechos Humanos y Derecho International Humanitario en el Marco del Conflicto Armado y de las Fumigaciones de los Cultivos de coca en el departmento del Putumayo,* October 9, 2002, p.30

21 Ibid., p.7

22 Carlos Higuera, 'El silencio de los fumigados, Nueve indígenas viajaron 875 kilómetros para asistir a un debate en el que no se les dio la palabra', *El Espectador,* Suplementos Medio Ambiente, 21 August 2001.

23 Gobernador de Nariño asegura que concentración de glifosato afecta la salud de la población', *El Tiempo,* Bogotá, 6 de septiembre de 2002.

24 Kintto Lucas reports from Nueva Loja, Ecuador, 'Plan Colombia herbicide spraying causes health and environmental problems', IPS, 17 October 2000

25 Kintto Lucas, IPS journalist in Ecuador, has provided excellent coverage of paramilitary violence and the impact of fumigation in the border regions

26 Elsa Neiva, op. cit.

27 Kintto Lucas, op. cit.

28 South Americans fear Plan Colombia contagion', Latin American Daily Report, August 31, 2000

29 'A verdade sobre a Colombia e as FARC - e o PT.' PT party statement, 16/10/02. Sent by email by Giancarlo Summa, Foreign Press Officer for President-elect Lula

30 'Toledo explica su gobierno', BBC Americas, June 7, 2001

31 Interview in *El Tiempo,* August 31, 2000

32 According to the president of the Venezuelan stockbreeders' federation, José Luis Betancourt, ELN guerrillas have been helping to evict Colombian trespassers. Latin American Daily Report, February 8, 2001

33 Controlling Cocaine: Supply Versus Demand Programs' by C. Peter Rydell and Susan S. Everingham, 1994

CHAPTER 6: THE UNITED STATES AND COLOMBIA

1   The most notorious case is the Eisenhower administration's close ties to United Fruit (which had extensive landholdings in Guatemala). His government helped to organise the 1954 coup which ousted a president who advocated minor agrarian reform. Today, many observers have highlighted the Bush administration's links with the oil industry.

2   Article in *Military Review*, February, 1987, pp.46-47, quoted in P. Dale Scott & J.
      Marshall, *Cocaine Politics*, University of California Press, 1998 p.198
3   C. Channel and R. Miller, 'Action Plan for 1986 Programs of the American
      Conservative Trust and The National Endowment for the Preservation of Liberty,' in
      Iran Contra Report, Appendix A, 686, quoted in ibid., p.23
4   R. Parry, 'Lost History: CIA Perception Management', The Consortium, 1996,
      www.consortium.com
5   P. Dale Scott & J. Marshall, op. cit.
6   Kerry Report. For the full story of the Contra scandal and CIA involvement in other
      drug trafficking scandals see op. cit. P. Dale Scott & J. Marshall.
7   Quoted in *Clear & Present Dangers: The US Military & the War on Drugs in the Andes*,
      Washington Office on Latin America (WOLA), 1991, p.32
8   Quoted in C. Youngers, *The War in the Andes: The Military Role in US International
      Drug Policy*, WOLA Briefing series: Issues in International Drug Policy, December
      1990, p.8
9   Ibid., p.19
10   US military aid was cut off in 1993-94, but was restored in 1995 after Fujimori won a
      landslide election victory. In 2000, Fujimori fled to Japan to avoid being put on trial
      for corruption in Peru.
11   P. Zirnite, *Reluctant Recruits: The US Military and the War on Drugs*, WOLA
      working paper, USA, 1997, p.4
12   Col. Robert Jacobelly told the Washington Office on Latin America in 1991: 'There is
      more of a latent insurgency in Bolivia at this point. Things will get worse, and that's
      related to the drug trade. I think that unless we provide counterinsurgency assistance
      [to Bolivia] the insurgency will get worse...,' *Clear and Present Danger*, WOLA, 1991,
      p.57
13   Speaking to Secretary of State John Hay in August 1903. Quoted in Stephen Randall
      Colombia and the United States: Hegemony and Interdependence, USA, 1992, pp.85-86
14   This paragraph is based on D. Dent *The legacy of the Monroe Doctrine: a reference
      guide to U.S. involvement in Latin America and the Caribbean*. Connecticut, Greenwood
      Press, 1999
15   Stephen Randall Colombia and the *United States: Hegemony and Interdependence*,
      USA, University of Georgia, 1992, p.209
16   From Statistical Abstract of Latin America, Vol 25. Totals calculated by author
17   Headquarters US Army Special Warfare School. Subject: 'Visit to Colombia by a Team
      from Special Warfare Center Fort Bragg, N Carolina, 26 February 1962' quoted in M.
      McClintock, *Instruments of Statecraft. US Guerrilla Warfare. Counterinsurgency &
      Counterterrorism*, 19 40-1990, Pantheon Books, USA, 1992, p.223
18   Ibid.
19   Ibid.
20   According to Richard Gott, 16,000 troops attacked Marquetalia, but this number
      seems exaggerated given the entire Colombian army totalled 23,000 men in 1964.
      Contemporary Colombian newspaper accounts do not state the number of troops used.
      Gott, Richard W. *Guerrilla movements in Latin America*. UK, Nelson, 1970
21   According to the FARC there were 48 guerrillas (46 men and 2 women)
22   Letter by Aid official Mathew J. Harvey to Senator James Abourezk, quoted in
      McClintock, op. cit., p.193
23   *Just the Facts. A civilian's guide to U.S. defense and security assistance to Latin America and
      the Caribbean*. A joint project of the Latin America Working Group and the Center for

International Policy. http://ciponline.org/facts

24 *El Terrorismo de Estado en Colombia* (Brussels: Ediciones NCOS, 1992) Report by: Organización Mundial Contra la Tortura (OMCT); Asociación Americana de Juristas; Federación Latinoamericana de Asociaciones de Familiares de Desaparecidos; Pax Christi Internacional; Commission of the Churches on International Affairs; Rechtvaardigheid en Vrede; Commission Justice et Paix; Centre National de Cooperation au Developpement; Nationaal Centrurn Voor Ontwikkelingsamenwerking; Servicio Paz y Justicia América Latina. The information in this section comes from School of the Americas Watch, which publishes full lists of SOA graduates. www.soawatch.org

25 M. Bowden, *Killing Pablo*, Atlantic Books, UK, 2001, pp.356-357

26 Interview in *El Espectador*, August 4, 1991, cited in Clear & Present Dangers: The US Military & the War on Drugs in the Andes, Washington Office on Latin America (WOLA), 1991, Chapter 3

27 Prepared statement of Gen. Barry R. McCaffrey, USA, commander in chief, U.S. Southern Command, before the House National Security Committee, March 8, 1995

28 Charles E. Wilhelm, Testimony the House Committee on Government Reform Subcommittee on Criminal Justice, Drug Policy and Human Resources, February 15, 2000

29 State Department Fact Sheet 'Is Plan Colombia a Colombian Plan?', 28 March 2000, Available on www.state.gov

30 Drug Control: International Counterdrug Sites Being Development, GAO report, December 2000

31 See 'U.S. security assistance to the Andean region, 2000-2001', Center for International Policy, http://www.ciponline.org/facts/co.htm#_edn5

32 CIA chief George Tenet remarks to the Senate Select Intelligence Committee on 'Worldwide Threats to National Security', February 7 2001

33 Brian E. Sheridan, Assistant Secretary of Defense for Special Operations and Low Intensity Conflict, United States House of Representatives Committee on Government Reform, Subcommittee on criminal Justice, Drug Policy and Human Resources, October 12, 2000, Statement for the Record.

34 Questioning of Gen. Peter Pace, commander-in-chief, U.S. Southern Command, by Senate Armed Services Committee, March 27, 2001

35 Ibid.

36 Resolución Defensorial nacional AL No.026. Derechos Humanos y Derecho International Humanitario en el Marco del Conflicto Armado y de las Fumigaciones de los Cultivos de coca en el departmento del Putumayo. 9 October 2002, p.14

37 Ibid., p.7

38 'End-Use Monitoring Report', INL, US Department of State, February 1997, cited in The Sixth Division Military-Paramilitary Ties and US Policy in Colombia, October 2001, p.87

39 All seven planes used in the attack were given by the US. Six came from the US government under military assistance and sales programs, and one by commercial purchase from a private manufacturer. The Sixth Division Military-Paramilitary Ties and US Policy in Colombia, October 2001, p.98

40 GAO, 'Drug Control: Challenges in Implementing Plan Colombia', October 12 2000, p.8. 'US Embassy officials stated that the [Colombian] National Police have not always provided necessary documents, such as budgetary and planning documents, to determine if the National Police are using the resources in accordance with eradication

and interdiction plans. In two instances, US Embassy officials said they observed the National Police using US-provided helicopters for purposes other than counternarcotics, but the Police did not co-operate in their attempts to clarify how the helicopters were being used.'

41 The Sixth Division Military-Paramilitary Ties and US Policy in Colombia, October 2001, p.102

42 'Fields of Battles: How Bogota Wooed Washington to a New War on Cocaine' by Carla Anne Robbins, *Wall Street Journal*, June 23, 2000

43 Officers cited on School of the Americas Watch website. The relatively high number of Colombian officers is partly due to the fact that more research has been done into the names of abusers in Colombia (particularly the 1992 inter-agency 'Black-Book' which listed hundreds of Colombian officers), whereas the names of officers who committed offences in other countries – particularly in Central America – are not all known.

44 School of the Americas Watch. www.soaw.org. This excellent site contains lists of SOA graduates, which can be matched up with human rights reports.

45 Interviewed by Coletta Youngers, *NACLA Report on the Americas*, Vol XXXI, March/April 1998

46 Los Peligros de la Ayuda Militar', by Ignacio Gómez, *El Espectador* February 27, 2000 http://www.elespectador.com/periodismo_inv/2000/febrero/nota1.htm

47 Interviewed by Coletta Youngers, *NACLA Report on the Americas*, Vol XXXI, March/April 1998, p.34

48 'Che Guevara and Guerrilla Warfare: Training for today's Nonlinear Battlefields' by Capt Steve Lewis, US Army, Military Review, Sep/Oct 2001, p.5. The article is discussing US actions worldwide including in Kosovo and Afghanistan.

49 Ibid., p.6

50 Testimony to Senate Caucus on International Narcotics control and the Senate Finance Subcomittee, 22 February 2000

51 Ibid.

52 Senate Armed Services Committee Hearing (confirmation of nominees), June 5, 2001

53 For full testimony see http://www.ciponline.org/colombia/021507.htm

54 ABC's *This Week*, September 23, 2001

55 Speech by U.S. Ambassador to Colombia Anne Patterson, Bogotá, Colombia, October 25, 2001; Speech by U.S. Ambassador to Colombia Anne Patterson, Cartagena, Colombia, October 24, 2001 http://usembassy.state.gov/colombia/wwwsprdc.shtml# Discursos

56 Cass Ballenger, October 10, 2001: Hearing of the Western Hemisphere Subcommittee of the House International Relations Committee on 'The Western Hemisphere's Response to the September 11th, 2001 Terrorist Attack on the United States'

57 Following President Pastrana's decision to end the FARC peace process, the US responded to Colombia's request for help by increasing intelligence support and expediting the delivery of Colombian-purchased spare parts for aircraft. Daily Press Briefing, State Department, Richard Boucher, Spokesman, Washington, DC, March 15, 2002

58 'US military in southern Colombia' *latinnewsdaily*, 26/2/2002, www.latinnews.com, The State Department admitted that 'four US personal, two military and two civilian' were present in San Vicente del Caguán on Sunday 24/2/2002, the day that President Andrés Pastrana had made a flying visit, but said that the men remained there only for one day (the duration of the President's visit).

59 Hearing of the House Appropriations Subcommittee on Commerce, Justice, State, the Judiciary and Related Agencies, March 6, 2002

CHAPTER 7: FACTS AND FIGURES

1   The Ministry of Defence figure for 2001 is 16,600 (from 8,200 in 1990) cited in Juan Carlos Echeverry, *Manejo de Riesgos del Estado: Violencia, Secuestro y Seguridad Personal*, Departamento Nacional de Planeación (DNP) 18.4.2002. http://www.dnp.gov.co/03_PROD/PRESEN/0p_dir.htm The expansion figures are cited in A. Rabasa and P. Chalk, *Colombian Labyrinth: The Synergy of Drugs and Insurgency and Its Implications for Regional Stability*, Rand Publications, USA, 2001 p.26, attributed to Alfredo Rangel Suárez, *Colombia: Guerra en el Fin de Siglo*, Tercer Mundo Editores, Bogotá, 1998. Rabasa and Chalk estimate the figure for FARC membership in 2001 is 18,000-20,000, p.26.

2   C. Echandía Castilla, *El Conflicto Armado y las Manifestaciones de Violencia en las Regiones de Colombia*, Presidencia de la República, Oficina del Alto Comisionado para la Paz, Observatorio de Violencia, Santa Fe de Bogotá, 1999

3   Ibid.

4   This section is based on essays by E. Pizarro and A. Molano in Colombia, in op. cit. C. Bergquist, R Peñaranda, G Sánchez (eds).; op. cit. J. Pearce; an essay by Ricardo Vargas Meza in *NACLA Report on the Americas*, Vol XXXI, March/April 1998; an essay by A. Molano in *NACLA Report on the Americas*,Vol XXXIV, Sep/Oct 2000, A Alape, *La Paz, La Violencia: Testigos de Excepción*, Planeta Colombiana Editorial, Bogotá 1999 and FARC website.

5   The ministry of defence figure for 2001 is 4,500 (compared with 2,300 in 1990) cited in Juan Carlos Echeverry, *Manejo de Riesgos del Estado: Violencia, Secuestro y Seguridad Personal*. Departamento Nacional de Planeación (DNP) 18.4.2002 http://www.dnp.gov.co/03_PROD/PRESEN/0p_dir.htm According to Center for International Policy Study, its numbers fell from a high of 5,000 in mid-1990s to 3,500 by end of the decade, due to the paramilitary advance. Rabasa and Chalk estimate it has 3,000-5,000 combatants, op. cit., p.26, attributed to Alfredo Rangel Suárez, *Colombia: Guerra en el Fin de Siglo*, Tercer Mundo Editores, Bogotá, 1998.

6   This section is based on essay by E. Pizarro in Colombia, in op. cit. C. Bergquist, R. Peñaranda, G. Sánchez (eds), op. cit. J. Pearce; essay by D. García Peña in *NACLA Report on the Americas*,Vol XXXIV, Sep/Oct 2000, A Alape, La Paz, *La Violencia: Testigos de Excepción*, Planeta Colombiana Editorial, Bogotá 1999 and ELN website.

7   Center for International Policy Colombian project, information about combatants. www.ciponline.org/colombia

8   C. Echandía Castilla, *El Conflicto Armado y las Manifestaciones de la Violencia en las Regiones de Colombia*, Presidencia de la República de Colombia, Oficina del Alto Comisionado para la Paz, Bogotá, 2000

9   William Calvo interview in Arturo Alape, *La Paz. La Violencia: Testigos de Excepción*, Planeta Colombiana Editorial, Bogotá 1999, p.311

10 M. Aranguren Molina, *Mi Confesión: Carlos Castaño revela sus secretos*, Editorial Oveja Negra, Colombia, 2001, p.222

11 Ibid. Other sources agree that EPL fronts joined the paramilitaries, see C. Echandía Castillo, op. cit.

12 This relies heavily on L. Boudon, 'Colombia's M19 Democratic Alliance: A Case Study in New-Party, Self Destruction', *Latin American Perspectives*, Issue 116, Vol 28, June 2001. See also M. Chernick and M. Jiménez, 'Popular Liberalism, Radical Democracy, and Marxism: Leftist Politics in Contemporary Colombia, 1974-1991', in B. Carr and S. Ellner, *The Latin American Left: from the Fall of Allende to Petrestroika*, Westview Press,

USA, 1993

14 'Historia del Movimiento Insurgente en Colombia', *Apuntes de Colombia*. *http://stes.es/llar/cosal/colomba/*. Some sources say the PRT was a breakaway from the ELN. (See C. Bergquist, R. Peñaranda, G. Sánchez, op. cit.).

15 The Ministry of Defence figure for 2001 was 10,600 (compared with 1,800 in 1990) cited in Juan Carlos Echeverry, *Manejo de Riesgos del Estado: Violencia, Secuestro y Seguridad Personal*, Departamento Nacional de Planeación (DNP) 18.4.2002 http://www.dnp.gov.co/03_PROD/PRESEN/0p_dir.htm A figure of 8,150 for 2000 was cited in the government's *Panorama de los Grupos de Autodefensa*, Vicepresidencia de la República/Programa Presidencial de los Derechos Humanos y DIH, Bogotá, December 2000, p.3. In an interview in 2002, Carlos Castaño said the AUC had 10,000 members. 'No soy la madre Teresa', Revista Poder, April 2002. The Center for International Policy estimates 'more than 8,000'. CIP Colombia Project Information about Combatants, www.ciponline/colombia

16 AUC Constitution, Capitulo dos: De los Principios Fundamentales, Article No 4: 'La propiedad privada es el fundamento esencial del sistema económico vigente. Su defensa y protección entraña deberes y derechos para el Estado y para los asociados.'

17 'In the Battalion: A Solider Speaks', *NACLA Report on the Americas*,Vol XXXIV, Sep/Oct 2000, p.42

18 M. Aranguren Molina, *Mi Confesión Carlos Castaño revela sus secretos*, Editorial Oveja Negra, Colombia, 2001, p.177

19 'In the Battalion: A Solider Speaks', *NACLA Report on the Americas*, Vol XXXIV, Sep/Oct 2000, p.42

20 M. Aranguren Molina, *Mi Confesión Carlos Castaño revela sus secretos*, Editorial Oveja Negra, Colombia, 2001, p.306

21 Ibid., p.177

22 Ibid.

23 Ibid., p.87. Castaño's contact in the MAS was major Alejandro Alvarez Henao of the Bombonà battalion, a School of the Americas graduate, who Castaño describes as 'one of the fathers of paramilitarism in Colombia'.

24 'Colombian death squad leader reveals his face', 2 March 2000, CNN Americas, cnn.com. Report about an interview shown on Colombian TV in February.

25 'Carlos Castaño responderá ante justicia de E.U', *El Tiempo*, 26.3.2002

26 He worked with the Cali Cartel in the PEPES death squad which targeted associates of Escobar. He says the Cali Cartel provided him with helicopters, but says the relationship with the Cartel was 'fleeting.' He describes Cali Cartel leader Gilberto Rodríguez as 'a gentleman, a *señor* — full stop', M. Aranguren Molina, *Mi Confesión Carlos Castaño revela sus secretos*, Editorial Oveja Negra, Colombia, 2001, p. 167

27 M. Aranguren Molina, op. cit. p.242

28 Maj. Alejandro de Jesus Alvarez Henao (1984, Joint Operations); LTC Virgilio Anzola Montero (1967, Cadet Orientation Course). Maj Julio Elias Barrera Bustos (1982 Joint Operations Course). Col Jaime Alberto Escobar Garzón (1981, Command and General Staff College). General Ramón Emilia Gil Bermúdez (1969 Maintenance Course, 1988 guest speaker) General Hernan Jose Guzman Rodriquez (1969, Maintenance Orientation, 1993, SOA Hall of Fame). For more see School of the Americas Watch, www.soaw.org

29 Alvaro Uribe Vélez, elected in 2002, is a dissident Liberal.

30 Cited by Fundación Hemera on www.etniasdecolombia.org. Date of Interior Ministry's figures not given.

31   The information on this page relies heavily on research done by the Center for
     International Policy http://www.ciponline.org/colombia/contractors.htm

32   'Drug Control: The Department of State's Contract Award for Its counternarcotics
     aviation Programme', US Congress, General Accounting Office report, 28 February
     2001

33   State Department spokesman Richard Boucher said guerrillas had fired at private
     contractors involved in fumigating missions 60 times in 2000. His comments to the
     press, on 22.02.01, were made after admitting that 'private US citizens' had been
     involved with a dogfight with FARC rebels on the weekend of 20.02.01.
     Latinnewsdaily, www.latinnews.com, 23.02.01

34   'Ollie North's Iran-Contra Gun Runners Now Work Plan Colombia, by Ken
     Guggenheim, Associated Press, June 5, 2001, published on
     http://www.commondreams.org/headlines01/0605-04.htm

35   http://www.mpri.com/subchannels/int_south.html

36   E.g. Ricardo Vargas, *Fumigación y conflicto*, executive summary, Transnational Institute.
     www.tni.org

37   'We have no accurate estimate of the extent of domestic marijuana cultivation, much of
     the marijuana smoked in the U.S. is cultivated domestically—commercially, privately,
     outdoors, and indoors.' March 12, 1997, Statement by Barry R. McCaffrey, Director,
     ONDCP, on U.S.-Mexico counterdrug cooperation, Senate Foreign Relations
     Committee, Subcommittee on Western Hemisphere and Peace Corps.

38   www.tni.org *Vicious Circle: The Chemical and Biological 'War on Drugs*,' March 2001

39   1998 Marijuana Crop Report, An Evaluation of Marijuana Production, Value, and
     Eradication Efforts in the United States prepared by Jon Gettman and Paul Armentano,
     http://www.norml.org/facts/crop/report.shtml#gettman

40   UNDCP, World Drug Report, 2000, Annex 2, Extracts from Table: Annual prevalence
     of abuse by substance, as percentage of the population aged 5 and above (unless
     otherwise indicated)

Bibliography

CHAPTER 1: HUMAN RIGHTS

Amnesty International Report: *Enough is Enough: Repression of Human Rights Defenders*, 1999

Amnesty International Report: *Colombia Protection of human rights defenders: One step forward, three steps back*, 2000

Amnesty International Report: *Colombia Return to Hope: Forcibly Displaced Communities of Urabá and Medio Atrato Region*, June 2000

Amnesty International Report: *Colombia. Barrancabermeja A City Under Siege*, May 1999

Avances y Resultados de la Política Sobre Derechos Humanos y Derecho Internacional Humanitario, Vicepresidencia del República de Colombia, Bogota, March 2000

Bitácora Informativa, Defensoría del Pueblo, Colombia, 1998

Bitácora Informativa, Defensoría del Pueblo, Colombia, 1999-2000

Codhes Informa 30, August 2000 *Boletín de la Consultoría para los Derechos Humanos y el Desplazamiento*

Codhes Informa 32, September 2000 *Boletín de la Consultoría para los Derechos Humanos y el Desplazamiento*

Codhes Informa 35, April 2001 *Boletín de la Consultoría para los Derechos Humanos y el Desplazamiento*

Codhes Informa: *Desplazados Rostros Anónimos de la Guerra. Resumen Ejecutivo 2001*, Bogota, 2001

COLOMBIA Human Rights and USA Military Aid to Colombia, joint report by Human Rights Watch, Amnesty International and Washington Office on Latin America, August 2000

COLOMBIA Human Rights and USA Military Aid to Colombia II, joint report by Human Rights Watch, Amnesty International and Washington Office on Latin America, January 2001

Colombia: Inseguridad, Violencia, y Desempeño Económico en las Areas Rurales,Consejería para la Paz de la Presidencia de la República, Colombia, 1999, Director de Investigación: Jesus Antonio Bejarano Avila.

Conflicto Armado en el Magdalena Medio, Diocesis de Barrancabermeja, July 2001

C. Echandía Castilla, *El Conflicto Armado y las Manifestaciones de Violencia en las Regiones de Colombia*, Presidencia de la República, Oficina del Alto Comisionado para la Paz, Observatorio de Violencia, Santa Fe de Bogotá, 1999

Human Rights Watch letter to Commander Manual Marulanda, July 10 2001

Human Rights Watch Report: *War Without Quarter: Colombia and International Humanitarian Law*, Oct 1998

Human Rights Watch Report: *The Sixth Division Military-Paramilitary Ties and US Policy in Colombia*, October 2001

Informe sobre situación de Derechos Humanos en Barrancabermeja y en el Magdalena Medio, Credhos/Christian Aid

Masacres Ocurridas en Colombia 1998-1999, Defensoría del Pueblo/ Naciones Unidas Alto Comisionado para los Refugiados, Santa Fe de Bogotá, 2000

Noche y Niebla 18, Oct-Dec 2000, Cinep y Justicia Paz, Colombia

Noche y Niebla 19, Jan-Mar 2001, Cinep y Justicia Paz, Colombia

Octavo Informe del Defensor Del Pueblo, Bogotá, Colombia, 2001

Panorama de los Grupos de Autodefensa, Vicepresidencia de la República/Programa Presidencial de los Derechos Humanos y DIH, Bogotá, December 2000

Report of the United Nations High Commissioner for Human Rights on the human rights situation in Colombia, published in English, 8 February 2001

Resultados Operacionales Fuerza Pública 1999 y 2000, Ministerio de Defensa Nacional, Colombia, March 2001

This Is Not Our War: Children and Forced Displacement in Colombia, Consultoria para el Desplazamiento Forzado y los Derechos Humanos (Codhes) and UNICEF, Santa Fe de Bogotá, March 2000

US State Department Annual Report on Human Rights: Colombia, 1999, 2000, 2001

CHAPTER 2: HISTORY

A. Alape, *La Paz. La Violencia: Testigos de Excepción*. Planeta Colombiana Editorial, Bogotá 1999

M. Aranguren Molina, *Mi Confesión Carlos Castaño revela sus secretos*, Editorial Oveja Negra, Colombia, 2001

L. Bethell (ed) Cambridge History of Latin America, Vols III, V and VIII

M. Bowden, *Killing Pablo*, Atlantic Books, London, 2001

B. Carr, S. Ellner (eds) *The Latin American Left*, Westview Press/LAB, 1993

C. Bergquist, R. Peñaranda, G. Sánchez G. (eds), *Violence in Colombia: The Contemporary Crisis in Historical Perspective*, Scholarly Resources, USA, 1992

C. Bergquist, R. Peñaranda, G. Sánchez G., (eds) *Violence in Colombia 1990-2000: Waging War and Negotiating Peace*, Scholarly Resources, USA, 2001

R. H. Davis, *Historical Dictionary of Colombia*. Metuchen, N.J., The Scarecrow Press, 1977. 280

M. García Durán, 'War, negotiations and mobilization for peace (1980-2002)' in Leal, C. and Bonilla D. (eds) *Colombia: Land in Turmoil*, Duke University Press.
'Veinte años buscando una salida negociada: aproximación a la dinamica del conflicto armado y procesos de paz en Colombia 1.980/2.000' in *Controversia*, No. 179, Diciembre 2001, pp. 11-41

G. García Márquez, *News of a Kidnapping*, Penguin, 1996

G. García Márquez, *One Hundred Years of Solitude*, Penguin, 2000

R. Gott. *Guerrilla Movements in Latin America*. UK, Nelson, 1970

H. Kline *Colombia: Democracy Under Assault*, Westview, Oxford, 1995

K. Lucas, *Plan Colombia: La Paz Armada*, Editorial Planeta del Ecuador, 2000

R. Maullin Solidiers, *Guerrillas & Politics in Colombia*, The Rand Corporation, USA, 1973

A. Molano, *Selva Adentro: Una Historia Oral de la Colonización del Guaviare*, El Ancora Editores, Bogotá, 1996

NACLA Report on the Americas.Vol XXXIV, Sep/Oct 2000

NACLA Report on the Americas. Vol XXXI, March/April 1998

E. Posada Carbó *Colombia: The Politics of Reforming the State*, ILAS/Macmillan, UK, 1998

J. Pearce, *Colombia: Inside the Labyrinth*, Latin America Bureau, London, 1990

A. Rabasa and P. Chalk, *Colombian Labyrinth: The Synergy of Drugs and Insurgency and Its Implications for Regional Stability*, Rand Publications, USA, 2001

F. Safford and M. Palacios, *Colombia: Fragmented Land & Divided Society*, Oxford University Press, 2002

CHAPTER 3: ECONOMY

E. Cardoso & A. Helwege *Latin America's Economy: Diversity, Trends and Conflicts*, Massachusetts Institute of Technology, 1992

R. Dornbusch and S. Edwards, *The Macroeconomics of populism in Latin America*, University of Chigaco Press, 1991

IMF Country Report No 01/68 Colombia: Selected Issues and Statistical Appendix

J. Orlando Melo (ed) *Colombia Hoy: Perspectivas Hacia el Siglo XXI*, Tercer Mundo Editores, Colombia, 1995

J. Sheahan, *Patterns of Development in Latin America. Poverty, Repression and Economic Strategy* Princeton University Press, 1987

United Nations Economic Commission for Latin America *The Equity Gap: A Second Assessment*, LC/G 2096, 8 May 200, English version

United Nations Economic Commission for Latin America & the Caribbean (ECLAC), *Foreign Investment in Latin America and the Caribbean*, 2000

United Nations Economic Commission for Latin America (ECLAC), *Preliminary Overview of the Economics of Latin America and the Caribbean*, 2000

United Nations Conference on Trade and Development (UNCTAD) *World Investment Report*, 2000

United Nations Conference on Trade and Development (UNCTAD) *Trade and Development Report*, 2000

Unpublished conference papers from seminar on the Colombian economy, Institute of Latin American Studies, University of London, 29 April 1996

M. Cárdenas & R. Córdoba 'Recent Economic Policy in Colombia: the View from Outside'

B. Grote 'The Challenges of Foreign Investment'

J. Fernández Riva, 'The Impact of Drugs on the Colombian Economy'

J. F. Isaza 'Oil Participation in the Colombian Economy'

R. Junguito 'The Management of Coffee Bonanzas and Crisis'

J. L. Londoño da Cuesta 'The Social Impact of the Colombian Economic Model'

J. A. Ocampo 'The Economic Policy of the Samper Administration'

M. Urrutia 'Institutions and Economic Policy Making'

CHAPTER 4: DRUGS

Cultivos ilícitos y proceso de paz en Colombia, Acción Andina/TNI, 2000

Evalucación Economica de la Propueta de Desarrollo: Granja Familiar Amazóncia, Cifisam, 2000

Fumigation & Conflict: In the Heat of the Debate, TNI, Netherlands 2001

D. González Posso (ed), *Cultivos Ilicitos, Narcotráfico y Agenda de Paz*, Agenda Ciudadana, 2000 (ed) *Opciones para el Desarrollo Rural*, Agenda Ciudadana, 1999

International Narcotics Control Strategy Report, 2000, Bureau for International Narcotics and Law, US State Department

E. Joyce & C. Malamud (ed) *Latin America and the multinational drug trade*. New York: St. Martin's Press, 1998

M. Jelsma, *Fungus Verus Coca: UNDCP and the Biological War on Drugs in Colombia*, TNI, Netherlands, February 2000

Las Claves Territoriales de la Guerra y La Paz, Agenda Ciudadana, 2000

Los Cultivos Ilícitos: Política Mundial y Realidad en Colombia, Defensoría del Pueblo, August 2000

A. Molano, *Selva Adentro, Una Historia Oral de la Colonización del Guaviare*, El Ancora Editore, 1996

The Revolutionary Armed Forces of Colombia and the Illict Drug Trade, TNI/Accion Andina, WOLA, June 1999

Sistematización de la Experiencia Cifisam y su Propuesta Grafam, Cifisam, 2000

Vicious Circle: The Chemical and Biological 'War on Drugs', Transnational Institute, March 2001

US *National Drug Control Strategy*, Office of National Drug Control Policy, 2001, ONDCP

UNDCP, World Drug Report, 2000

R. Vargas Meza, *Fumigación y Conflicto: Políticas Antidrogas y Deslegitimación del Estado en Colombia*, Tercer Mundo, 1999

CHAPTER 6: THE UNITED STATES AND COLOMBIA

B. Bagley & W. O. Walker (eds), *Drug Trafficking in the Americas*. Coral Gables, Fla.: Univ. of Miami, North-South Center; New Brunswick, N.J.: Transaction Publishers, 1994.

—*Myths of militarization: The Role of the Military in the War on Drugs in the Americas*. Miami: North-South Center, Univ. of Miami, 1991.

V. Bulmer-Thomas and J. Dunkerley, *The United States and Latin America: The New Agenda*, ILAS, London, 1999

Clear & Present Dangers: The US Military & the War on Drugs in the Andes, Washington Office on Latin America (WOLA), 1991

P. Dale Scott & J. Marshall, *Cocaine Politics*, University of California Press, 1998

D. Dent, *The Legacy of the Monroe Doctrine: A Reference Guide to U.S. Involvement in Latin America and the Caribbean*. Westport, Conn.: Greenwood Press, 1999

M. McClintock, *Instruments of Statecraft. US Guerrilla Warfare, Counterinsurgency & Counter-terrorism*, 1940-1990, Pantheon Books, USA, 1992

S. Randall, *Colombia and the United States*, University of Georgia Press, 1992

C. Youngers, *The War in the Andes: The Military Role in US International Drug Policy*, WOLA Briefing series: Issues in International Drug Policy, December 1990

P. Zirnite, *Reluctant Recruits: The US Military and the War on Drugs*, WOLA working paper, USA, August 1997

Index

Printed in the United States
59443LVS00003B/106-306

9 780813 534435